GREATER
GRAND RAPIDS
THE CITY THAT WORKS

URBAN
TAPESTRY
SERIES
TOWERY
PUBLISHING, INC.

GREATER GRAND RAPIDS: THE CITY THAT WORKS

BY *Gerald R. Ford* AND *John Corriveau*

PROFILES IN EXCELLENCE BY *Peggy J. Parks*

CAPTIONS BY *Jennifer Ward*

ART DIRECTION BY *Jil Foutch*

LIBRARY OF CONGRESS CATALOGING-IN-PUBLICATION DATA

Ford, Gerald R., 1913-
  Greater Grand Rapids : the city that works / by Gerald R. Ford and
John Corriveau ; profiles in excellence by Peggy J. Parks ; captions
by Jennifer Ward ; art direction by Jil Foutch.
    p. cm. — (Urban tapestry series)
  Includes index.
  ISBN 1-881096-52-1 (alk. paper)
    1. Grand Rapids Region (Mich.)—Civilization.   2. Grand Rapids
Region (Mich.)—Pictorial works.   3. Business enterprises—Michigan-
-Grand Rapids Region.   4. Grand Rapids Region (Mich.)—Economic
conditions.   I. Corriveau, John, 1954-   . II. Parks, Peggy J.,
1951-   . III. Title. IV. Series.
F574.G7F67 1998
977.4'56—dc21   98-18339

TOWERY PUBLISHING, INC.
1835 UNION AVENUE
MEMPHIS, TN 38104

Copyright © 1998 by Towery Publishing, Inc.

Publisher: J. Robert Towery
Executive Publisher: Jenny McDowell
National Sales Manager: Stephen Hung
Marketing Director: Carol Culpepper
Project Directors: Henry Hintermeister, Al Mateus

Executive Editor: David B. Dawson
Managing Editor: Michael C. James
Senior Editors: Lynn Conlee, Carlisle Hacker
Editor/Project Manager: Lori Bond
Editors: Mary Jane Adams, Jana Files, Susan Hesson,
  Brian Johnston
Assistant Editor: Becky Green

Editorial Assistants: Allison Ring, Sunni Thompson
Editorial Consultants: Jeff Kosloski, Peggy J. Parks

Creative Director: Brian Groppe
Profile Designers: Laurie Beck, Kelley Pratt, Ann Ward
Digital Color Supervisor: Brenda Pattat
Digital Color Technicians: Jack Griffith, Darin Ipema,
  Jason Moak
Production Resources Manager: Dave Dunlap Jr.
Production Assistants: Geoffrey Ellis, Enrique Espinosa,
  Robin McGehee
Print Coordinator: Tonda Thomas

WILLIAM J. HEBERT / INSIGHT / FPG IMAGERY

"Grand Rapids was built by the hands of honest, hardworking people whose

values and work ethic were matched only by their generosity."

A look at the corporations, businesses, professional groups, and community

service organizations that have made this book possible.

LTHOUGH I HAVE LIVED IN A LOT OF PLACES, I HAVE ALWAYS considered Grand Rapids to be my home. My career and personal life have presented me with a number of addresses, from college dorms to the vice president's mansion, and from a cramped bunk aboard an aircraft carrier to the most famous address in the world, the White House at 1600 Pennsylvania Avenue.

All of these addresses are—and have been—important to me. Yet whenever Betty and I think of home, our thoughts invariably turn to Grand Rapids.

It was here that I lived during the formative years of my life, at a time in our country's history when the circumstances of daily life were much different from what they are now. It was here that my values took shape. And it was here that I learned the lessons that have served me well throughout my career as an attorney, as a congressman, and as president of the United States.

Grand Rapids, throughout my lifetime, has offered a kind of bedrock that has remained very much the same even though the city itself has grown and prospered beyond my wildest imagination. Those who live in Grand Rapids know what I mean: There has always been something about the city—something familiar and down-to-

Though its rapids have slowed over the years, the Grand River still lives up to its name. Cutting a path through the heart of the city, the waterway is spanned by nine bridges of varying ages and styles.

earth—that has helped its residents to keep their feet on the ground no matter where their dreams and careers might take them. In my case, the people of Grand Rapids have always been the ones to encourage me to dream as large as possible and to accomplish all that I could, and they have supported me no matter what came of my efforts.

Whenever I return to Grand Rapids, I am always so delighted to see that the city has maintained its feet-on-the-ground values while continuing to thrive and build. Today, Grand Rapids—like all of West Michigan—is very healthy economically. In fact, there's actually a labor shortage. What's more, the community is growing in a broad and constructive way, not just in one predominant sector, as a result of a well-diversified economic base.

Grand Rapids' recent—and continued—prosperity is no accident. The city has excellent local leadership, concerned with blending what's best about the past with the bright promise of the future. And the people of Grand Rapids who have been blessed with wealth have remained immensely generous in donating money for worthwhile community projects. The result has been a steady rise in the quality of living for Grand Rapids, a solid business climate, and an abundance of opportunities for meaningful growth in the years to come. ☞

Signs of patriotism are easy to spot in Grand Rapids, whether you're cruising the city's leafy pocket neighborhoods (LEFT) or strolling past Veterans Memorial Park along Monroe Avenue (OPPO-SITE). Pictured here in 1941, the downtown boulevard and long-time retail center today lures shoppers and strollers with its bright lighting and wide sidewalks that feature snow-melting technology underneath.

MOVED TO GRAND RAPIDS IN 1914. I WAS LESS THAN A YEAR OLD, SO IN A REAL sense, I consider myself a native of the city. My family lived first on Madison Avenue SE, in what is now referred to as Heritage Hill in downtown Grand Rapids. I have a number of vivid memories of this early period of my life. One of the most powerful of these has to do with the horse-drawn fire equipment from Firehouse No. 7, which was across the street from Madison School. There was a sense of real excitement and power whenever my grade school friends and I heard the alarm bells go off and saw those horses come charging out of the firehouse. Back in 1918, this was the last firehouse in Grand Rapids to employ horse-drawn equipment.

Needless to say, any dreams I might have had of becoming a fireman on a horse-drawn wagon remained the fantasy of a young boy. But ever since, I've carried with me a desire to protect and serve the city and people of Grand Rapids. In my youth, the seeds of a career in public service were firmly planted. And Grand Rapids proved to be the ideal ground in which to encourage these seeds to grow.

In 1919, my parents moved to Rosewood Street in East Grand Rapids, where we lived for two years. When my family lost that house because of financial difficulties, we rented a place at 649 Union Avenue—which was considered a moderate area economically. We lived there until 1930. ☞

Much of Grand Rapids' strength comes from its neighborhoods, each with its own sense of community and history. The landmark Heritage Hill District showcases such architectural gems as the Voigt House Victorian Museum, built in 1895 by local businessman Carl Voigt (OPPOSITE), and this distinctive Gothic cottage on Union Street (LEFT). Other homes in the neighborhood run the spectrum of architecture's delights and vagaries.

My memories of Grand Rapids during the 1920s—the years I lived on Union—are of an exciting, progressive city that epitomized the Roaring Twenties as well as any city could. Businesses thrived as downtown bustled with people day and night. Throughout my youth, one of my favorite things to do was swim. Families enjoyed trips to amusement parks like Ramona Park, and my friends and I spent as much time as we could swimming in various municipal pools—like Franklin Park and Garfield Park— that were within a mile or two from our home. Then, when we really wanted to show our swimming prowess, we'd go out to Reeds Lake in East Grand Rapids.

Looking back, Union was a perfect location for me to grow up and learn to live in a diverse, modern world. It was an area that had a number of children roughly my age, as well as an active Boy Scout troop. My involvement with the Boy Scouts provided a valuable perspective, and had a tremendous impact on my life. Just two-and-a-half years after I joined Troop No. 3, I became an Eagle Scout. ☞

There would certainly be bigger fish to fry for the boy who would become president, but like generations of children before and since, young Gerald Ford, pictured here with cousin Gardner James, found happiness in the day's catch (LEFT). In and around Grand Rapids, youngsters follow a similar recipe for the good life, as they enjoy the last light of day on Lake Michigan (OPPOSITE).

Autumn's glow provides a perfect backdrop for life's simple pleasures.

The neighborhood was unusual in that it was right on the dividing line between three schools. The oldest was Central High; this was where the people with large incomes traditionally sent their children. Ottawa Hills was considered a nouveau riche high school. And then there was South High, which had a very diverse and cosmopolitan student body, with rich, poor, black, white, Polish, Italian, Dutch, and just about any other kind of student you can imagine. On the whole, it was very down-to-earth.

Because anyone who lived on my block could choose which of the three high schools they wanted to attend, my parents had a tough decision to make. Fortunately, they were very good friends of a man named Ralph Conger, who was the basketball coach at Central High. When I was about to decide where I wanted to go to high school, my parents talked to Conger. To our surprise, he said that I should go not to

Central, where he taught, but to South High, because that's where I would not only get a good education, but also learn to live with people of all backgrounds.

So South is where I went, and Conger's advice turned out to be 100 percent correct. When I came back from the military and ran for Congress, the friends I had made during my time at South High served me well. Some of my best political supporters were the people I had gone to high school with. They were working in factories and plants, or were union members, and their vigorous support helped me tremendously, both in terms of getting votes and in terms of staying in touch with the people of the district. If I had gone to Central or Ottawa, I wouldn't have had that support and that feedback from the city's down-to-earth, solid people, and I wouldn't have been as good a representative of all of the constituents I was elected to serve. ☞

Home of the West Michigan Whitecaps, Old Kent Park is a hot spot for family fun. For some fans, getting soaked by a water balloon between innings rivals the thrill of catching a homer in the stands.

THE GREAT DEPRESSION HAD BEGUN TO TAKE ITS TOLL ON GRAND RAPIDS by the late 1920s. Economic conditions were terrible. Unemployment was very high. Parents of good friends of mine were on welfare. It was a tough period.

In 1931, I enrolled as a freshman at the University of Michigan, where I was on the Wolverines varsity football team from 1932 to 1934. While I was no longer in Grand Rapids every day to witness the tough times firsthand, my frequent trips home from Ann Arbor kept me painfully aware of how bad things were.

Yet, in spite of the grim news in the daily papers, what I saw at home also encouraged me. Rather than allowing themselves to become helpless and hopeless victims, the people of Grand Rapids banded together as the community they had always been. Not only did people work two and three jobs to support their own families, but they also

There's no place like home: That sentiment was all too familiar during World War II, as local servicemen said their reluctant goodbyes from Union Station (OPPOSITE). Gerald Ford (BELOW, FAR RIGHT) first got to know the feeling when he attended the University of Michigan in Ann Arbor. The welcoming familiarity of his hometown lured Ford back to Grand Rapids often, as it does even today.

did whatever they could to help those even less fortunate than themselves. For the people who survived, it was a strengthening experience.

In January 1941, I returned to Grand Rapids after completing law school. I passed the bar exams and opened a law firm with Phil Buchen, one of my University of Michigan fraternity brothers. Almost immediately, World War II caused me to put my law career in Grand Rapids on hold. On January 1, 1942, I volunteered and served the next four years of my life as a naval officer, ending up as a lieutenant commander. Much

of this time was spent on an aircraft carrier—the USS *Monterey*—in the Pacific.

Grand Rapids' manufacturers banded together to join in the war effort, providing such essential material as the wooden stocks for rifles, parts for airplanes, or parachutes. Everyone from church groups to school organizations to the Boy Scouts pitched in to collect such necessities as paper, scrap metal, and rubber. All along, I was proud that Grand Rapids was a leader in the effort to win the war on the home front. ☞

Patriotism runs deep in this all-American community, where students sold war bonds during World War II to raise money for jeeps and other equipment. Not only did local Boy Scouts help fuel an extensive bottle-recycling drive (OPPOSITE), but in 1943, the students of South High School raised $375,000 to purchase a B-17 Flying Fortress, christened *The Spirit of South High* (ABOVE).

**W**HEN THE WAR ENDED, I CAME BACK HOME TO GRAND RAPIDS and found that the city had undergone quite a bit of growth. Automobile plants and auto parts manufacturing facilities now stood beside the traditional furniture factories. Union membership had always been important in Grand Rapids, but with these new manufacturing jobs, the unions grew tremendously, becoming a potent political constituency. The city's population had become much more diverse as well, with many African-American families moving up from the South.

The law firm that I had established with Buchen had disbanded while the war was raging. Now, back home, I found that my friend and partner had joined Butterfield, Keeney & Amberg, a prestigious Grand Rapids firm. While Buchen and I thought about setting up our own firm again, I decided to accept an offer to join the Butterfield firm and begin the life of an attorney.

Both before and after the war, I had received offers to practice law in Philadelphia and New York, but I always felt that I could do better and would be happier in the environment and the city where I grew up. Also, I wanted to be a part of the community in other ways, mainly by getting involved with such organizations as the American Red Cross and its local board of trustees, the United Way, the Kent County Farm Bureau, the NAACP, and—close to my heart—the Boy Scouts. I was also active in various veterans organizations such as the American Legion, VFW, and AMVETS.

All of this community activity seemed to lead

Thanks in part to the top-quality household furnishings produced by the Phoenix Furniture Factory (BELOW), Grand Rapids earned the moniker Furniture City in the early 20th century. Today, locals still work hard, but they also know how to throw a party. When the day is done, residents come together and celebrate at traditional holiday parades, countless festivals, and the annual Fourth of July fireworks display (OPPOSITE).

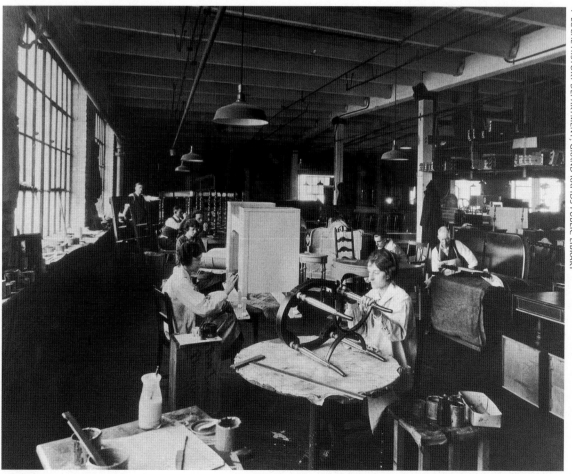

naturally into a life of public service, especially as I got to know more about the array of people from Grand Rapids who came from various backgrounds.

A couple of years after the war, a group of us Young Turks decided that the Old Guard in the Republican Party in West Michigan was out of tune and poorly led. We felt that our incumbent congressman—Bartel J. Jonkman, an isolationist who had been elected with the help of the Old Guard political bosses—was undercutting Senator Arthur Vandenburg, who came from Grand Rapids. We were idealists, and thought there should be new, internationalist attitudes after the war. But no one would run against Jonkman because of how entrenched the old political machine had become.

So I decided to challenge him in the Fifth District primary, and ended up beating him about two-to-one. For support, I turned to old friends from South High, as well as the people I had met in my college days or through my community activities. By then, these people were working in all walks of life, from businesses and professions to factories and farms.

Looking at the diversity of the group that elected me, in 1948, to represent them in Congress, I am gratified that people of such varying backgrounds were on my team. From them, and from my upbringing in Grand Rapids, I knew I would represent the values and work ethic that make up such a strong part of West Michigan's spirit. ☛

Nature's beauty coexists with man-made masterpieces at the Frederik Meijer Gardens on the city's eastern edge. Located amid the glorious flora, the Meijer Sculpture Park displays works of art that are meant to be experienced by more than just the eye.

 REMAINED IN WASHINGTON FOR NEARLY 30 YEARS. AS A U.S. REPRESENTATIVE, I served for 25 and a half years. Then, I served as vice president from December 1973 until August 1974, and as president of the United States (with my old friend Buchen as my chief legal counselor) from August 1974 until January 1977.

I missed Grand Rapids the whole time. Having grown up here, Betty—whom I had met and married shortly after the war—and I had many, many friends in Grand Rapids. We used to get back as often as we could, whenever Congress was not in session. Even when Congress was in session, I would return to Grand Rapids at least every other weekend, something that I felt was necessary for me to be a good representative. After all, you don't just go off to Washington and never go back to your hometown.

In January 1977, Betty and I moved to California, where we built a house in Rancho Mirage. We wanted to retire to a place with a warmer climate, and to be closer to our children. But we never stopped thinking of Grand Rapids as home. This is where I

There's no shortage of ways to spend your leisure time in and around Grand Rapids. A stroll down the Grand Haven Pier reveals the beauty of Lake Michigan (BELOW), while a visit to the Gerald R. Ford Museum will teach you a thing or two about the city's most famous son (OPPOSITE). Chronicling the life and times of the former U.S. president, whose homegrown values helped heal America during some of its most difficult days, the museum features 10 permanent galleries on the west bank of the Grand River.

chose to build the Gerald R. Ford Museum to house many of the official papers and memorabilia from my presidency.

These days, Betty and I still come back to visit as often as we can. Every time we return, we are amazed at how much Grand Rapids has changed and grown.

Part of the reason for this, I'm sure, is that families have long been able to obtain houses and apartments in safe, clean neighborhoods with excellent schools. In other cities, comparable housing costs three and four times as much as it does in Grand Rapids. One area with which I am familiar is Heritage Hill on the east side of downtown. This historic district is filled with beautiful turn-of-the-century homes, many of which have been restored by young families who want to live in the wonderfully diverse and culturally rich urban landscape of Grand Rapids. ☛

When it opened in 1996, the Van Andel Arena marked the dawn of a downtown renaissance (OPPOSITE). The venue has quickly become a showplace for top-notch entertainment, offering everything from sports to opera to rock 'n' roll.

For a fresh-air alternative, nothing says summertime quite like the Picnic Pops series at the Cannonsburg Ski Area. The popular concerts feature glorious music courtesy of the Grand Rapids Symphony, considered one of the best orchestras of its size in the nation.

It's not just affordable housing. For as long as I can remember, there have always been things for a family to do in Grand Rapids. Theaters, parks, festivals, churches, recreational events, and pro sports teams—like the West Michigan Whitecaps baseball team and the Grand Rapids Griffins hockey team, which plays in the new Van Andel Arena—are only a few examples.

Recreational activities are also extremely important in making Grand Rapids an attractive city. Cross-country skiing and ice-skating are popular in the wintertime, while swimming, waterskiing, biking, and hiking are among summer's favorite activities. From Reeds Lake, where I swam when I was young, to nearby Lake Michigan, you can find plenty of people sailing, fishing, floating, or soaking up the sun. And, as an avid golfer, I've got to add that Grand Rapids has some of the finest public and private golf courses in the country.

Local sports fans hunger for action, and Grand Rapids is only too happy to satisfy their appetites. Sharing space at the Van Andel Arena are the Hoops, who hold their own in the Continental Basketball Association (RIGHT), and the Griffins, a minor-league hockey team that started play in the 1996-1997 season (OPPOSITE).

Grand Rapids was built by the hands of honest, hardworking people whose values and work ethic were matched only by their generosity. While thousands of businesses have helped to keep the city economically strong and supply its residents with products and services, those who have accumulated wealth are also generous in donating money for good community projects. Many attractions in the city were made possible by such donations,

A diligent goalkeeper for the Grand Rapids Griffins, Eldon "Pokey" Reddick was a crowd favorite during his tenure with the team. Much to the disappointment of loyal fans, Reddick was traded early in the 1997-1998 season.

or by private donations in conjunction with public funding.

The Van Andel sports arena that seats 14,000 is an example of this kind of community support. We have a brand-new, beautiful public library. And we have a gorgeous garden donated by one of the successful families in town.

There is a remarkable amount of support for the performing arts, drawing people from all over the state of Michigan, as well as neighboring states, to see performances

n Grand Rapids. Museums abound, along with an excellent zoo, nature center, parks, and a planetarium. Several theater groups, the opera, the ballet, and the Grand Rapids Symphony are just a few of the choices. Or, for those who like popular music, there are plenty of clubs and, in the summertime, many open-air concerts right in the center of downtown.

It is this wonderful community atmosphere that makes me proudest of Grand Rapids. Without this attitude, and the involvement of the city's entire population, none of the rest would have been possible. From the bustle of the 1920s through the depths of the Great Depression and the war years, and through the decades I served Grand Rapids and West Michigan in government, the area has steadily blossomed.

And yet, through all the years and all the changes, it's still what it always was. It's home. ■

As the home of the Public Museum of Grand Rapids, the Van Andel Museum Center is one of the brightest spots downtown (OPPOSITE). There, kids of all ages can travel back in time, thanks to exhibits about Native American culture and the region's furniture-making heritage, as well as a magnificently restored 1928 carousel (ABOVE).

Ever since 1826, when French-
man Louis Campau established a
trading post on the site, Campau
Square has been the heart of
Grand Rapids' business district.
Pictured here in 1873 (ABOVE),
the plaza is today the center of
a thriving downtown economy
(OPPOSITE).

STRETCHING BOLDLY INTO THE morning sky, the 29-story glass tower of the Amway Grand Plaza Hotel complex is a focal point of the city skyline (PAGES 34 AND 35).

▲ JOHN CORRIVEAU

ON THE EVE OF THE AUTOMOBILE age, circa 1900, a streetcar shuttles riders through Campau Square, past Sweet's Hotel and the Tower Clock Building (PAGES 36 AND 37). Sweet's opened in 1869, became the Pantlind Hotel in 1902, and was revived and expanded in the late 1970s as the luxurious Amway Grand Plaza. Unfortunately, the clock tower fell prey to progress in 1939.

ELEGANT ARCHES AND OTHER EYE-catching details recall the beauty of a bygone era in downtown Grand Rapids.

OH, THE STORIES THEY COULD tell! Generations of progress have come and gone—all under the watchful eye of the city's historic architecture.

IN THE CITY'S HEARTSIDE DISTRICT, historic appeal has endured, even as recent renewal has spread. Although some old favorites look a little the worse for wear, a host of apartments, offices, and restaurants now occupy many of the neighborhood's century-old structures.

ATTENTION TO HISTORIC PRESERVA-
tion has given downtown Grand
Rapids an intriguing blend of old
and new, with windows to the past
around every architectural corner.

THE SLEEK, 384-FOOT TOWER OF the Amway Grand Plaza cuts a dramatic shape in any light. The Mobil four-star, AAA four-diamond hotel is equally impressive on the inside, where Austrian crystal chandeliers and glittering gold-leaf ceilings are among the numerous luxuries awaiting guests.

ALL WORK AND NO PLAY? NOT IN Grand Rapids. The reflection of a giant butterfly mural on a nearby office building injects a bit of whimsy into downtown's workaday world.

THOUGH DISTORTED BY THE SHINY glass of its more modern neighbor, the historic McKay Tower still shimmers majestically. Standing on the site of the first frame house in the Grand River Valley, the "tower" opened in 1915 as the two-story Grand Rapids National Bank Building, and grew to its current stature when 14 floors were added between 1926 and 1927.

AT HOME IN THE CLOUDS: MANY locals who work downtown also call the business district home. Anchoring the north end of the city's skyline is Bridgewater Place, a 17-story, glass-and-steel building whose tenants include professional firms, retail merchants, and a restaurant (ABOVE). Nearby, on the Grand River's east bank, the 32-story Plaza Towers boasts apartments and condominiums, a Courtyard by Marriott hotel, and an enclosed skywalk with access to the Van Andel Arena and the Amway Grand Plaza Hotel (OPPOSITE).

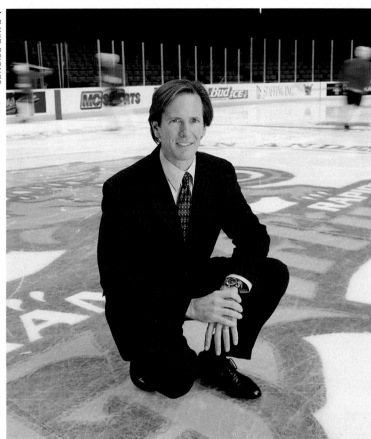

▶ DAVID DEJONGE

▶ FRED L. KLEIBOER

A FORMIDABLE PRESENCE ON Fulton Street, the Van Andel Arena packs 'em in with top-flight sports and entertainment. Helping secure Grand Rapids' status as a model midwestern city for the 21st century, the venue's success—and the resulting reemergence of downtown—is in large part due to a new generation of leadership that includes Dan DeVos, a principal owner of West Michigan Hockey, Inc. (TOP RIGHT).

THE CONSTRUCTION OF THE VAN Andel Museum Center created a sparkling anchor on Pearl Street's Museum Row and broadened the cultural corridor that includes Grand Valley State University's local campus and the Gerald R. Ford Museum. In addition to its intriguing history and natural science exhibits, the facility serves as a monument to the civic generosity of Jay Van Andel, cofounder of Amway Corporation (ABOVE).

THE KALEIDOSCOPE OF LIFE IS always in motion in Grand Rapids, where steady growth keeps local laborers on the move. At Union High School (left), a mural depict-ing the city's history—from Native American life to modern manufac-turing—is dismantled for the trip to its new home in the Van Andel Museum Center.

MICHAEL MORIN ▶ ANDREW C. TERZES

SPARKS FLY AS A WELDER GETS
down to business at Hydraulic
Technology, an area manufacturer
of hydraulic cylinders.

All spit and polish: Motorcycle authority Brett Beimers—a guru of sorts in this town—takes pleasure in keeping the pistons firing on sleek, classic bikes.

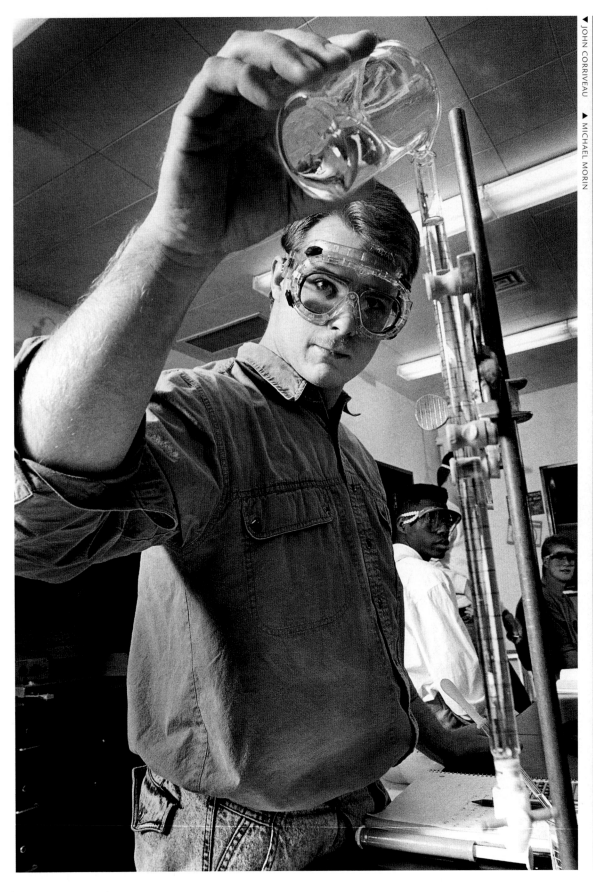

▼ JOHN CORRIVEAU ▲ MICHAEL MORIN

GREATER GRAND RAPIDS

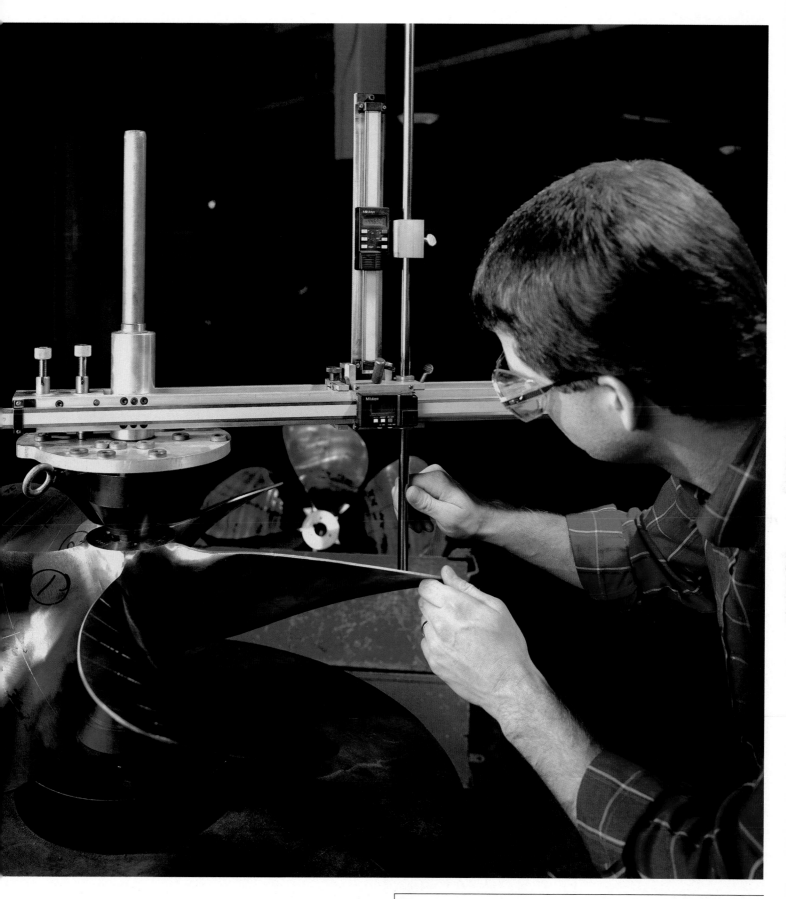

THE WEALTH OF TOP-NOTCH EDU-
cational institutions in and around
Grand Rapids ensures a well-
trained, professional workforce
for West Michigan's science- and
technology-driven manufacturing
community.

GETTING SOAKED: WHETHER it's a company of firefighters practicing for the real thing or carefree children enjoying the simple pleasures of a garden sprinkler, turning down the heat is sometimes the only way to go.

SINCE 1994, THE VAN ANDEL Museum Center, home of the Roger B. Chaffee Planetarium, has made a striking addition to the west bank of the Grand River. Among the facility's attractions are a 76-foot-long whale skeleton suspended ominously overhead, the restored Spillman Carousel, and a permanent exhibit tracing the colorful history of Furniture City.

By the light of a silvery moon, the Gerald R. Ford Museum breathes with life (RIGHT), while Judson Nelson's *Man in Space*, a bronze sculpture located outside the facility, appears to step into the heavens (OPPOSITE). A long-time supporter of the nation's journey into the final frontier, President Ford was minority leader of the U.S. House of Representatives during America's adventures into space in the 1960s and early 1970s.

BY DAY, A STROLL ABOUT THE well-manicured grounds of the Ford Museum offers a peaceful perspective (PAGES 68 AND 69).

THE CITY THAT WORKS

OVER THE YEARS, THE CITY'S PUB-
lic transportation system has
seen its ups and downs. Early on,
horse-drawn streetcars gave way
to steam-powered vehicles, and by
the early 1890s, an efficient electric system shuttled residents
around town. At its peak size in
the 1920s, Grand Rapids' streetcar
line boasted more than 70 miles
of track that linked most parts of
the city and the surrounding areas.

WHEN IT FIRST ROLLED OFF THE presses in March 1855, the daily *Grand Rapids Herald* joined a journalistic tradition begun by the *Grand River Times* in 1837, the year Michigan achieved statehood. In the 1900s, the *Herald* was hit hard by the success of the *Grand Rapids Press*, one of eight Michigan dailies owned by George C. Booth. Although Booth added the ailing *Herald* to his lineup in 1958, the paper published its final issue early in 1959.

PEOPLE ON THE MOVE FIND EASY access to all points in West Michigan and beyond via the expressway system that crisscrosses Grand Rapids.

IN THE WEE HOURS, DOWNTOWN enjoys a few moments of calm as it awaits another day of hustle and bustle.

OPULENT LIVING, EVIDENT IN THIS
1880s view of Washington Street,
was a by-product of Grand Rapids'
boom times—first in lumber, then
in furniture.

EYEING HER HISTORY-RICH SUR-
roundings, Heritage Hill resident
and vintage clothing collector
Barbara Van Wienen pauses before
a backdrop of bittersweet and
roses.

THERE'S BEAUTY IN THE DETAILS: The Heritage Hill District's marvelous collection of homes, reflecting the fanciful and ornate taste of their original 18th- and early-19th-century owners, is on display during the Tour of Homes, held the first weekend in October.

One striking member of the Heritage Hill family is the Fox House, a chateauesque mansion built in the late 1880s by Colonel Ethelbert Crofton Fox and his brother, Charles. Designed by local architect William G. Robinson, the Castle, as it's affectionately called, is constructed of granite block imported from Scotland.

83

In 1870, Indiana resident and native Prussian Carl Voigt opened a dry goods store in Grand Rapids with his business partner, William O. Herpolsheimer. Prosperity soon followed, and in 1895, Voigt built a new home, designed by William G. Robinson. Now part of the Public Museum of Grand Rapids, the Voigt House Victorian Museum—still filled with the Voigt family's furniture and personal belongings—draws visitors into the opulent world of a wealthy turn-of-the-century family.

GREATER GRAND RAPIDS

WHATEVER YOUR FANCY, HERITAGE Hill has it all. And somehow, the palette of shapes and colors links the neighborhood's more than 60 different architectural styles. In the mid-1960s, when developers threatened to wipe out parts of the historically significant area, residents succeeded in halting the encroachment, and a 350-acre section of Heritage Hill joined the National Register of Historic Places in 1971.

BEYOND EXTERIOR DESIGN AND interior decor, detailed window frames add a touch of elegance to historic homes in Grand Rapids.

FRANK LLOYD WRIGHT DESIGNED this early-20th-century home for Grand Rapids clothing retailer Meyer May. Today owned by Steelcase Inc., the prairie-style Madison Avenue house was thoroughly restored by fall 1987, complete with original furnishings as well as reproductions crafted from original plans. Regular public tours make the Meyer May House a top attraction in Heritage Hill.

FRANK LLOYD WRIGHT'S TRADE-
mark stained-glass work appears
in light fixtures and windows
throughout the Meyer May House.
Characteristic of the architect's
thorough approach to design,
these details incorporate the au-
tumnal tones used in other decorative elements in the house.

THE ARTFULLY DESIGNED DINING room of the Meyer May House demonstrates Wright's dedication to organic architecture—the intertwining of living space with nature. Small pots of ivy flourish under lights integrated into the table's design, and a stylized floral wall mural mimics the natural beauty of a garden just outside the room.

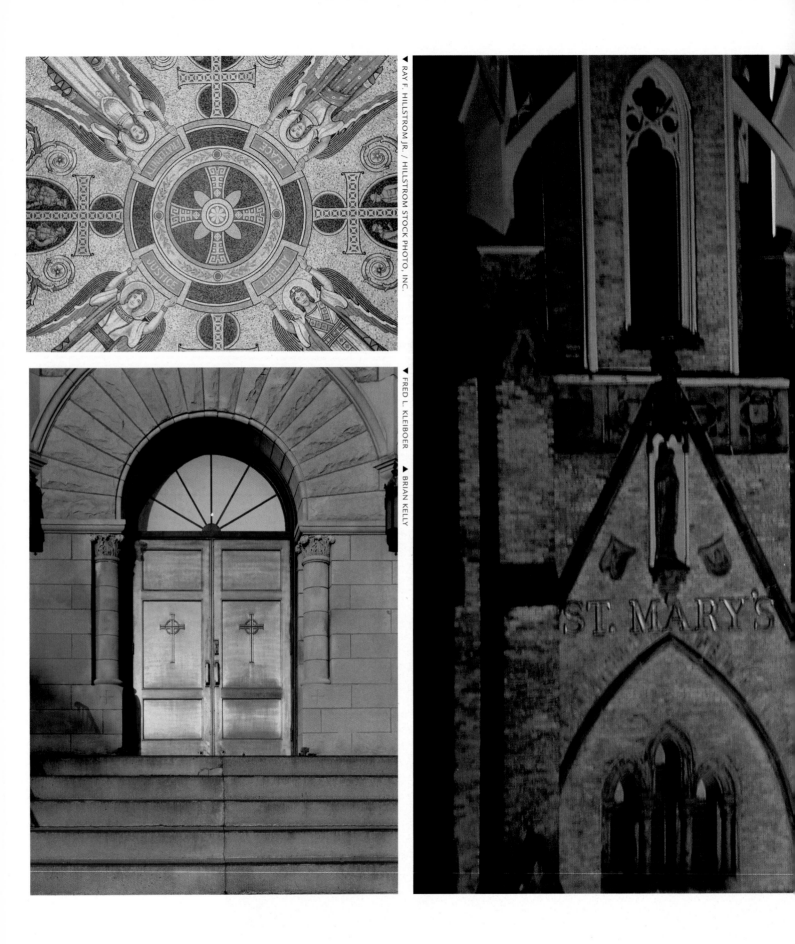

ST. MARY'S

THE LOCAL LANDSCAPE IS EN-
riched by the architectural symbols
of this diverse, deeply religious
community. On the west side,
members of the neighborhood's
historically Polish population
worship within the gold-plated
doors of the 1913 Basilica of St.
Adalbert (OPPOSITE BOTTOM).
Within view of its imposing
Byzantine domes is beautiful St.
Mary's Catholic Church, which
originally served descendants of
German immigrants who were
drawn to Grand Rapids' thriving
furniture industry in the late 1800s
(ABOVE). Also striking is the ornate
ceiling that looms overhead in the
symbolically rich Fountain Street
Church (OPPOSITE TOP).

DEMOGRAPHIC TRENDS ASIDE, downtown churches have kept a guiding hand in metropolitan life. Known for its sky-piercing steeples and distinctive limestone dredged from the Grand River, St. Mark's Episcopal Church has overlooked Pearl Street since the early 1850s (OPPOSITE). Nearby, the imposing facade of Immanuel Lutheran Church frames a sliver of moon in the night sky (LEFT).

THE CITY THAT WORKS

WITH PLENTY OF CHANCES TO
make a splash, take a tumble, or
soak up the spectacle at a Fourth
of July parade, summer is indeed a
fun-filled time for local children.

GREATER GRAND RAPIDS

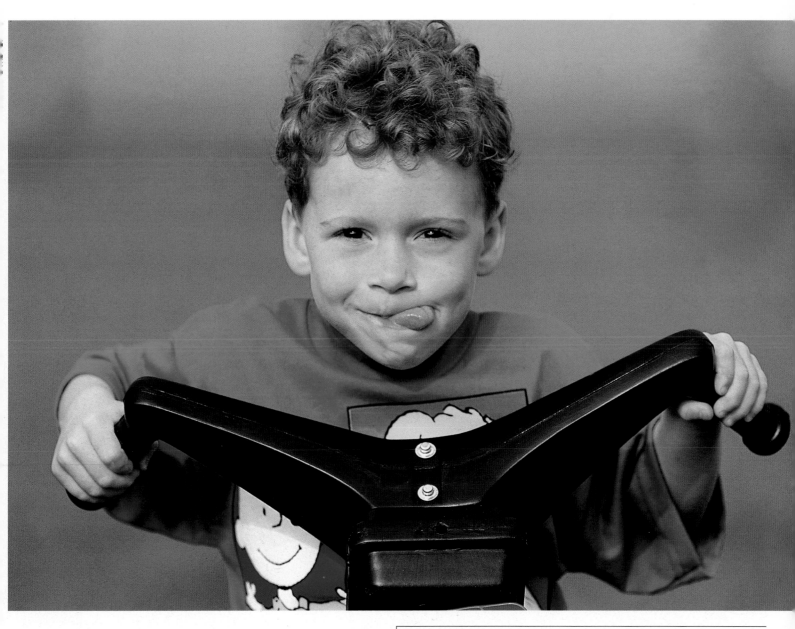

AS SUMMER DRAWS TO A CLOSE, the appearance of the familiar crossing guard signals the start of another school year in Grand Rapids. With older brother and sister back in class, future students can get in their last licks and spins before autumn's chill sets in.

STUDENTS KNOW HOW TO ENJOY the great outdoors every chance they get, whether they're taking a shortcut across Wilcox Park (OPPOSITE), making friends during recess at Madison Park School (TOP), or just hanging out at Oakdale Christian Elementary (BOTTOM).

COME RAIN OR COME SHINE, MOST residents embrace the community's staunch work ethic. Here, a *Grand Rapids Press* carrier prepares her deliveries in spite of a wet afternoon.

WITH THE EYE OF THE TIGER, these young boxers exercise great precision while preparing for their next big bout.

HOOPS HOOPLA: EXPLODING WITH energy, kids take over the court during halftime at an Explorer Elementary fund-raiser, featuring a contest between fifth graders and school staffers.

INSPIRING YOUNG AUDIENCES TO reach new heights, the Grand Rapids Ballet leads an after-school dance instruction program at Oakdale Elementary.

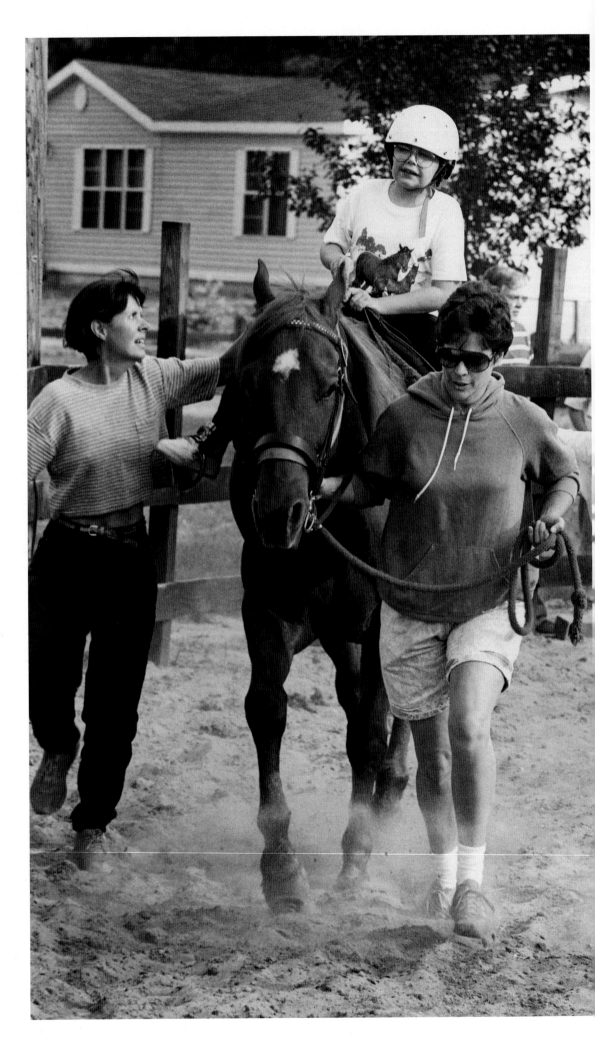

THE CITY THAT WORKS

GETTING A MOVE ON: A PASSEL OF young runners pound the pavement during the Children's Run portion of the annual Pietro's Run Fasta, Eat Pasta race, sponsored by one of the city's most popular Italian eateries.

Each June, more than 2,000 runners compete in the Reeds Lake Run, sponsored by the East Grand Rapids Parks and Recreation Department. There's an event for everyone in the 20-year-old contest, including 5K and 10K runs, a 5K walk, and a kids' race.

LOOK AT HIM GO! A YOUNG MAN with a mission makes a run for it in a peewee football match (TOP). Love for the gridiron starts early in West Michigan, thanks in large part to the summer camps sponsored by the Grand Rapids Parks and Recreation Department. Here, Eric Lynch, a former member of the Detroit Lions and a standout during his days at Grand Valley State University, gives pointers to young football fanatics (BOTTOM).

WHETHER YOU FAVOR POM-POMS or shin guards, there are plenty of ways to get your kicks on playing fields throughout Grand Rapids. Some athletes opt to hit the streets in the Old Kent River Bank Run, which got its start in 1978 with 1,000 participants (PAGES 118 AND 119). Today, the event is the largest 25K race in the United States, drawing some 7,500 runners and more than 20,000 spectators to downtown Grand Rapids each May.

IF YOU'RE TOUGH AND YOU KNOW it, you might as well show it. A popular show of athletic prowess is the Reeds Lake Triathlon, sponsored each September by the East Grand Rapids Parks and Recreation Department. Contestants begin with a half-mile swim in the lake, then race 18 miles on bike and five miles on foot.

SNAGGING A SALMON NEAR THE Sixth Street Dam is the payoff of patience. As the Grand River runs through downtown, the shallow waters invite anglers aplenty to wade in and go for the big prize.

124

THE CITY THAT WORKS

GREATER GRAND RAPIDS

THE SPORTING LIFE TAKES ON AN artful air in and around Grand Rapids, where a picture-perfect autumn backdrop is the ideal inspiration for an afternoon of fly-fishing (OPPOSITE). At nearby Reeds Lake, hardy souls can take advantage of the year-round bounty, snagging their catch in the clear winter waters beneath the ice (TOP). And back in town, the functional *Grand Rapids River Sculpture and Fish Ladder*, created by multimedia artist Joseph Kinnebrew, intrigues the eye as it aids salmon in their struggle up the Sixth Street Dam to spawn (BOTTOM).

GREATER GRAND RAPIDS

THE FIRST OF AMERICA CLASSIC, Grand Rapids' biggest summertime golf event, has become a hot stop on the PGA Senior Tour. Taking a time-out from the action, legend Lee Trevino shares a moment with former President Gerald Ford, one of the biggest golf fans this town has ever produced (OPPOSITE LEFT). Other "Classic" moments include the unwavering concentration of Dave Stockton as he sinks a putt (LEFT) and Chi Chi's cha-cha, demonstrated by the inimitable Mr. Rodriguez (RIGHT).

SINCE STARTING PLAY IN 1994, THE West Michigan Whitecaps have produced some of the Midwest League's top players, including pitcher Jamey Price, MVP of the 1996 play-offs (TOP), and All-Star left fielder Duane Filchner (BOTTOM). Displaying his undying dedication to earning runs, outfielder Mat Reese hits the dirt as he tries to beat the throw to third (OPPOSITE).

At OLD KENT PARK, THE FUN never stops for young Whitecaps fans. After kids collect the autographs of their hometown heroes (TOP), they can try their hand at running the bases. Between innings, a youngster is pitted against team mascot Crash, the River Rascal, who's lagging so far behind that he's not even pictured (BOTTOM). And on Baseball Buddies Night, Little Leaguers are invited to stand alongside the 'Caps during the national anthem (OPPOSITE, BOTTOM LEFT).

THERE'S NO BETTER PLACE TO BEAT summer's heat than Old Kent Park during a Whitecaps game. While these "hosers" espouse one cool-off cure (TOP), a coterie of cowboys support another, slinging wet foam baseballs into the stands on Western Night (BOTTOM RIGHT).

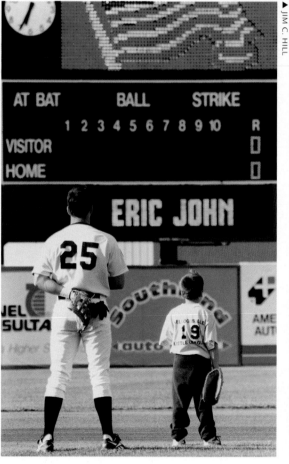

▲ JIM C. HILL

WHEN THE GRAND RAPIDS HOOPS take to the court, their high-flying acrobatics heat up fall and winter nights downtown. At home in the Van Andel Arena since 1996, the CBA franchise began play in 1989.

For Griffins fans, hockey night at the Van Andel Arena means plenty of action both on and off the ice. As Travis Richards and Glen Metropolit line up to help defend their goal (TOP), Darcy Simon introduces an opponent to the rest of his teammates (BOTTOM RIGHT). In the meantime, mascot Griff and the ever present Trumpet Man keep the place hopping (BOTTOM LEFT).

AirTouch Cellular

THEY MAY HAVE GREAT FANS AND a state-of-the-art venue, but the real secret to the Griffins' success has been the nonstop action provided by a steady stream of solid players, including Travis Richards (BOTTOM LEFT) and Brian Sullivan (BOTTOM RIGHT).

▶ JIM C. HILL

GREATER GRAND RAPIDS

IT TAKES MORE THAN A LITTLE SNOW to send folks indoors in West Michigan, where cross-country skiers hit the path in Seidman Park (OPPOSITE TOP), locals marvel at the city's new wintry blanket (OPPOSITE BOTTOM), and one of the region's younger residents packs a snowball destined for an unsuspecting target (LEFT).

GREATER GRAND RAPIDS

WHEN FRIGID TEMPERATURES descend on the city, even the Grand River begins to look like one big skating rink (OPPOSITE). But don't lace up your skates too fast: For a much safer turn on the ice, head to Monroe Center, where spectacular views of downtown are the major attraction (ABOVE).

SPANNING THE FLAT RIVER out-side Grand Rapids, White's Bridge provides a vista frozen in time. In use for well over a century, the bridge is held together by wooden pegs and hand-cut iron nails.

142

THE CITY THAT WORKS

A SHORT DRIVE OUT OF THE city brings living reminders of a simpler time. The pastoral surroundings are a bit deceptive, though; as the state's second-largest industry, agriculture is big business in West Michigan.

GREATER GRAND RAPIDS

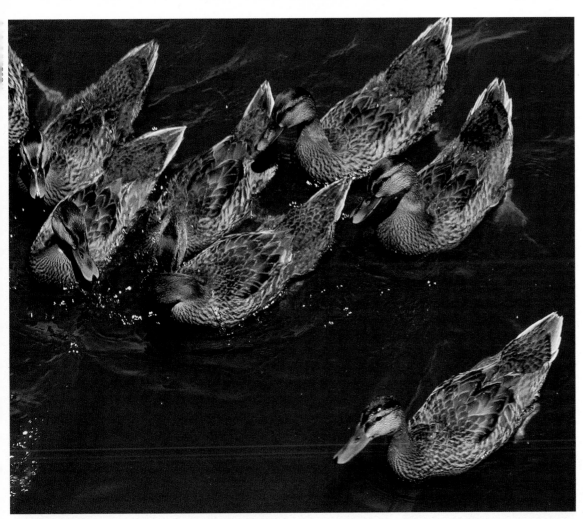

WILDLIFE AND OTHER NATURAL wonders abound throughout the Grand River region, where bird-watchers can delight in spotting a red-tailed hawk, several varieties of ducks, and the ever graceful swan.

DIANE BOSLEY TAYLOR / HILLSTROM STOCK PHOTO, INC.

STEVE HUYSER-HONIG

FROM A SWAMPY STRETCH OF Reeds Lake (LEFT) to the 235-acre Frederik Meijer Nature Preserve (RIGHT), Mother Nature shows off her colors in and around Grand Rapids. One of the best ways to take in her magical canvas is a walk along Kent Trails, a 15-mile system of reclaimed rail beds that winds from John Ball Zoo to Byron Center (OPPOSITE).

THE SUN ADDS ITS WARM GLOW TO area pastures, from a soaked corn-field curtsying before a rainbow (PAGES 150 AND 151) to a field of golden wheat welcoming morning's earliest light (PAGES 152 AND 153).

WHETHER THEY'RE STRAIGHT FROM the field or packed for sale at a roadside stand, juicy blueberries are always a blessing in July's heat. Michigan is the nation's top blueberry producer, thanks in large part to growers in and around Grand Rapids.

GREATER GRAND RAPIDS

SPRING'S SHOW OF DELICATE APPLE blossoms fills the air with their sweet scent and foretells the bountiful harvest to come.

GREATER GRAND RAPIDS

MCINTOSH, ROME, EMPIRE, Jonathan, Winesap—they're all delicious! In a state where apples are the king of the fruit crop, Kent County is the number one producer.

GREATER GRAND RAPIDS

WITH A RAINBOW OF HARVEST colors, downtown Grand Rapids gets a dose of the country every Thursday from May through October when Monroe Mall becomes a vast farmer's market.

WHEN AUTUMN'S COOL DAYS PAINT the landscape with warm colors, city streets glow under a golden canopy, area lakes come alive with fiery hues, and harvesttime offers its rich delights. As the days grow even shorter, a blanket of frosty leaves forecasts winter's approach (PAGES 164 AND 165).

AN 1871 SIGN AT THE ENTRANCE to the Fallasburg Covered Bridge warns, "$5 Fine for Riding or Driving on This Bridge Faster Than a Walk." Crossing the Flat River in Vergennes Township, the span is as hardworking today as ever, accommodating automobiles, pedestrians, and even the occasional wagon.

THE CITY THAT WORKS

Several generations ago, education likely meant McGuffey Eclectic Readers and a one-room schoolhouse. Recalling those times is the 1853 Star School, moved from Ottawa County to become part of the Blandford Nature Center's Heritage Complex, a collection of carefully preserved, 19th-century buildings.

BUILT IN 1866, THE HISTORIC Robinson-Kuhtic Cabin (ABOVE) is a major attraction at the Blandford Nature Center, which offers 143 acres of exquisite flora and fauna. At the center's Fall Harvest Fair, visitors of all ages can travel back to a time when spinning, weaving, cider pressing, candle dipping, blacksmithing, and corn shelling were part of everyday life (OPPOSITE).

HELD EVERY MAY SINCE 1930, THE Tulip Time Festival in nearby Holland celebrates West Michigan's strong Dutch heritage. The 10-day event draws more than a million visitors with its Tulip Trolley, beautiful blossoms, and lively parades (PAGES 174 AND 175).

IMPORTED FROM THE NETHER-lands, DeZwaan is a 230-year-old, working windmill that punctuates Windmill Island in Holland, offering a glimpse of the Old Country and commemorating the region's Dutch influence (TOP).

It's easy speculation that West Michigan leads the world in wooden shoes per capita during Holland's Tulip Time, when Klompen dancers take to the streets in traditional Dutch costumes (LEFT). In and among the flowers, a pair of "two-lips" lend their own charm to the unique festival (OPPOSITE BOTTOM).

A FAVORITE DESTINATION FOR many of the tourists who visit Holland each year is Veldheer's Tulip Gardens, which features an authentic windmill and wooden shoes of every size. Of course, the garden's vast fields of colorful blossoms are Tulip Time's top attraction (PAGES 180 AND 181).

STEVE HUYSER-HONIG

ANDREW C. TERZES

NATURE LOVERS YOUNG AND OLD enjoy West Michigan's scenic foliage, brought into colorful focus each spring and summer (PAGES 182-185).

GREATER GRAND RAPIDS

As the seasons change, Mother Nature reveals her diverse splendor. Turning leaves begin their autumn dance at the Blandford Nature Center (OPPOSITE), and trillium shows its fresh face in the spring air at Aman Park (ABOVE).

THE SWEET, HUMID AIR OF THE rain forest at the Frederik Meijer Gardens transports visitors to the tropics, where a two-story waterfall cascades over a rock cliff, turtles swim in misty pools, and bronze frogs and other sculpted creatures hide under a canopy of banana and palm trees.

OPENED IN 1995, THE FREDERIK Meijer Gardens is home to the impressive Lena Meijer Conservatory. The largest facility of its kind in the state, the five-story structure is surrounded by beautifully manicured green spaces and an array of distinctive sculptures.

Lᴉᴏɴs ᴀɴᴅ ᴛɪɢᴇʀs ᴀɴᴅ ʙᴇᴀʀs, ᴏғ course! But more than 225 other species also live peacefully in John Ball Zoological Gardens. The col-lection of more than 1,000 animals includes American cougars (ᴛᴏᴘ ʟᴇꜰᴛ), African bongo (ʙᴏᴛᴛᴏᴍ ʟᴇꜰᴛ), and South American capy-baras—the world's largest rodent (ʙᴏᴛᴛᴏᴍ ʀɪɢʜᴛ). Early Grand Rap-ids resident John Ball, a Renais-sance man by all accounts, donated the original acreage for the zoo in 1884. In commemoration, a bronze sculpture of Ball and two of his children was erected in 1925 (ᴏᴘᴘᴏsɪᴛᴇ).

GREATER GRAND RAPIDS

MODERN SCULPTURE HAS MADE its mark on the local landscape. Accenting downtown's Vandenburg Center since 1969, Alexander Calder's *La Grande Vitesse*, which means "the great swiftness" or "the grand rapids" is embraced as a symbol of the city (OPPOSITE). At Lacks Park on Grand Valley State University's downtown campus, well-formed fish and birds cavort among the waves of *The River's Edge*, a 1988 sculpture by Jim Clover (LEFT).

THE CITY THAT WORKS

THE GRANDEST OF ALL THE CITY'S downtown gatherings, the fun-filled Festival of the Arts draws more than a half-million people to Calder Plaza each year. Started in 1962, the event is the largest all-volunteer arts festival in the nation.

GREATER GRAND RAPIDS

ALTHOUGH FESTIVAL OF THE ARTS certainly highlights the talents of the city's many accomplished artists and performers, it's a special favorite among children for its numerous hands-on creative activities.

GOING UP? A DETERMINED CLIMBER in Lincoln Park reaches new heights during National Night Out, an event sponsored by the National Association of Town Watch to help strengthen community spirit while elevating crime awareness.

GOING DOWN? ALEXANDER Calder's famous downtown sculpture may not have been built for sliding, but more than one fun-seeker has found the space between form and function.

Up, up, and away: Balloonists take advantage of a nearly cloud-less day as they travel skyward for a bird's-eye view of the city.

An appreciation for the arts pervades Grand Rapids year-round, as local youth put their creativity to the test in area schools and museums (TOP). But everyone gets into the act during Festival of the Arts. Here, a young man does his best to ward away the squirms, as he sits tight for a quick portrait (OPPOSITE). Nearby, a concrete canvas leaves no doubt as to Josh's love for dinosaurs—proclaimed for all time, or at least until the next rain (BOTTOM).

HUMANS AND ANIMALS SHARE common ground in West Michigan. While a kitten returns one child's curiosity (OPPOSITE), a tame dove finds a haven in the gentle hand of Newaygo potter George DeVries (ABOVE).

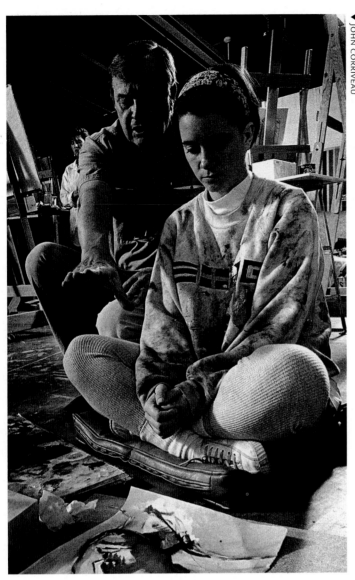

VINTAGE CLOTHING DEALER
Barbara Van Wienen readies her
treasures for display at Nobody's
Sweetheart, a haven for lovers of
yesterday's couture and other
antiques.

HIDING BEHIND RETRO SHADES, a modish mannequin beckons window-shoppers as she models a frothy white gown.

HEADS DOWN IN PURPOSEFUL PLAY, creative kids make their own mark on the city during Festival of the Arts.

BOWING REVERENTLY OVER THEIR work, Tibetan monks created a richly colored sand mandala during a 1995 visit to Grand Rapids. As soon as the millions of grains were in place, the mandala, believed to heal living beings and their environment, was ceremoniously destroyed, with some of the sand poured into the Grand River.

GRAND RAPIDS IS HOME TO AN active community of artists, including (CLOCKWISE FROM OPPOSITE TOP) abstract painter José Narezo, artist/architect Gretchen Minnhaar, world-famous artist Paul Collins, and watercolorist Mark Wilkens.

ALL ACROSS THE CITY, AT ANY GIVEN moment, you'll find voices, spirits, and even arms lifted in celebration of the arts. The Grand Rapids Ballet has brought its elegant style and precision to the stage for more than 25 years (OPPOSITE TOP). Equally disciplined are the techniques of tai chi, learned by these senior citizens through the Gerontology Network of Kent County (OPPOSITE BOTTOM). And at Grand Valley State University, music students train their voices under the direction of faculty member Ellen Pool (LEFT).

GREATER GRAND RAPIDS

EACH WEDNESDAY NIGHT DURING the summer, nearly 10,000 music lovers get into the groove as local radio station WLAV hosts *Blues on the Mall*, featuring bands from across the country.

SHOPS, COFFEE BARS, AND NEIGH-
borhood cafés abound in Eastown,
one of Grand Rapids' hippest and
quirkiest districts. Each summer,
the Eastown Street Fair promises
music, food, and oodles of fun,
thanks in part to traveling per-
former "Crazy Richard" (TOP).

GREATER GRAND RAPIDS

EMBRACING ETHNIC DIVERSITY has long been an important part of Grand Rapids life. The region celebrates its Native American heritage through traditional pow-wows and ceremonial dress (LEFT AND OPPOSITE TOP). And in 1995, a group of Tibetan monks were welcomed to town with a public ceremony at the Urban Institute for Contemporary Arts (OPPOSITE BOTTOM).

STIRRING UP APPETITES IS THE specialty of the house at San Chez, downtown's popular purveyor of tapas delights.

GREATER GRAND RAPIDS

ANY TIME IS THE RIGHT TIME TO enjoy one of the city's many restaurants and cafés. In East Grand Rapids, Crisan's Coffee Company fits the bill on a quiet afternoon (OPPOSITE), Jersey Junction serves up sandwiches and ice cream to the after-school and weekend crowd (TOP LEFT), and Rose's offers alfresco eats with striking views of Reeds Lake (TOP RIGHT). Further west is Gibson's, where sophisticated dining makes for a spectacular Sunday brunch (BOTTOM LEFT). And gone but not forgotten, Socrates Newscenter was a longtime favorite of Eastown's hip, literate, and chess-loving locals (BOTTOM RIGHT).

GREATER GRAND RAPIDS

WHEN THE SUN GOES DOWN, downtown Grand Rapids lights up with entertainment options, from Dr. J's Jazz Emporium, owned by trombonist and local music icon John Hair (OPPOSITE), to the Rhythm Kitchen Café, where soulful sounds fill the darkness (ABOVE).

THE DIM GLOW OF THE OLD GREY-hound station—now part of the city's past—belies its former role as a gateway to destinations near and far.

GREATER GRAND RAPIDS

WITH A TRADITION OF HIGH-quality productions that dates to the 1920s, the Grand Rapids Civic Theatre is the oldest community theater in Michigan and the third-oldest in the nation. Having occu-pied a number of venues over the years, the organization today makes its home at the former Majestic Theatre, a turn-of-the-century auditorium on Division Avenue downtown.

TRANQUIL AS EVER, REEDS LAKE in East Grand Rapids has been a favorite spot for pleasure-seekers since the late 1800s, when it became a popular resort (RIGHT). Long gone are the clubhouse and steamboats, but the friendly waters still welcome sailors, swimmers, and fishers (PAGES 232 AND 233).

THE QUIET WATERS OF WEST Michigan offer a warm invitation to those who want to relax with their fishing poles, feel the waves lap against their legs, or merely enjoy the sun-drenched vistas (PAGES 236-239).

THE CITY THAT WORKS

GREATER GRAND RAPIDS

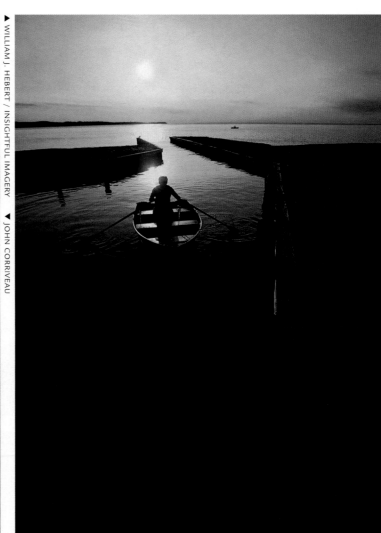

AS THE SINKING SUN SPILLS ITS golden glow onto a watery canvas, solitary rowers revel in the serenity of day's end.

GREATER GRAND RAPIDS

Only an hour's drive from Grand Rapids, picturesque Saugatuck entices visitors with an abundance of charm. After a day of shopping in the town's dozens of elegant and eclectic boutiques, a sunny seat on the shore of the Kalamazoo River offers much-needed rest for weary feet (OPPOSITE). Perhaps nothing is as relaxing, though, as a slow ride across the water on North America's only remaining hand-cranked chain ferry (ABOVE).

MOUNTAINOUS SAND DUNES ALONG
Lake Michigan's shore challenge
even the most determined climbers, and every sinking step up the
slopes testifies to Mother Nature's
imposing dominance (PAGES 246
AND 247).

THE LIVING DOESN'T GET ANY
easier than summertime on the
Big Lake, as sun worshippers flock
to the sandy beaches of Charles
Mears State Park in Pentwater.

IN HOLLAND, THE NORTH PIERHEAD
challenges fishers to try their luck
by day (ABOVE), while the historic
lighthouse known as Big Red invites strollers to admire the water
by night (PAGES 250 AND 251).

A FIERY SUN SETS GRAND HAVEN'S pier and lighthouse aglow, giving creedance to the old adage: red sky at night, sailor's delight (PAGES 252 AND 253). Back in the city, dusk silhouettes the sharp angles of corporate Grand Rapids (ABOVE) and the elegant curves of the Basilica of St. Adalbert (OPPOSITE).

PROFILES IN EXCELLENCE

A LOOK AT THE CORPORATIONS, BUSINESSES, PROFESSIONAL GROUPS, AND COMMUNITY SERVICE ORGANIZATIONS THAT HAVE MADE THIS BOOK POSSIBLE. THEIR STORIES—OFFERING AN INFORMAL CHRONICLE OF THE LOCAL BUSINESS COMMUNITY—ARE ARRANGED ACCORDING TO THE DATE THEY WERE ESTABLISHED IN GREATER GRAND RAPIDS.

ADAC ■ AMERICAN SEATING ■ AMWAY CORPORATION ■ AMWAY GRAND PLAZA HOTEL ■ AQUINAS COLLEGE ■ AUTOCAM CORPORATION ■ BELWITH INTERNATIONAL, LTD. ■ BENTELER AUTOMOTIVE CORPORATION ■ BERTSCH COMPANY ■ BETZ INDUSTRIES ■ BLUE CROSS/BLUE SHIELD OF MICHIGAN ■ BULMAN PRODUCTS, INC. ■ BUTTERBALL FARMS, INC. ■ CALVIN COLLEGE ■ CALVIN THEOLOGICAL SEMINARY ■ THE CHRISTIAN REFORMED CHURCH IN NORTH AMERICA ■ CITY OF GRAND RAPIDS ■ CONSUMERS ENERGY ■ COUNTRY FRESH, INC. ■ CPR/MICROAGE ■ CUSTER OFFICE ENVIRONMENTS ■ DAVENPORT COLLEGE ■ DEVRIES COMPANIES ■ DIESEL TECHNOLOGY COMPANY ■ DISTRIBUTION PLANNING INCORPORATED (DPI) ■ DVK CONSTRUCTION, INC. ■ FALCON FOAM ■ FEYEN-ZYLSTRA ■ FOREMOST CORPORATION OF AMERICA ■ G&T INDUSTRIES, INC. ■ GEMINI PUBLICATIONS ■ GORDON FOOD SERVICE ■ GRAND RAPIDS COMMUNITY COLLEGE ■ GRAND VALLEY STATE UNIVERSITY ■ GUARDSMAN PRODUCTS, A UNIT OF LILLY INDUSTRIES, INC. ■ GUS MACKER ENTERPRISES ■ HAVILAND ENTERPRISES, INC. ■ HOLLAND AMERICAN WAFER COMPANY ■ HOPE COLLEGE ■ HOPE NETWORK ■ HS DIE & ENGINEERING INC. ■ HUNGERFORD, ALDRIN, NICHOLS & CARTER, P.C. ■ THE HUNTINGTON NATIONAL BANK ■ INTERFACEAR ■ IRWIN SEATING COMPANY ■ J.W. MESSNER INC. ■ KENDALL COLLEGE OF ART & DESIGN ■ KENT COUNTY INTERNATIONAL AIRPORT ■ LEEDY MANUFACTURING CO. ■ LEITZ TOOLING SYSTEMS, INC. ■ LIGHT METALS CORPORATION ■ MARY FREE BED HOSPITAL AND REHABILITATION CENTER ■ MASTER FINISH CO. ■ METRO HEALTH ■ MICHIGAN WIRE PROCESSING COMPANY, INC. ■ MILLER, JOHNSON, SNELL & CUMMISKEY, P.L.C. ■ MOORE & BRUGGINK, INC. ■ NATIONAL CITY BANK ■ OLD KENT BANK ■ OLIVER PRODUCTS COMPANY ■ OWENS-AMES-KIMBALL CO. ■ PAULSTRA CRC ■ PIONEER INCORPORATED ■ PLASTIC MOLD TECHNOLOGY ■ PRICE, HENEVELD, COOPER, DEWITT & LITTON ■ PRIDGEON & CLAY, INC. ■ PROGRESSIVE DIE & AUTOMATION, INC. ■ PUBLIC MUSEUM OF GRAND RAPIDS ■ RAMBLEWOOD EXECUTIVE SUITES ■ RAPID DIE & ENGINEERING ■ RAPISTAN SYSTEMS, DIVISION MANNESMANN DEMATIC, A.G. ■ THE RIGHT PLACE PROGRAM ■ ROBERT GROOTERS DEVELOPMENT COMPANY ■ ROHDE CONSTRUCTION COMPANY ■ SAINT MARY'S HEALTH SERVICES ■ S.J. WISINSKI & COMPANY ■ SMITHS INDUSTRIES AEROSPACE ■ SPARTAN STORES, INC. ■ SPECTRUM HEALTH ■ SPECTRUM INDUSTRIES INC. ■ STEELCASE INC. ■ STILES MACHINERY, INC. ■ SUSPA INCORPORATED ■ TOOLING SYSTEMS GROUP ■ TWOHEY MAGGINI, PLC ■ VAN'S DELIVERY SERVICE, INC. ■ VICKERS ELECTROMECHANICAL DIVISION ■ WINKELMANN ASSOCIATES-ARCHITECTS, P.C. ■ WKLQ, WLAV, WBBL/MICHIGAN MEDIA, INC. ■ WOLVERINE BUILDING GROUP ■ WOLVERINE WORLD WIDE, INC. ■ WOOD TV8 ■ WORLDCOM ■ YAMAHA CORPORATION OF AMERICA

1847-1939

SPECTRUM HEALTH MIGHT BE WEST MICHIGAN'S NEWEST HEALTH care system, but it is far from being a newcomer to the area. Quite the contrary, Spectrum Health represents the union of two long-established, award-winning hospitals—Blodgett Memorial Medical Center and Butterworth Hospital.

Separately, the two facilities were consistently rated among the finest in the country. Together, as Spectrum Health, they form a partnership that makes the hospitals even stronger than they were before.

Spectrum Health was founded in 1997, but it is already recognized as one of the finest health systems in the country. With a network of more than 1,200 primary care physicians and specialists, Spectrum Health has a total of four acute care hospitals, including West Michigan's only recognized children's hospital. The system has four subacute care skilled nursing facilities, and a variety of clinics offering multiple services in more than two dozen regional community hospitals. Spectrum also has the largest managed care plan in the region, and a state-of-the-art research and education facility that brings the latest technologies to area clinicians and educators.

A LONG HISTORY OF CARING

On a cold December day in 1846, a small group of women from several area churches gathered in a one-room schoolhouse on Prospect Hill. Their mission was clearly defined: they would pull together a plan to help ease the human suffering they saw around them. The women agreed to pool their volunteer efforts to help feed, house, and clothe needy people in their village—a village that would later become the city of Grand Rapids. And three weeks later, they signed a formal consti-

Spectrum Health's mission is to improve the health of the community by serving each individual and family with superior quality personal care.

The Spectrum Health-Downtown Campus continues to be a beacon of hope for West Michigan.

tution creating the Female Union Charitable Association, an organization devoted to looking after the needs of the poor and sick people in its community. Little did these women know that 150 years later, the organization they had founded in a drafty old schoolhouse would become Blodgett Memorial Medical Center, a major teaching hospital known as one of the leading health care facilities in the country.

By the 1870s, Grand Rapids had grown immensely, with improvements in transportation and technology and a diverse variety of new manufacturing plants. The result was an exploding labor market that lured many workers and their families to move to Grand Rapids, causing the city's population to swell by more than 750 percent in a 20-year period. Of course, along with that rapid growth came an increase in Grand Rapids' population of sick, poor, and needy.

The year was 1873 when Reverend Samuel Earp asked the ladies of his congregation to help care for several elderly members of his parish, and they responded by founding St. Mark's Church Home. Just like the founders of the Female Union Charitable Association 26 years before, these women had no way of knowing that the facility they founded, which served a total of six elderly women in its first year, would someday become a major hospital called Butterworth. All they knew was that people needed them, and they wanted to help. This dedication to caring was the legacy of these founders, and it has continued to live on as the heart and soul of Butterworth Hospital.

By coming together to form Spectrum Health, Blodgett and Butterworth have combined their strengths, and now offer West Michigan top-quality health care. Spectrum Health's mission is "to improve the health of the community by serving each individual with superior quality personal care." And this commitment is shared by everyone in the organization. "What we had before were two high-quality, award-winning

organizations that have now joined together to become one, which greatly increases our benefit to the community," says Terrence M. O'Rourke, Spectrum Health's president and CEO. "It's our goal to set the standard for superior quality and cost-effective personal care—to ultimately become West Michigan's recognized leader in health care and medicine."

PEOPLE WHO CARE

As Butterworth and Blodgett grew through the years, the spirit of caring increased along with them, and it's that spirit that forms the foundation of Spectrum Health. It's a health system where patients and visitors are treated with sensitivity, understanding, and warmth by staff members for whom the art of caring is as important as their professional training. The physicians, nurses, technicians, and other health care professionals at Spectrum Health comprise a team of highly talented people who have been repeatedly recognized for the quality of care they provide.

Spectrum Health's focus is on providing the highest level of personal attention and care available today, qualities that are often

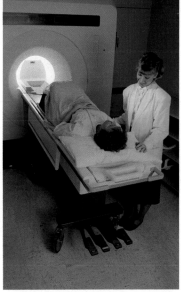

missing from a large health system. "Health care is often an emotional issue for people," O'Rourke says, "so it's up to us to show patients we genuinely care about them, and will do everything possible to make their stay a positive experience. We're proud of the statistics that rate us at the top of the scale, but we believe the only true measurement of our service is how our patients feel about us."

William G. Gonzalez, former Butterworth president and now Spectrum Health's chief health system officer, notes that what

The Spectrum Health-East Campus symbolizes a 150-year tradition of medical excellence (top).

Spectrum Health's focus is on providing the highest level of personal attention and care available today (bottom).

Spectrum Health offers West Michigan far surpasses what either Blodgett or Butterworth was able to do separately. "We'll continue to learn from each other and build on each other's strengths, and in the process will keep raising our own levels of quality," he says. "Plus, by combining financial resources, we're able to invest in more costly technology and the highest levels of specialized medicine—while still being able to control our costs.

"There's something else we can offer too," Gonzalez adds, "and that's increased opportunities for our employees. We want to serve them in the same way we serve our patients, so that Spectrum Health will continually attract the very best health care professionals in the business."

SUPERIOR HEALTH CARE

The main Spectrum Health facilities include the Downtown Campus, East Campus, South Campus, and Surgical Center-East Paris. The Downtown and East campus hospitals provide highly specialized services such as a comprehensive orthopedic program, including arthritis and reconstructive surgery, and spe-

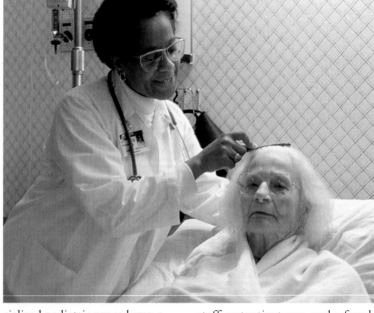

Spectrum Health's nurses, physicians, and support staff have been repeatedly recognized for the quality of care they provide (top).

Spectrum Health's trauma staff specializes in treating critically injured or ill patients (bottom).

cialized pediatric procedures; a widely recognized heart and vascular program; neurosciences, including a neuro intensive care unit for patients with head and spine injuries; obstetric, high-risk obstetric, perinatal, and infertility programs; neonatal services; cancer treatment and screening programs; a digestive diseases program, which offers medical and surgical specialties; a regional burn center, with extensive inpatient services,

staff, outpatient care, and referral resources; and DeVos Children's Hospital, which is completely dedicated to serving the unique needs of children and includes the only pediatric cancer center on this side of the state.

The Spectrum Health trauma services include a Level I trauma center, which is the first of its kind in West Michigan and specializes in treating patients who are critically injured or ill. Open for treatment seven days a week, 24 hours a day, the center is staffed by teams of physicians, nurses, respiratory therapists, and radiology and medical technologists—all highly trained in the field of critical care. And because time plays such an urgent role in the treatment of critically ill or injured patients, Spectrum Health owns and operates the Aero Med helicopter, which was one of the first hospital-owned and -operated air medical services in the country.

The Surgical Center-East Paris site offers day surgery suites, physician offices, and other general or specialized patient services. And the South Campus, another Spectrum Health facility, is a unique integrated health center that offers a variety of services for the whole family, including outpatient surgery, a laboratory, a radiology department, both physical and occupational therapy, a pharmacy, a child care center, and a community room.

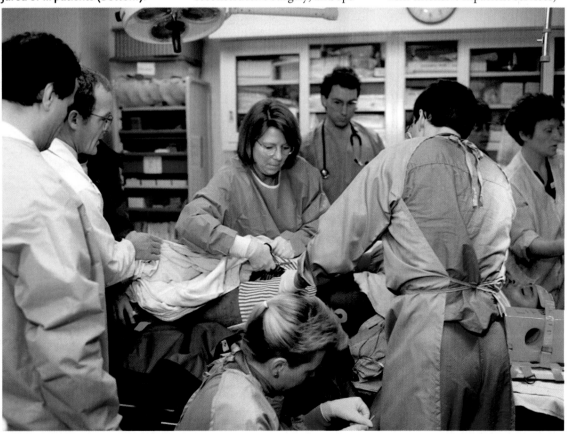

By mid-1999, one of the finest research and education centers in the United States, the Van Andel Institute for Medical Education and Research, will open on the Downtown Campus. The facility will be led by Dr. Luis Tomatis, a well-known cardiologist and surgeon who helped pioneer cardiac bypass surgery in West Michigan. The institute's scientific board of advisers will include four Nobel Prize winners, and it will be dedicated to "preserving, enhancing, and expanding the frontiers of medical science."

HEALTH CARE WHERE IT'S NEEDED

Spectrum Health's mission of caring for the people of West Michigan goes far beyond treating those who are inside the hospital. "We have beautiful facilities here, the best in the country," Gonzalez says. "But there's a whole population out there we're not able to reach, either because they don't have insurance, don't have transportation, or just don't have knowledge about health care. It's our job to reach out and try to find a way to help these people."

As president of Butterworth, Gonzalez was instrumental in helping Cherry Street Health Services get back on its feet, and the clinic now provides a full range of health care services to patients on a sliding-fee basis. Cherry Street also set up another neighborhood clinic, the West Side Health Center, and Gonzalez says Spectrum Health will continue to work toward breaking down the barriers to health care until all geographic areas are served.

"We're really on the threshold of a wonderful opportunity for this community," O'Rourke says, "because at Spectrum Health, we're able to provide an unparalleled array of highly specialized services, superior quality, and cost-effective personal care. When we were separate, as Blodgett Memorial Medical Center and Butterworth Hospital, we were both superior health care organizations. Together, we'll be better than we ever were before."

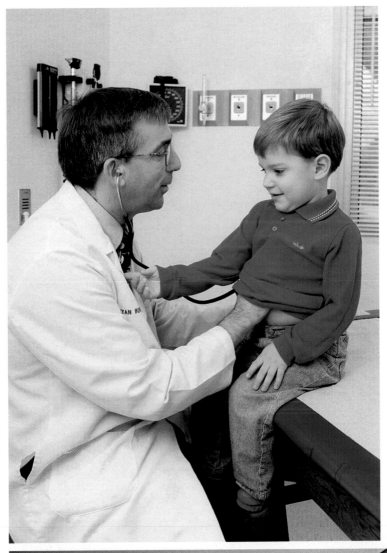

Spectrum Health provides West Michigan with highly specialized services such as comprehensive pediatric care (top).

Aero Med was one of the first hospital-owned and -operated air medical services in the country (bottom).

s MICHIGAN'S SECOND-LARGEST CITY, GRAND RAPIDS OFFERS A small-town quality of life with a big-city atmosphere. Grand Rapids is an ethnically and racially diverse community that serves as the economic, legal, health care, and cultural center of West Michigan. A three-time All-America City, Grand

Rapids is proud of its vitality, work ethic, innovation, social responsibility, and skilled workforce. Grand Rapids attributes its continuing growth to a diverse manufacturing base, low unemployment, low health care costs, affordable housing, and a reputation as a good place to raise a family.

Grand Rapids has been called the driving force behind the high performance of Michigan's renaissance. A highly diversified and growing economy helps small businesses thrive. Known at one time as the Furniture City, for its concentration of wood finishing, today it is home to the world's largest office furniture manufacturers. In the past 10 years, employment has grown by nearly 40 percent and manufacturing job growth has increased by 17 percent, compared to a national decline of 3 percent. Grand Rapids' unemployment rate is less than 4 percent. To encourage redevelopment, Grand Rapids' 800-acre Renaissance Zone has eliminated state and city taxes for 15 years, while new state laws are making it easier for property owners to reuse environmentally damaged sites.

In the last few years, downtown Grand Rapids has undergone un-

Clockwise from top left:
A renovated Victorian home depicts the heart of the Heritage Hill neighborhood.

One of Grand Rapids' attractions is the Gerald R. Ford Museum.

A three-time All-America City, Grand Rapids is proud of its vitality, work ethic, innovation, social responsibility, and skilled workforce. The city attributes its continuing growth to a diverse manufacturing base, low unemployment, low health care costs, affordable housing, and a reputation as a good place to raise a family.

A half-million people gather in Calder Plaza every June for the Festival of the Arts.

precedented growth. Much of this is due to the construction of the Van Andel Arena, a 10,000-seat, state-of-the-art facility that is home to the Grand Rapids Griffins of the International Hockey League; the Grand Rapids Hoops of the Continental Basketball Association; and the Grand Rapids Rampage, the city's new arena football team. The arena is also one of the Midwest's hottest venues for concerts and other attractions, prompting millions of dollars to be poured into the conversion of surround-

ing older buildings and warehouses into new restaurants, clubs, shops, and luxurious loft apartments and condominiums.

With one of the country's 10 most affordable housing markets, Grand Rapids boasts high home ownership and a nationally registered historic district of restored, turn-of-the-century Victorian homes. Grand Rapids has more than 100 neighborhood parks, 10 public swimming pools, a public museum, the Gerald R. Ford Museum, the Children's Museum, a zoo and aquarium, and an art museum.

The city has eight hospitals, including the DeVos Women and Children's Hospital and Spectrum Health, a recent merger of two of the nation's top 100 hospitals. Plans are under way for Grand Rapids to become a major medical research center with the opening of the Van Andel Institute. Grand Rapids is also home to 13 colleges and universities, with a $100 million addition to Grand Valley State University's campus planned in 2000.

The people, the institutions, and all of the activity provide the substance behind Grand Rapids' slogan, Building a Better Grand Rapids by Design.

ESTABLISHED IN 1854, THE PUBLIC MUSEUM OF GRAND RAPIDS IS Michigan's largest and oldest general museum. ■ The Public Museum's exhibitions and programs can be experienced at four principal and separate sites: the flagship Van Andel Museum Center, which also houses the Roger B. Chaffee

Planetarium; Blandford Nature Center; and the Voigt House Victorian Museum. These four sites collectively attract more than 400,000 visitors per year.

VAN ANDEL MUSEUM CENTER

Located in the heart of downtown Grand Rapids, this amazing, 150,000-square-foot facility features such exhibitions as a life-size re-creation of urban Grand Rapids at the turn of the century. *Anishinabek: People of this Place* has been called the finest Great Lakes Indian exhibition to be found in Michigan. *The Furniture City*, the museum's largest exhibit, show-

cases Grand Rapids' manufacturing heritage. And, a fully restored and operating antique carousel features 1,200 lights; elaborately jeweled, carved, and painted wooden horses; two chariots; and six menagerie animals.

ROGER B. CHAFFEE PLANETARIUM

Named in honor of the Grand Rapids astronaut who lost his life in the 1967 Apollo spacecraft fire, the Roger B. Chaffee Planetarium is a 21st-century space exploration theater. The domed multimedia experience features high-powered digital sound, a battery of special effects and video projectors, a 360-degree domed screen, and an impressive three-dimensional simulation device that carries visitors on exotic journeys from interplanetary space to the miniature universe of the atom.

VOIGT HOUSE VICTORIAN MUSEUM

A carefully preserved, turreted mansion and its quaint carriage house and period garden transport visitors back in time to soak in the fascinating details of everyday life during the late 19th century at Voigt House Victorian Museum. Located in the heart of Heritage Hill, Grand

Rapids' National Register of Historic Places district, this unique 1895 home has been preserved along with its original furnishings and the personal possessions of the Carl G.A. Voigt family.

BLANDFORD NATURE CENTER

The Public Museum not only collects and exhibits natural history specimens, but at its Blandford Nature Center, it preserves within the city limits a beautiful hardwood forest, fields, ponds, and streams, connected by nearly 4.5 miles of interpretive hiking trails. Open year-round, Blandford Nature Center allows visitors to explore a variety of habitats, enjoy an array of colorful wildflowers in the spring, observe native wildlife in the summer, relish the vibrant colors of autumn, and even cross-country ski in the winter.

For nearly 150 years, the Public Museum of Grand Rapids has contributed to the quality of life in West Michigan by providing visitors with opportunities to learn from yesterday, analyze today, and dream about tomorrow. The community's investment of more than $45 million into its properties ensures that the museum's second 150 years will be as vital as its first.

Clockwise from top:
Overlooking the Grand River, the Public Museum's new Van Andel Museum Center houses interactive exhibitions that make history and natural science come alive. Its Cook Carousel Pavilion, jutting out over the river, is a distinctive architectural feature.

More than four miles of interpretive trails, many of which are wheelchair accessible, traverse 143 acres of forest, ponds, and streams at the Public Museum's Blandford Nature Center.

Resembling a French château, Voigt House preserves a treasure trove of Victoriana in the heart of Heritage Hill, Grand Rapids' National Register of Historic Places neighborhood.

SOME LANDMARKS IN GRAND RAPIDS ARE SO FAMILIAR THAT THEIR names are practically synonymous with the city's. A few that fit this description are the Grand River, Pearl Street Bridge, Gerald R. Ford Museum, Heritage Hill, and, of course, Old Kent Bank. Chartered in 1853 as the Daniel Ball Exchange Bank,

Old Kent is well known in Grand Rapids, as well as throughout Michigan and Illinois, for its dependability, quality products and services, and ongoing commitment to continuously exceed its customers' expectations.

A REPUTATION FOR CONSISTENT PERFORMANCE

Old Kent prides itself on providing customers with the widest range of products and services, while continuing to keep customer service on a personal level. Tanya Berg, vice president, marketing communications, says the bank is highly customer driven. "It's our goal to earn and retain the respect, confidence, and loyalty of our customers," says Berg, "and

to serve them so they'll benefit from their association with us."

Old Kent serves its customers with a wide variety of quality business and personal banking products and services. The corporation specializes in five lines of business: investment and insurance services, which include trusts, asset management programs, 401(k) programs, and others; retail banking, including branch banking, consumer loans, electronic banking, and small-business banking; corporate banking, which includes commercial lending, deposit services, cash management products, leasing programs, and international services; mortgage banking, including mortgage origination and relocation services; and community banking,

which offers banking products and services to retail and commercial customers in smaller markets, and focuses on providing full-service, person-to-person banking.

A FULL-SERVICE FINANCIAL SERVICES ORGANIZATION

As a premier financial institution, Old Kent has a large market share in its core markets, and its presence and reputation are steadily growing, not only in West Michigan, but also in the metro Detroit and suburban Chicago areas. To best serve those markets, the bank has shifted from being a commercial bank to a full-service company that offers an array of financial services.

Over the years, Old Kent's growth has steadily continued. When Old Kent Financial Corporation (OKFC) was first formed in 1972, it was a $340 million bank with 27 offices. By 1988, it had grown into an $8 billion regional bank holding company with nearly 200 offices in Michigan and Illinois. By year-end, 1997 assets were worth $13.8 billion, and OKFC was operating 228 full-service banking offices, including a growing number of supermarket branches, as well as more than 100 mortgage offices in 25 states throughout the country. In addition, the Old Kent Insurance Group has grown to become the largest independent insurance agency in western Michigan and one of the top 50 independent insurance agencies in the United States.

DISTINCTIONS AND HONORS, COMMUNITY EFFORTS

Over the years, Old Kent's performance has won the bank repeated recognition and acknowledgments. In 1997, *Money* magazine listed Old Kent as an All-Star stock. In recognition of its Small Business Association (SBA) lending activity

In 1964, the Old Kent Bank Building was constructed as the first new downtown office building in 40 years, kicking off Grand Rapids' Urban Renewal Project.

in the same year, Old Kent was ranked as the number two SBA lender in Michigan and was named SBA Lender of the Year in Illinois. In April 1994, *U.S. Banker* magazine rated Old Kent first in Michigan and 11th nationally for Top 100 Performance. It was also rated the top-performing bank holding company in Michigan and was ranked 18th nationally in *Bank Management* magazine's 1993 annual rating of the nation's 100 largest bank holding companies. Old Kent had also previously won the distinction of top performing bank in 1989. In 1988, OKFC ranked third in the United States in overall performance in *U.S. Banker*'s report on the nation's top 100 bank holding companies. And as for Old Kent's record of continued financial success, it speaks for itself: 1997 was the 39th consecutive year that Old Kent achieved record earnings and increased dividends, ranking the bank eighth among 16,000 publicly traded companies in the United States in that category.

Something Old Kent has long been known and respected for is its history of active community involvement. In 1964, the bank constructed the Old Kent Bank Building, the first new downtown office building in 40 years, which kicked off Grand Rapids' Urban Renewal Project. The bank continues to exceed Community Reinvestment Act (CRA) requirements, serving as primary mortgage lender for the Inner City Christian Federation, a Grand Rapids group that finds housing for low- to moderate-income persons. Old Kent is also a primary investor in the Pleasant-Prospect Dividend Housing Partnership, and is involved in the Local Initiatives Support Coalition, a consortium of Grand Rapids banks and foundations that have contributed seed money for new business and revitalization projects. In 1997 alone, nearly 1,000 families benefited from Old Kent's participation in seminars and workshops on such topics as credit and credit repair, home ownership and maintenance, budgeting, small-business management, and individual money management.

For many years, Old Kent has provided active support for other community organizations, charities, and events, including annual support of United Way campaigns and an ongoing tutoring program with neighborhood schools. And, of course, for the past 20 years Old Kent has sponsored the famous Old Kent River Bank Run, which has become the top 25K road race in the country.

Continuing to Grow, Continuing to Serve

Berg says that, in the future, Old Kent will continue to pursue its mission of being a high-performing, independent financial services company, and will maintain its commitment to providing exceptional service to customers. "We're a progressive organization that's looking to build long-term, multi-service customer relationships," she says. "We'll continue to pursue new products that better meet our customers' needs, and we'll

For the past 20 years, Old Kent has sponsored the famous Old Kent River Bank Run, which has become the top 25K road race in the country (top).

Old Kent Park is the home of the West Michigan Whitecaps minor-league baseball team (bottom).

continue to grow and expand our presence. But one thing we won't lose is the thing we've been known for since the beginning: our commitment to offer the products, resources, and expertise of a large financial services company, combined with the responsiveness and personal service of a smaller bank."

"**A**S PEOPLE CALLED BY GOD, WE SEE THE CHURCH AS A GROWING, diverse family of vibrant congregations in which thousands worship God celebratively, grow in His Word, and honor the Creator as Lord." These words are from the mission statement of the Christian Reformed Church in North America (CRC), a denomination that was founded in Grand Rapids in 1857. Beginning with fewer than 10 congregations, the CRC's membership has increased during the decades that have followed, initially due to continued immigration from Europe, and in more recent decades through outreach and community service. Today, the CRC has 200 congregations in West Michigan, has nearly 1,000 throughout the United States and Canada, and is known and respected for its significant ministry in 30 countries around the world.

Although based in Grand Rapids, the work of the people of the Christian Reformed Church is diverse and impacts people worldwide through missions and relief work, multilingual publications, and radio and television broadcasts.

PHIL SCHAAFSMA PHOTOGRAPHY

A RICH HISTORY

Many settlers migrated to the United States during the 1840s and initially joined the congregations of the Reformed Church in America, a denomination with similar historical and theological roots that had established itself in the United States in the 1600s. To this day, the Reformed Church remains a sister denomination of the CRC. Continued immigration into the United States, supplemented in the 20th century by immigration into Canada, sustained the growth of the CRC well into the 1950s.

After its formation, the CRC expanded its ministry beyond the member congregations by establishing Calvin College and Seminary in 1876. In the 1890s, the CRC initiated its outreach efforts by establishing its World Missions and Home Missions agencies. In the century that followed, additional agencies were added, such as CRC Publications, *The Back to God Hour/Faith 20*, Christian Reformed World Relief Committee (CRWRC), and Pastoral Ministries. All of these agencies and institutions function under the auspices of the synod of the Christian Reformed Church, and are governed by the board of trustees of the church.

CHANGES IN THE CRC

While the basic values and beliefs of the Christian Reformed Church have not changed over time, many practices, emphases, and circumstances, as well as the culture and general mind-set of church members, have changed greatly. One particularly significant change is the fact that today, within the boundaries of the United States and Canada, the CRC worships in 14 different language groups—a far cry from the Dutch-only preaching that was customary until the early part of the twentieth century.

Another difference is that the CRC has moved toward the mainstream of Protestantism in North America, and is moving away from its European influences of previous decades. Yet, according to Dr. Peter Borgdorff, executive director of ministries, the mission of the CRC has remained the same in spite of its many changes. "The Christian Reformed Church preaches a faith that recognizes the sovereignty of God over all of creation," he says, "and calls people to personal faith and commitment to a personal God. And though we believe that change is essential for us to remain a healthy, vibrant denomination, our mission and core values will not change. It's an essential part of who we are, and what we are trying to achieve."

Borgdorff says the CRC has adopted a strategic plan that will help the denomination in looking toward its future. "We intend to continue being a dynamic church," he says, "one that seeks diversity and celebrates it, and one that plants many new congregations. I am very optimistic about the CRC because it has been given fantastic resources—both human and financial—which will allow us to be an active and responsive organization. At the same time, because the church is always God's; our future is in His hands."

ORIGINALLY FOUNDED IN 1876 AS THE DENOMINATIONAL seminary of the Christian Reformed Church in North America, Calvin Theological Seminary trains pastors and other leaders for the church, while welcoming others from all denominations who wish to receive theological education or pastoral preparation.

Today—along with its affiliate, Calvin College—Calvin Theological Seminary is situated on the spacious, attractive Knollcrest Campus in southeast Grand Rapids, which can be accessed from both Burton Street and the East Beltline. The seminary building was dedicated in 1960 and has been expanded twice since. Its serene setting and dignified, contemporary character make the seminary a favored spot for retreats, conferences, and weddings.

FOSTERING THE STUDY OF THEOLOGY

Well known for its academic rigor and excellence, Calvin Theological Seminary offers six degrees, including two at the graduate level—the master of theology and the doctor of philosophy. Its graduates serve on numerous theological faculties worldwide, and a number are well-known theological leaders. The school attracts students from around the world—particularly in its graduate programs—from countries in Asia, Africa, Latin America, and Eastern Europe. Some 20 percent of its 300 students are from overseas, and 40 percent have a non-Christian Reformed background.

Calvin's student body is served by 30 full-time and part-time faculty. The interaction between students and faculty is warm, intimate, engaging, and rewarding, and special attention is given to limiting class size for maximum interaction for a quality education.

Calvin Theological Seminary's superbly trained faculty hold degrees from recognized North American and European universities. A number are widely published and respected in their fields, and they are all distinguished spokespersons for the Reformed faith.

The international and ecumenical character of the Calvin seminary makes it a stimulating environment for theological education. The Hekman Library, which serves both Calvin College and Calvin Seminary, exceeds 600,000 titles in its holdings, a third of which are in theology. In addition, such special collections as the H. Henry Meeter Center for Calvin Studies and the Heritage Hall Collection enhance the myriad research opportunities on campus. The Meeter Center is one of the world's leading centers for Reformation and post-Reformation study, particularly the life and influence of John Calvin. The Heritage Collection specializes in Dutch immigration and Reformed religious history.

Since opening its doors, Calvin Theological Seminary has prepared men and women to be outstanding church leaders, and its status as a valuable member of the Grand Rapids community is well recognized.

DELBRIDGE LANGDON JR.

DELBRIDGE LANGDON JR.

Clockwise from top:
Calvin Theological Seminary's serene setting and dignified, contemporary character make the seminary a favored spot for retreats, conferences, and weddings.

Calvin Theological Seminary's superbly trained faculty hold degrees from recognized North American and European universities.

Well known for its academic rigor and excellence, Calvin Theological Seminary offers six degrees, including two at the graduate level—the master of theology and the doctor of philosophy.

ALVIN COLLEGE, FOUNDED IN 1876, IS ONE OF NORTH AMERICA'S largest Christian colleges, offering a comprehensive and diverse liberal arts education that features more than 80 majors and programs. The profile of Calvin's 4,100 students reflects the international draw of the institution: All 50 states plus 38 countries are represented, with 45 percent of the student body coming from outside the state of Michigan. Calvin College has mapped out a bold path for those students—a journey that is both distinctively Christian and academically excellent—as it

Calvin College boasts one of the prettiest campuses in the country. Its 375 rolling acres include an architecturally unified assortment of residence halls, academic buildings, a chapel, an administrative center, and a large athletic facility, as well as a 200-acre ecological preserve (top).

Calvin students enjoy the personal attention of accomplished professors, most of whom hold doctorates or the highest degrees in their respective fields. With small classes, it doesn't take long for professors and students to get to know each other (bottom).

purposefully integrates faith and learning in every class.

Affiliated with the Christian Reformed Church in North America, Calvin's purpose is to engage in vigorous liberal arts education that promotes lifelong Christian service. This aim is reflected in the college's mission statement: "We offer education that is shaped by Christian faith, thought, and practice. We aim to develop knowledge, understanding, and critical inquiry; encourage insightful and creative participation in society; and foster thoughtful, passionate Christian commitments."

CARING AND ACCOMPLISHED PROFESSORS

Calvin students enjoy the personal attention of accomplished professors, most of whom hold doctorates or the highest degrees in their respective fields. The teacher-pupil

relationship at Calvin has many components, but one that students seem to notice and appreciate most is that Calvin professors know their students by name. With small classes, it doesn't take long for professors and students to get to know each other.

Many Calvin professors extend themselves to students beyond the classroom, and maintain contact with current and former students through activities ranging from writing postcards to having pizza parties. Some professors invite foreign students to their homes for holiday celebrations such as Thanksgiving, during which the students would otherwise be alone.

Faculty-student interactions also take place in the academic disciplines. Students in the sciences have many opportunities to do hands-on research with Calvin faculty. Often, these opportunities result in published research papers, allowing students to get a jump-start on becoming published themselves. Students in more classical liberal arts disciplines also have opportunities for hands-on experience. Philosophy students, for example, have worked on indexes for books written by Calvin professors. English students have helped organize the biennial Faith & Writing Conference at Calvin, an event that has featured Nobel and Pulitzer prize winners.

BEAUTIFUL CAMPUS, DIVERSE CLASSES

Calvin boasts one of the prettiest campuses in the country. Its 375 rolling acres include an architecturally unified assortment of residence halls, academic buildings, a chapel, an administrative center, and a large athletic facility, as well as a 200-acre ecological preserve.

The college's curriculum has been expanded to 80 programs and

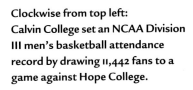

majors. Students can earn a bachelor of arts or a bachelor of science degree in such subjects as biology, business, economics, English, French, German, history, music, philosophy, political science, religion, and sociology. Calvin's professional programs also have grown, and students can earn a bachelor of science degree in accountancy, communication disorders, engineering, nursing, medical technology, occupational therapy, social work, and recreation, as well as a bachelor of fine arts degree. Calvin also offers preprofessional education in such areas as optometry, pharmacy, physical therapy, architecture, and natural resources.

National Recognition

Calvin has been one of the top schools in the Midwest in nine of the last 11 years, according to *U.S. News & World Report*. The magazine's methodical survey is based on everything from faculty resources to alumni satisfaction to class size to library resources. Calvin's efforts to remain superb and affordable have met with approval, as well. Both *Fiske Guide to Colleges* and *U.S. News & World Report* give kudos to Calvin's cost-to-benefit ratio, praising the school for providing an outstanding education at a reasonable price. Calvin's Christian commitment has been well received by the Templeton Foundation, which, over the years, has named Calvin to all seven of its Honor Rolls for Character Building Colleges.

A lively mix of art, lectures, music, athletics, and more provides a wealth of opportunities for students away from the classroom. Classical music is a staple on campus, but so are visits from artists on today's pop charts. Visiting lecturers are common, and in January the school offers its heralded January Series, twice voted the best college lecture series in the country. Sporting events are also a draw, and the basketball rivalry between Calvin and Hope College prompted Calvin to move its 1997 home game to the Van Andel Arena in Grand Rapids, where Calvin promptly set an NCAA Division III attendance record with 11,442 fans.

Calvin is well known in the Grand Rapids community for its emphasis on service. The Service-Learning Center, the school's largest student organization, sets the stage for students during freshman orientation with a massive service project titled StreetFest. During StreetFest, all Calvin first-year students hit the streets of Grand Rapids to serve others, even before they buy their books or take their first class. Each year, some 1,000 Calvin students make a difference in the community through various volunteer projects.

Many Calvin alumni have chosen to live and work in the Grand Rapids area, making a strong impact in the social service, educational, medical, business, religious, and governmental sectors of community life, thus living out Calvin's vision to graduate "agents of renewal" in the academy, church, and society. Through such leadership, both in Grand Rapids and beyond, the graduates of Calvin College will carry out the institution's ideals in their work, their service, and their lives.

N 1866, A YOUNG UNION ARMY VETERAN NAMED CONRAD SWENSBURG came to Grand Rapids and started the state's first college devoted exclusively to business. Initially called Grand Rapids Business College, the school opened with a total of 16 students and a small offering of standard office subjects, such as bookkeeping, penman-

ship, business law, and arithmetic. Today, the school is known as Davenport College, and has more than 16,000 students at multiple locations in Michigan and Indiana.

Davenport is the largest private college in Michigan and offers more than 30 different majors, including marketing, accounting, computer information systems, health care administration, and international business. More than 90 percent of Davenport graduates find work in their chosen fields.

PROGRAMS THAT WORK FOR BUSY ADULTS

Not only does Davenport specialize in helping students prepare for careers, it also helps students find ways to fit college into their lives. Davenport offers flexible class schedules; day, evening, and weekend classes; opportunities to earn credits for prior learning experiences, community leadership, or specialized training; and independent study programs that do not require classroom attendance. On-line classes are also available throughout the year.

Davenport's Adult Accelerated Career Education (AACE) program is designed for busy adults who want to complete their education more quickly. Concentrated, five-

week courses meet once per week in the evening or on the weekend. These courses are also offered in the on-line format. Through the AACE program, students can earn a bachelor's degree in business, management, marketing, or human resources, or they can opt to concentrate on clusters of five to six classes that focus on a specific technical area.

PROGRAMS BUILT AROUND BUSINESS

Davenport College has long been respected as one of the leading business colleges in the Midwest, and according to Cathy Yared, Davenport's director of public relations, a big factor in Davenport's success and growth has been the college's relationships with area businesses. "We have a long history of relationships with local business and industry," she says, "and we constantly put their input to use when we design our programs and courses. This real-world focus is one of the main reasons employers recommend Davenport College to their employees, and why they seek to hire Davenport graduates."

Davenport's School for Business and Industry (SBI) is one example of the school's partnering with local businesses. Located in the W.A.

Lettinga Business Training Center, the school works hand in hand with businesses and corporations to identify organizational needs, and then provides seminars, customized training, and on-site programs and certifications for employees.

Davenport's Career Center, located on Eastern Avenue in Grand Rapids, is designed to offer adults short-term results in upgrading job skills or entering new careers. Various one-year programs are offered in business and health care, and the center features highly flexible scheduling and personalized attention, as well as free brushup classes and lifetime job placement services.

With its real-world focus, multiple program and degree options for busy adults, and solid history of helping students succeed in their chosen careers, Davenport College is an excellent choice for busy, career-focused students. "We have specialized in educating people for the business world for more than 130 years," says Yared, "and that's what really makes us unique. Lots of colleges specialize in educating students. We specialize in educating them throughout their careers."

Davenport's School for Business and Industry (SBI) is located in the W.A. Lettinga Business Training Center. The school works hand in hand with businesses and corporations to identify organizational needs, and then provides seminars, customized training, and on-site programs and certifications for employees (left).

Mabel Engle Hall is the home of the Adult Accelerated Career Education (AACE) program designed for busy adults who want to complete their education more quickly by taking concentrated, five-week courses that meet once per week in the evening or on the weekend (right).

TO THE AVERAGE VISITOR, HOPE COLLEGE QUICKLY REVEALS itself as a truly unique academic institution. It is a caring and supportive place where students feel at home, a Christian college that reaches out and welcomes students of different religious faiths, and a school that encourages

students to strive for their fullest potential, spiritually as well as academically. Hope is also a small college where professors have a deep concern for the growth and development of students, where values and ethics are still very much a priority, and where the goal is to provide an education that helps students grow through knowledge, creativity, and compassion for others.

THEN AND NOW
In 1851, four years after settlers from the Netherlands founded the town of Holland, they formed a secondary school called the Pioneer School to provide education for their children. It was later renamed Holland Academy, and in 1862 the school's first college class was enrolled. In May 1866, the institution was chartered as Hope College, and later that summer the first class of eight students graduated.

Today, Hope has approximately 2,900 students, and offers a variety of courses in 53 majors leading to bachelor of arts, bachelor of music, bachelor of science, and bachelor of science in nursing degrees. Hope is known for academic excellence, and nowhere is this more apparent than in the success rate of its students.

Approximately one-third of Hope's graduates enter graduate schools to pursue advanced training for careers in medicine, science, business, education, economics, the humanities, psychology, and many areas of performing and fine arts. Hope students are accepted into law and medical schools at a rate that's well above the national average. And Hope is among a handful of small colleges that have had four or more graduates begin study through prestigious Rhodes and Marshall scholarships since 1987.

NATIONAL RECOGNITION
Hope College has long been recognized as one of the nation's outstanding liberal arts schools. Designated by the Carnegie Foundation as a national liberal arts college, Hope is the only private, four-year liberal arts college in the United States with national accreditation in art, dance, music, and theater.

A *New York Times* article referred to Hope as "Michigan's well-protected treasure," and *U.S. News & World Report*'s 1998 issue on America's Best Colleges ranked it among the nation's 159 best liberal arts schools. The first edition of *Peterson's Top Colleges for Science* includes Hope among its top 190 four-year programs in the biological, chemical, geological, mathematical, and physical sciences, and the college's science and mathematics program was also recognized as a Program That Works by Project Kaleidoscope of Washington, D.C. Also, in the John Templeton Foundation's biennial Honor Roll for Character-Building Colleges, Hope has been listed seven consecutive times.

CLOSE COMMUNITY CONNECTION
Hope College has maintained a very close connection with the

Holland community. In 1988, the school acquired the historic Knickerbocker Theatre, which has been fully restored and provides the Holland community with movies, concerts, and events. In addition, Hope's new, $15 million Haworth Conference and Learning Center offers businesses a deluxe convention and meeting facility, as well as hotel accommodations.

Hope College has grown and thrived for nearly 150 years, and through its dedication to the academic and personal development of each student, the college will continue its path of excellence for future generations.

Hope College's Dimnent Memorial Chapel, with its 120-foot tower and abundant stained glass, is a community landmark (left).

The Gordon J. and Margaret D. Van Wylen Library provides new technologies, including a computerized public catalog and circulation system (above).

Haworth Conference and Learning Center is the newest addition to the Hope College campus.

I N A 1911 PRODUCT CATALOG PUBLISHED FOR THE BARCLAY, AYERS & Bertsch Company, some of the products advertised included Hoyt's Turtle Brand Waterproof Leather Belting; steam and hot water radiators (both three-column and four-column); Buffalo propeller fans (the quickest and most economical method of ventilating factories,

shops, offices, stores, restaurants, laundries, and private residences); and whitewashing and painting machines.

Today, the company's core business is pipes, valves, and fittings (known as PVF), and the product line differs greatly from the vintage catalog of more than 85 years ago—now including more than 55,000 line items. The company name has been shortened to Bertsch Company, and it is one of the country's leading suppliers for the chemical, pharmaceutical, pulp and paper, automotive, power generation (major utilities companies), food processing, light manufacturing, marine, mining, and mechanical contracting industries.

EXPANDED SERVICES

Bertsch Company was founded in Grand Rapids in 1875 as an industrial supplier to a West Michigan customer base. From the very beginning, the company's specialty product was process piping, which was originally made of wood and has now evolved into materials such as steel, plastic, copper, stainless steel, and fiberglass, among others. Although PVF still forms the Bertsch Company's core business, it has formed four specialty divisions and provides customers with a variety of industrial-related products.

Bertsch Instrumentation Technology (BIT) designs and sells a full range of sophisticated components and systems for monitoring and controlling flow, temperature, level, and pressure. BIT's products include a variety of control valves, level sensors, flow controllers, pressure gauges, digital displays, temperature controllers, turbine flow meters, and variable-speed drives.

Bertsch Pump division sells industrial process pumps to virtually any company that uses pumps

(which applies to most manufacturers). The division sells centrifugal pumps, which are commonly used for pumping water and light liquids; air diaphragm pumps, which are used for heavier liquids that are more viscous; and positive displacement pumps, which pump extremely dense liquids that resemble the consistency of cold molasses.

Bertsch Fluid Sealing division sells mechanical seals and packing, as well as sheet packing and gaskets. According to John Bertsch, a fourth-generation Bertsch and the company's president, this division has extremely high growth potential because the seals help control emissions. "In the old days," he says, "rotating shafts leaked because of their design. With modern sealing technology, there is zero leakage, which is an enormous deterrent to air pollution from emissions."

The fourth division is Bertsch Fire Protection, which supplies all the valves, fittings, piping, and other component parts for commercial sprinkling systems.

A TEAM OF TECHNICAL EXPERTS

Bertsch says the company takes a great deal of pride in having a reputation as an outstanding supplier in the PVF business, and provides customers with not only products, but also high-level technical expertise. "We're known for our problem-solving capabilities," he says, "and that's because our people are so skilled and highly qualified. We have more than 50 technical people on staff, including engineers and other specialists. It's our goal to be perceived as a company that's easy to do business with. We can provide customers with whatever they need, from onetime technical consultation to the whole single-source package." Bertsch says the company serves

more than 3,500 customers, from small companies to industry giants, and many of them—especially large companies like Dow Chemical, Steelcase, Upjohn, and Dow Corning—use Bertsch Company's full range of services, turning to the company for help with design and overall technical consultation, as well as the needed products.

Today, Bertsch Company is the nation's 13th-largest distributor of PVF, and has earned ISO 9002 certification from the International Organization for Standardization. The company has 400 employees located in its 24 branch locations in Michigan, Wisconsin, Ohio, and Indiana. In the past five years, sales have doubled, and today annual sales well exceed $100 million. Bertsch says the company has a virtually nonexistent turnover rate: "I'm a firm believer in hiring capable, talented people, and then providing an environment that keeps them motivated and empowers them to make decisions about the best way to do their jobs.

Around here, we were empowering people before the term became an industry buzzword."

Bertsch Company provides its employees with many opportunities for career growth, including on-the-job training and 100 percent tuition reimbursement. Employees are encouraged to participate on problem-solving and TQM (total quality management) teams, as well as offer feedback on how the company can exceed current quality levels and improve customer service.

Vision for the Future

Bertsch says he expects the company to continue its pattern of growth and expansion, and to concentrate on becoming even more valuable to its customers by forming meaningful partnerships with them. "Our industry is experiencing rapid consolidation," he says, "which means it's getting more and more difficult for small distributors to survive in the marketplace. Our challenge will be to continue getting even better at what we're known for: providing customers with an expansive product line, the highest possible levels of technical expertise, and the best possible value. It's worked for more than 125 years, and I'm confident it will keep working in the future."

JOHN CORRIVEAU

THE HUNTINGTON NAME IS RELATIVELY NEW IN GRAND RAPIDS, but it is attached to more than a century of West Michigan banking tradition. In 1997, Huntington Bancshares Incorporated merged with First Michigan Bank (FMB) Corporation. The merger brought together two companies with a similar

commitment to personal service, the same dedication to meeting the needs of small businesses, and a common legacy as a family-owned institution.

The Huntington selected Grand Rapids as the site of its Northwest Region headquarters, connecting the banking offices in the former FMB network with offices in eastern Michigan and northwestern Ohio. The Huntington leased administrative office space at Monroe Center in downtown Grand Rapids, while the former FMB headquarters building in Holland was con-

verted to a regional operations and service center for the company.

KEEPING IT IN THE FAMILY

The FMB story begins with Jacob Den Herder, one of Zeeland, Michigan's leading citizens in the late 1800s. He was the insurance agent, the township clerk, a church elder, and, in 1878, the community's first banker. He opened the Den Herder Bank in the back of a clothing store, and changed the name to Zeeland State Bank 22 years later when he moved into a new building on Main Street.

The Huntington story is much the same, except the family name stayed over the door. Pelatiah Webster Huntington, known as P.W., came to Columbus, Ohio, in 1853 and found work as a messenger in the State Bank of Ohio. In 1866, P.W. formed a partnership with his father-in-law and opened P.W. Huntington & Company, a private banking house. In 1905, the company was incorporated as The Huntington National Bank, with P.W. as president and his four sons comprising the remainder of the board of directors. Three of those sons would serve a term as the bank's chief executive officer, keeping the company in family hands until 1958.

Meanwhile, back in Michigan, three more generations of the Den Herder family would run the Zeeland bank, which became First Michigan Bank and Trust Company in 1958. Fifteen years later, First Michigan Bank Corporation was formed under new bank holding company laws. That opened the door for growth, and FMB started an affiliate bank in the Grand Rapids area in 1975. At the time, state laws prevented a bank from opening an office in a community where another bank was already chartered, so FMB could not stake a claim within the Grand Rapids city limits. The bank was located in the suburb of Walker until the laws were relaxed.

FMB-Grand Rapids grew rapidly during the 1980s, with its main office at Ottawa Avenue and Lyon Street in the downtown business district, and 10 other branches in Kent County by 1997. First Michigan Bank Corporation continued to expand through acquisitions and internal growth in its thriving markets. By 1997, the company had $3.5 billion in assets and 91 offices stretching from the Indiana line to the Canadian border.

The Huntington National Bank signs now appear in front of 90 former First Michigan Bank offices throughout West Michigan.

The Huntington was also growing during this period. From its central Ohio base, The Huntington acquired banks in Cleveland, Cincinnati, and other parts of Ohio; Indiana; West Virginia; Florida; and the suburban counties to the north and west of Detroit. Looking to expand its Michigan franchise, The Huntington made a successful bid to acquire FMB in May 1997. When the transaction was completed, The Huntington stood as one of the nation's 35 largest banks, with total assets in excess of $26 billion.

A FRIEND TO SMALL BUSINESS

Since its establishment, The Huntington has focused on meeting the needs of small- and medium-sized businesses. More than 95 percent of the bank's commercial lending goes to companies with annual sales of less than $5 million. In the early days of the bank, P.W. Huntington shied away from at least one large customer. He refused a then-massive deposit of $500,000 from one of the railroads because, he said, "We should not owe that much money to anyone." The Huntington family's conservative business practices enabled the bank to survive and remain stable during economic hard times.

On the bank's 50th anniversary, P.W. declared, "The Huntington National Bank aims to unite what is best in modern practice with strict adherence to ethical standards." Technological innovations continue to change the definition of modern practice, but the philosophy—as applied to both commercial and individual customers—remains firmly in place.

The Huntington has always been at the forefront of banking technology. The bank opened the world's first 24-hour, fully automated banking office, known as the Handy Bank, in 1972. The Huntington was one of the first banks in the nation to provide customers with the option of banking via the Internet. Commercial customers have a menu of electronic cash management options to help them better manage their finances.

Technology plays a major role in making banking easier, but it is still no substitute for the customer-focused personal service that is a tradition of both The Huntington and FMB. As Frank Wobst, chairman of Huntington Bancshares Incorporated, wrote in the company's 1997 annual report, "Each customer defines service differently, but at The Huntington, we define service as meeting customer expectations. To succeed, we must provide superior personal service, but we must provide it in new ways and new places." The ways and places may change, but the principles established by Jacob Den Herder and P.W. Huntington remain the driving force behind The Huntington's success in West Michigan.

The Huntington National Bank moved its regional headquarters to Grand Rapids in the spring of 1998.

Customer-focused personal service has been a tradition at The Huntington for more than 100 years.

WOLVERINE WORLD WIDE, INC. IS THE WORLD'S LARGEST marketer and manufacturer of casual, work, and outdoor footwear. Since the company's beginnings in 1883, it has grown from a pioneer tannery and workboot maker into a global company whose

brands are sold in more than 100 countries. Last year, nearly 38 million men, women, and children walked in new Wolverine World Wide footwear—and the growing popularity of the company's brands has been successfully extended to apparel, watches, eyewear, handbags, work clothing, and accessories. The company's latest brand—Harley Davidson Footwear—will be brought to market in 1998 under a newly acquired global license.

AN INDUSTRY LEADER

Wolverine World Wide's success has brought it many awards and has made the company a pacesetter in the footwear industry. Wolverine World Wide was voted Footwear Company of the Year in 1995 by U.S. shoe retailers, suppliers, and marketers; Hush Puppies® shoes were named Fashion Accessory of the Year by the Council of Fashion Designers of America; and on Wall Street, *USA Today* ranks Wolverine stock among the 25 stocks that have risen the most in value since the bull market began in 1990. The company has ranked among the top 10 performing stocks in Michigan for four of the last five years according to *Crain's Detroit Business*; it achieved this high standing on the basis of stock performance, sales growth, profits, and return on equity.

The company's 12 factories in Michigan, Arkansas, Missouri,

New York, and Puerto Rico produce more "Made in the U.S.A." footwear than any other U.S.-based manufacturer. Since 1992, the company has added nearly 1,200 new jobs in Michigan alone, and in Europe, Latin America, and Asia, Wolverine World Wide brands of boots and shoes are made in 19 contract factories. Through innovative licensing and distribution agreements, footwear bearing the company's brands is produced for retailers on six continents.

A STRONG FAMILY OF GLOBAL BRANDS

Tough, horsehide Wolverine workboots were Wolverine World Wide's first product, and their popularity fueled the company's growth until the phenomenon of Hush Puppies shoes first struck the nation in 1958. Both of the products were manufactured from leathers invented in the company's Rockford tannery—now a modern, high-capacity facility that produces high-performance leathers for Wolverine and other major brands. Wolverine World Wide—originally known as the Hirth-Krause Company—took its name from the Wolverine work boot, and built the Hush Puppies brand into one of the world's most recognized trademarks. Since then, the diverse line of Wolverine-made boots and shoes has evolved into a family of global brands that provide casual,

work, and rugged outdoor footwear for men, women, and children in more than 100 countries.

Wolverine strengthened its position in the growing market for hiking and adventure footwear with the acquisition of the Merrell brand in 1997. Merrell is an admired name among dedicated outdoor adventurers, known for its uncompromising attention to quality and high-performance design. In a move to further consolidate its position in this market, Wolverine World Wide also negotiated rights to produce and market Coleman footwear globally. Wolverine has marketed the brand in the United States, Canada, and Japan since 1987, with an emphasis on value and family adventure. Wolverine Boots and Shoes' rugged outdoor footwear brings Coleman's unique qualities to this mix of footwear styles and allows Wolverine World Wide to serve the outdoor market through every distribution channel and price level.

Wolverine World Wide's brand-globalization strategy began with Hush Puppies shoes when the brand was introduced in Canada and the United Kingdom in 1959. The casual appeal of this brand has since made it a favorite worldwide for shoes, apparel, and accessories. In 1997, Hush Puppies shoes were voted Footwear Brand of the Year by *FHM Magazine*, the leading menswear magazine in the United Kingdom.

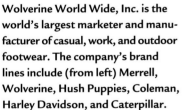

Wolverine World Wide, Inc. is the world's largest marketer and manufacturer of casual, work, and outdoor footwear. The company's brand lines include (from left) Merrell, Wolverine, Hush Puppies, Coleman, Harley Davidson, and Caterpillar.

Wolverine's Bates uniform footwear has been worn by U.S. military personnel, police, and firefighters since 1885. The official footwear of the U.S. Naval Academy and the U.S. Navy Seals, U.S.-made Bates shoes and boots have been exported to military units in 51 nations. Recent innovations in the brand have been aimed at meeting the growing needs of law enforcement and security markets: Bates Enforcer Series footwear was introduced in 1995 and provides these men and women with high-performance boots and shoes.

Wolverine World Wide's headquarters is located in Rockford, Michigan.

Hush Puppies shoes debuted in 12 new countries in 1997, and in 1998, consumers in countries as diverse as Russia, France, China, Germany, and Scandinavia will be able to take home the fun, casual style, and comfort that Hush Puppies invented.

FOOTWEAR FOR WORKERS

Workers who depend on high performance and durability favor the Wolverine brand for work, outdoor sport, and rugged casual footwear. The brand's flagship technology, the DuraShocks Comfort System, was developed in the biomechanical labs of Michigan State University and revolutionized workboot construction and comfort. New slip-resistant technologies and a unique Women's Fit workboot program were introduced in 1997, the latest innovations brought to market by the brand known for pioneering products. In recognition of the unique Women's Fit, the National Association of Women in Construction has endorsed Wolverine Boots and Shoes.

Acquisition of the Hy-Test Boots and Shoes brand in 1996 consolidated Wolverine World Wide's position as the leading domestic supplier of occupation and safety footwear—the fastest-growing segment of the U.S. workboot industry. Hy-Test footwear is known for technological leadership, and its most recent breakthrough is the dramatic Inferno fire-resistant boot, capable of withstanding immersion in molten steel for twice the reaction time of most workers involved in an accident with this superheated material. The Hy-Test brand moved overseas for the first time in 1997 with its launch of the boots in Japan by the Asahi Company.

Wolverine World Wide has produced Caterpillar boots and shoes since 1994, when it acquired the global license to market footwear under this powerful name. Rated as the fastest-growing footwear brand in the world, Caterpillar sales have expanded to nearly 8 million pairs of work and lifestyle boots and shoes in 97 countries. The rugged styling and empowering attitudes of the Caterpillar brand give it special strength with young, urban men and women and their counterparts on work sites everywhere.

COMFORT AT HOME

The Wolverine Slipper Group ranks as the leading domestic supplier of upscale, private-label slippers with the At Home products of the Tru-Stitch division. Since 1940, these high-quality shearling and moose-hide slippers and moccasins have been produced for leading U.S. retail catalog and department store customers at Wolverine's New York factories—and in 1996, a new line of Hush Puppies slippers was introduced in major U.S. department stores. Hush Puppies slippers feature the popular colors of Wolverine performance leathers popularized by Hush Puppies shoes.

Wolverine World Wide has laid the foundation—in its brand family, its manufacturing and marketing capacity, and its global business strategy—to continue its growth and industry leadership. With record sales and earnings for the 22nd consecutive quarter, there is every reason to believe the firm will enter the next millennium as the great global company it has positioned itself to become.

RAND RAPIDS SCHOOL FURNITURE COMPANY BEGAN ITS OPERA-
tions in 1886 in Grand Rapids with 50 employees. The
company's product was a combination student desk that
joined a desktop and book box with a seat and back. This
desk was developed because students spent approximately

15,000 hours sitting in classrooms between kindergarten and college, and the founders believed that desks should be designed to enhance students' productivity and physical development. The desk design was an immediate success, and the following year, the company expanded its line to include folding chairs and church furniture.

In 1889, Grand Rapids School Furniture Company made its way into the entertainment seating market by furnishing the Tabor Opera House in Leadville, Colorado. Although far different from school furniture, this type of product was intended to serve the same purpose: to provide comfortable, dependable seating, designed to withstand hours of sitting. By 1892, the company was manufacturing the greatest number of chairs of any furniture producer in the world—more than 81,000 annually—and in 1926, the company's name was changed to American Seating.

PRODUCT SHIFT DURING WARTIME

During World War II, American Seating supported the war effort by producing aircraft wings for airplane trainers and pilot ejection seats, as well as folding chairs. In fact, the company manufactured more than 5 million folding chairs at a rate of 10,000 per day. A common joke around the company then was that it was "in charge of seating the standing army."

With peacetime came the baby boom, which brought increased demand for American Seating's classroom furniture. The company developed new flip-up desk lids, study carrels, and other products for schools. In the 1950s, the company began serving the transportation market with a newly developed cantilevered bus seat.

THREE MARKETS SERVED

Today, American Seating has three divisions that serve three distinct markets: Transportation Products, providing coach and city bus seating; Architectural Products, providing auditorium, stadium, arena, and theater seating; and Interior Systems, providing contract seating, tables, and systems furniture for offices and laboratory settings.

The Transportation Products division is the recognized leader in mass transit seating. The division designs seating primarily for buses and railcars, and its products are known for outstanding quality, long life, and designs that provide passengers with exceptional safety and comfort.

The Architectural Products division designs public seating for stadiums, arenas, auditoriums, and theaters. These products can be found in many of the country's most prestigious public venues. Among them are Detroit's Tiger Stadium and the Silverdome; New York City's Lincoln Center for the Performing Arts, Metropolitan Opera House, and Yankee Stadium; Denver's Mile High Stadium; the Los Angeles Coliseum; Wrigley Field in Chicago; Riverfront Stadium in Cincinnati; Oriole Park at Camden Yards and the new Baltimore Ravens Stadium; Cleveland's Jacobs Field; and the long-awaited Van Andel Arena in Grand Rapids.

American Seating's Interior Systems division provides a full line of high-quality office seating and a versatile interior furniture

American Seating's Framework Access™ system is engineered for the information workplace, and can be adapted to a variety of work environments, including office and laboratory settings (left).

The GeoMetrix™ table system responds to changing needs in the office with access to power/telecommunications at the desktop for increased flexibility, while the Cue™ chair provides active ergonomic support (right).

system called Framework Access™, which can adapt to the needs of the individual worker. This product features a wide array of integrated components and a unique panel design that allows it to be easily reconfigured or expanded. The Framework Laboratory System offers fixed and freestanding components with specialized work surfaces, equipment support, storage, and utilities for technical environments.

A Company of Firsts

Since introducing the first tilt-back opera chair in 1893, American Seating has continued to lead the industry in state-of-the-art product design. The company was the first to take the squeak out of folding chairs with a nylon bearing-and-spring assembly—a matter of special significance for symphony hall fans. Thanks to American Seating's three-quarter safety fold stadium seat, sports fans can easily back into a folded seat while holding food and beverages. After Dutch elm disease ravaged supplies for major-league stadium seats that were traditionally made of steam-bent elm, American Seating led the industry in developing molded plastic seats. In addition, the company was the first to develop seating that complied with requirements of the Americans with Disabilities Act. The com-

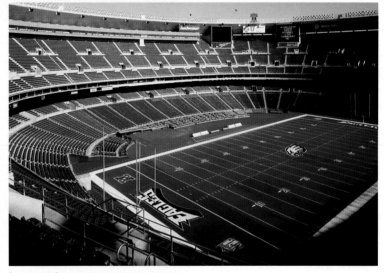

pany also developed the first removable panel systems insert that can be refurbished on-site without disturbing adjoining furniture or wiring and cabling.

American Seating employs 800 people at its main facility in Grand Rapids. In addition, the company has manufacturing operations in Winchester, Tennessee, and Orillia, Ontario, in Canada. For a three-year period, the company was owned by Atlanta-based Fuqua Industries, until it was purchased by the management team in 1987. "We had an opportunity to become owners of American Seating a little over 10 years ago," says Edward Clark, American Seating's president and CEO. "Since that time, we have experienced steady growth and

have made a major commitment to building our company in the city of Grand Rapids."

Clark says the company's excellent relationship with its employees is key to its success, now and in the future. "We have a great team of people here, and a relationship that is based on trust," he says. "Basically, we let our employees do their jobs and make many of the decisions that affect those jobs. We've put a very high priority on communicating with our people, and we share information regularly. Because of their efforts, we've become a thriving, revitalized company. In the coming years, we look forward to continued success while maintaining our tradition of excellence and industry leadership."

CHALLENGING CONVENTIONAL THINKING MAY NOT BE A PRACTICE one typically associates with a small Catholic college, but at Aquinas College, it is a way of life. Aquinas is a school where critical thinking plays a vital role in every classroom and is woven into every subject taught at the school. It is a place

where spirit and energy abound and where there is a firm belief that passion has the power to transform lives, perhaps even change the world. Aquinas is a place where students of every age and nationality are welcomed, yet feel challenged, and where they learn that the only limits to success are those they place on themselves.

A CATHOLIC HERITAGE, A CHRISTIAN TRADITION

Aquinas College has its roots in a normal novitiate school founded by the Dominican Sisters of Grand Rapids in 1886. In 1931, the college, then known as Catholic Junior College, became the first coedu-

cational Catholic college in the United States. In 1941, the Dominicans renamed the school after Saint Thomas Aquinas, a revered preacher, scholar, and teacher of the Dominican order whose teachings stressed the importance of combining faith with reason and continuously learning from our own life experiences. The Dominican tradition of "open mind, open heart" lives on at Aquinas College today. A values-centered learning community, Aquinas strives to graduate students of competence, conscience, compassion, and commitment.

Students of all religions, outlooks, races, and backgrounds are warmly welcomed. Students come

to Aquinas from 22 U.S. states and 15 foreign countries. More than 40 percent of the student body is non-Catholic. "Our students are drawn to Aquinas because it offers a diverse but inclusive learning community, one that enables them to increase their knowledge, hone their competencies, develop their character, and use their God-given talents to make a positive difference in our world through their lives, work, and service," says Harry Knopke, president of Aquinas.

AN EDUCATION FOR A LIFETIME

Consistently ranked one of the top liberal arts colleges in the Midwest by *U.S. News & World Report*, Aquinas offers an approach to learning and living that teaches students unlimited ways of seeing the world. The college offers more than 40 undergraduate majors and four graduate degrees. Students study a rich variety of subjects, and acquire skills that help them become critical thinkers, articulate speakers, strong writers, and effective problem solvers.

Students are urged to participate in field experiences and internship opportunities in Grand Rapids, as well as in other parts of the country and world. Each year more than 2,000 local, national, and international business and government agencies, from Grand Rapids to Washington, D.C., offer field experience to Aquinas students. "We're one of the few liberal arts colleges that strongly encourage students to participate in internships because we believe that kind of real-world experience is an invaluable part of our students' total learning experience," says Sharon Smith, director of career and counseling services.

Because Aquinas has long recognized that different students have different needs, it was the first college in the country to offer

Clockwise from top:
The Aquinas College campus is the former Holmdene estate of Edward and Susan Blodgett Lowe. The property was purchased by the Dominican Sisters of Grand Rapids in 1945 as the new home for Aquinas College. The English Tudor Renaissance-style manor house, built in the early 1900s, now houses administrative and faculty offices.

Aquinas is more than an intellectual journey. The college wants students to do more than think deeply; they are encouraged to experience life.

Aquinas is considered one of the most beautiful small college campuses in Michigan. Consistently ranked one of the top liberal arts colleges in the Midwest by *U.S. News & World Report*, the college draws students from more than 22 states and 15 foreign countries.

a continuing education program specifically geared toward working adults. Of the school's 2,500 students, approximately 700 currently are enrolled in the continuing education program. Classes are held on weekdays, evenings, and weekends, and may be taken on either a semester or a "quadmester" basis, offering students the choice of an accelerated format. Classes at Aquinas are small; the average size is about 15 students, which means professors can offer plenty of personalized attention, while at the same time encouraging students to participate in frequent classroom discussions.

Aquinas also was the first college in Michigan to offer a Master of Management degree program. Unlike quantitative MBA programs, the Aquinas program focuses on people, not numbers. Developed in concert with area business leaders, it was designed to meet the community's workforce requirements. The skills they seek include leadership, team building, communication, problem solving, and ethics. All are emphasized in the Aquinas program, which graduates masters of management. Other graduate programs include the Master in Education/Initial Certification for recent graduates or career changers seeking certification as elementary or secondary teachers; a Master in the Art of Teaching program for certified teachers that focuses on theory, practical applications, and a humanistic approach to education; and a Master in Science Education, geared to certified teachers seeking to enhance their teaching skills in the sciences.

Understanding that many older adults are interested in expanding their knowledge, without necessarily pursuing a degree, Aquinas also offers the Emeritus program. Designed for adult learners aged 55 and older, the program offers students opportunities to study a variety of subjects such as computers, the human brain, mythology, and improving listening skills.

A COMMITMENT TO THE COMMUNITY

From mentorship programs for local youth at risk to service

learning projects in Appalachia and in Mexico and Haiti, as well as other countries, students demonstrate their commitment to the community and the world around them. The college also is engaged in collaborations with institutions serving the Grand Rapids community. Through a collaboration with Saint Mary's Health Services, Aquinas faculty and staff are working with health care professionals to establish new health care training and delivery programs, as well as ongoing professional in-service training. In turn, Saint Mary's provides valuable field opportunities for Aquinas students and faculty. Each institution benefits, and the community benefits from an improved continuum of care. A similar collaboration has long been under way with Lake Michigan Academy, through which Aquinas education students and area teachers become better equipped to diagnose and assist learning-disabled children.

STATISTICS THAT SPEAK FOR THEMSELVES

Aquinas graduates not only are well educated, they also have a way of being successful at whatever they choose to do with their lives. Nine out of 10 applicants recommended by the Aquinas premedical advisory committee are admitted to medical school, and 19 out of 20 are accepted into other graduate programs. Aquinas has the highest percentage of

teacher placement in the state and one of the highest in the country. Each year, 98 percent of Aquinas graduates are employed in full-time jobs or are enrolled in professional schools of law, medicine, or dentistry, or in a master or doctoral program within six months of graduation.

Sister Rosemary O'Donnell, one of Aquinas' popular professors, describes the college as a place that "challenges untruths, questions new truths, and analyzes old truths in new ways." That is an apt description of a school that has always prided itself on its passion, its spirit, and its willingness to explore knowledge to its fullest. At Aquinas, open-minded thinking and the willingness to express controversial opinions are not only accepted, they are expected. Students are inspired to think critically, and then act with conviction.

As a career-oriented liberal arts institution, Aquinas prepares students for their future by offering many opportunities to learn and grow, both inside and outside of the classroom (top).

Students come to Aquinas from as far away as Indonesia and France, and as nearby as Detroit and Chicago (bottom).

F MOST PEOPLE IN GRAND RAPIDS WERE ASKED WHO SUPPLIES THEIR electricity, most likely they would answer "Consumers Energy." After all, Consumers provides electric service to more than 6 million customers in Michigan's Lower Peninsula. It is the fourth-largest combination electric and gas utility in the country. But some people might be

surprised to hear of the company's contributions to West Michigan's diverse, thriving economy. In addition to providing customers with electric and natural gas value-added services that deliver comfort, convenience, safety, and security, Consumers Energy is committed to being a good corporate citizen and a strong contributing member of the Grand Rapids community.

THE ROOTS OF CONSUMERS ENERGY

The story of Consumers Energy began more than 110 years ago with a man named W.A. Foote in the small southeastern Michigan town of Adrian. After becoming fascinated with how electricity lit up the shops and streets of his hometown, Foote moved to Jackson, where the downtown area was still illuminated by gas-lights. He received permission to erect poles, stretch wires, and install a few electric lights, known as "dishpan lights," which were actually carbon points set behind large tin reflectors that magnified light. This led to Foote's founding the Jackson Electric Light Works in 1886. Through the ensuing years, he formed and acquired similar businesses throughout Michigan. Among them was Grand Rapids Electric Light and Power Company. Foote eventually consolidated all

of his companies into a single entity that he named Consumers Power Company.

Today, the company is called Consumers Energy and is a principal subsidiary of CMS Energy, an international energy company that provides energy services and develops, owns, and operates a variety of energy facilities around the world. CMS Energy is active in 26 countries on five continents, with broad expertise and experience in electric and gas utility operations; oil and gas exploration and production; electric power production; natural gas transmission, storage, and processing; international energy distribution; and energy marketing, services, and trading.

INSTRUMENTAL IN ECONOMIC DEVELOPMENT

Doug Buikema, Consumers Energy's director for domestic

Carl English (top), vice president of transmission and distribution for the utility and a member of the Right Place Board, believes there's exciting growth ahead for Consumers Energy. "Not only will our company continue to provide customers with the most reliable electricity and natural gas service, we'll also continue to play a major role in community and state economic development."

economic development, says the company has a strong commitment to Michigan's economic development and works closely with Grand Rapids' Right Place Program in its efforts to reach out to new businesses. "It's doubtful that people are aware of how instrumental Consumers Energy is in helping companies relocate to West Michigan. It's one of the areas we focus heavily on," he says.

Buikema gives three primary reasons for the company's interest in West Michigan's economic development: "First, we feel it's important to diversify the economy in Michigan. Over the past several years, Michigan has been extremely successful in attracting a variety of businesses. Our concentration is on further developing several key industries, including furniture, plastics, food processing, and automotive. We also want to help create jobs to keep our state's unemployment level as low as possible and to prepare our growing younger workforce for the demand of high-tech jobs.

"And there's a third reason: It's just good business for Consumers Energy," Buikema added. "We need to be successful just like any business or industry, and we do that through growth. If we can help the state's economy grow, then we grow as well, and constantly increase the size of our market."

Consumers Energy works closely with the Michigan Jobs Commission, an organization whose mission is to attract businesses from other states and other countries. The two organizations work jointly to help businesses qualify for state and federal grants and locate sites for their businesses. They also help with funding, attracting, and training qualified employees; identifying tax considerations; and other services that help businesses see Michigan as a desirable place.

A Good Corporate Citizen, a Good Neighbor

Consumers Energy takes its corporate citizenship very seriously. Its philanthropic arm, the Consumers Energy Foundation, has a strategic goal of enhancing the economic, social, and environmental progress of the communities the company serves. The foundation has committed $1.5 million annually to community and statewide groups for a variety of causes, including the United Way, local food banks, literacy programs, educational grants, environmental programs, culture and the arts, social services, and other community and civic efforts. The foundation also sponsors the Volunteer Investment Program (VIP); employees who volunteer more than 60 personal

hours to nonprofit organizations are eligible to apply for grants to benefit their groups.

Carl English, vice president of transmission and distribution for the utility and a member of the Right Place Board, believes there's exciting growth ahead for Consumers Energy. "For many reasons, West Michigan is a highly desirable place to live, and to grow and develop a business," he says. "Not only will our company continue to provide customers with the most reliable electricity and natural gas service, we'll also continue to play a major role in community and state economic development. By doing that, we'll help our state continue to grow and thrive. We'll all benefit from that."

In addition to providing customers with electric and natural gas value-added services that deliver comfort, convenience, safety, and security, Consumers Energy is committed to being a good corporate citizen and a strong contributing member of the Grand Rapids community.

MOST PEOPLE HAVE HEARD THE OLD PHRASE "IT'S THE greatest thing since sliced bread." Oliver Products Company has a special fondness for this saying, having produced one of the very first retail bread slicers in 1932 for a pastry kitchen in Grand Rapids. "We're not sure

we can actually say we invented sliced bread," chuckles Oliver President and CEO Bob Porter, "but we certainly made the bread slicer a reality."

ROOTS THAT BEGAN MORE THAN A CENTURY AGO

In 1890, the furniture industry in Grand Rapids was prolific. To answer the need for precision, high-speed cutting technology, Joseph W. Oliver, a successful salesman, formed American Machinery Company. By 1904, Oliver's company had grown significantly and was producing an extensive line of state-of-the-art woodworking machinery for furniture manufacturers.

In 1932, when the entire country was caught in the grips of the Great Depression, the new owners of the company—the Baldwin and Tuthill families—renamed the company Oliver Machinery. The company needed to reinvent itself in

order to survive, and, applying the same level of expertise and knowledge used in woodworking machinery, Oliver turned to another industry—food. The company developed the bread slicer, a highly advanced product that was very much ahead of its time. Even today, the third slicer built by the company actually still operates.

In order to continue responding to the needs of the retail bakery industry, Oliver went on to develop

better and more sophisticated products, including machinery to package sliced bread, and new adhesives to seal packages and attach labels. Oliver Machinery grew into Oliver Products, a company known internationally for its expertise not only in bakery equipment, but also in packaging equipment, converted package materials for the food and medical industries, and materials for major companies specializing in photographics and office copiers.

DIVERSIFIED TALENTS

Today, Oliver Products is the leading supplier of slicer equipment for the retail baking industry. In addition to variable-thickness bread slicers that can slice bread from thin to extra thick, Oliver develops and manufactures precision slicers for bagels, buns, rolls, and baguettes. The company also specializes in a variety of mixers and dough preparation equipment, such as French bread molders that shape baguettes, and sheeters and rollers designed to shape pastries, pizza dough, tortillas, and bagels.

In addition to the bakery industry, Oliver Products serves major food retailers all over the country by providing see-through packaging for store-brand convenience foods. Porter says Oliver was first approached by D&W Foods with this need. "D&W wanted a way to showcase its homemade lasagna,

In the future, Oliver Products Company plans to continue serving the unique market needs of retail bakeries, retail food establishments, and medical device manufacturers, as well as expanding its technological expertise in the photographic and reprographic industries (top).

Oliver's pouching machines produce a variety of pouches used by device manufacturers to package medical instruments (bottom).

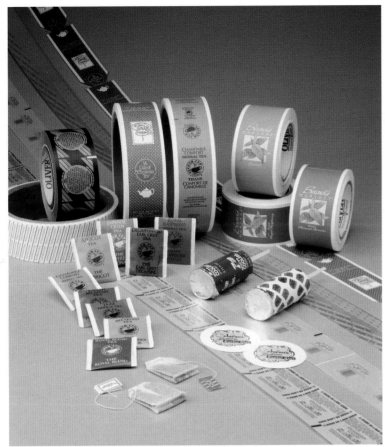

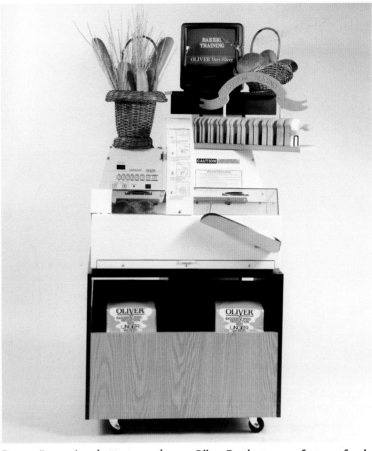

quiche, and various salads," says Porter, "so we developed heat seal film lids with see-through tops. This packaging lets customers see the product they're buying, and it makes the product much more appealing."

Today, Oliver sells this type of packaging to West Michigan grocery giants D&W and Meijer, as well as food retailers all over the country, such as Winn Dixie, Publix, and Kroger. Oliver packaging is also used by major brand frozen foods, such as Banquet chicken and Stouffer's Lean Cuisine. In addition, Oliver makes tea tags and envelopes used by Twinings, Bigelow, and Celestial Seasonings.

Oliver Products also makes specialty products, including adhesive coated and printed labels for major photographic companies like Kodak, as well as custom-coated materials used on photocopier toner cartridges for Xerox and other companies specializing in reprographics.

SERVING THE MEDICAL INDUSTRY

Oliver Products is a major supplier of high-quality medical packaging used for devices and supplies such as heart catheters, implantable heart valves, pacemakers, sterile eye solutions, and prosthetics. Oliver's custom adhesive coating allows packages to withstand the severe process of sterilization, including extremely high heat and pressure, as well as the rigors of product distribution and transportation.

Used worldwide by medical companies such as Johnson & Johnson, U.S. Surgical, 3-M, and Alcon Surgical, Oliver Products packaging can be found in every corner of the world, from a clinic in Romania to a hospital in Africa to medical centers in Grand Rapids. No matter where the packaging travels, medical personnel can be assured that the products inside will remain completely sterile until opened.

COMMITMENT TO EMPLOYEES AND THE CUSTOMER

According to Porter, Oliver Products is very aware of how important its employees are to the company's success. Several employees at Oliver have worked there for more than 40 years; 44 people have worked there for more than 20 years, 19 of whom have passed the 30-year mark.

"To us, the idea of continuous improvement is a way of life," says Porter, "so we involve our people and draw on their collective wisdom." The company asks employees to participate in regular quality-of-work-life surveys, and also regularly brings key customers to the plant to meet face-to-face with employees.

LOOKING TOWARD TOMORROW

Oliver Products is ready to tackle future challenges. The company plans to continue serving the unique market needs of retail bakeries, retail food establishments, and medical device manufacturers, as well as expanding its technological expertise in the photographic and reprographic industries. Currently certified by the British Standards Institution (BSI) as an ISO 9001 company and a winner of multiple awards for customer service, Oliver plans to continue its growth by focusing on continuous improvement in quality and customer service.

"We believe in what we do," says Porter. "And we're committed to our employees, our customers, and our community. And as we move toward the end of this century, we fully intend to keep strengthening those commitments."

Oliver Products manufactures food packaging machines and materials, such as tea envelopes, tea tags, and ice-cream novelty lids, and home meal replacement packaging systems (left).

In-store bakeries and delis use Oliver's Model 2003 Vari-Slicer bread slicer (right).

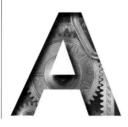

AN INITIAL GLANCE AT MARY FREE BED HOSPITAL AND Rehabilitation Center might lead one to believe that it is like any other hospital—but nothing could be further from the truth. In this unique health care setting, spaces are open and patients are active, moving with determination. Some patients move on wheels while others walk on limbs of polymer and steel. At Mary Free Bed, there are workshops and laboratories that mold material into anatomical designs that imitate bone and muscle. There are also schoolrooms, gyms, and a large pool for therapy. Mary Free Bed offers independence through rehabilitation and a new chance at life for its patients. Often it gives hope to those who might otherwise have given up.

IN THE NAME OF ALL MARYS
In 1891, a group of women identified the need for a free bed in one of the local hospitals for patients of limited financial means. The women initially solicited financial support through teas and fundraisers, asking for contributions from everyone named Mary and from those with relatives named Mary. Soon, enough money was raised to endow a free bed, which subsequently became known as the Mary Free Bed.

Much of the group's initial work involved caring for children with birth defects, serious injuries, and polio. As the fund continued to grow, along with the needs of the community, the women's group became incorporated as the Mary Free Bed Guild of Grand Rapids. Today, through the expanded services of Mary Free Bed Hospital and Rehabilitation Center, the Marys continue to serve both children and adults challenged by injuries, disease, or birth defects—helping them realize their potential.

INDEPENDENCE THROUGH REHABILITATION
Mary Free Bed Hospital and Rehabilitation Center is an 80-bed, nonprofit hospital, and is the only freestanding rehabilitation center in West Michigan. Mary Free Bed is devoted exclusively to comprehensive rehabilitation for adults and children, and programs are designed to help individuals learn to live as independently as possible at home, at work, and within the community.

The hospital's rehabilitative care begins with a team approach. Every patient receives individualized care from a team of experts representing various disciplines. Children and adults with physical limitations may feel fear and anxiety. The Mary Free Bed staff helps alleviate these fears with encouragement and a warm, caring approach.

◄ GEORGE GRYZENIA

At Mary Free Bed Hospital and Rehabilitation Center, the Toy and Technology Library provides physically challenged children with play experiences using specially adapted, customized toys. Youngsters like Rebecca Hayes will become used to special adaptations, and through the years will adapt more easily to new customizations and assistive devices.

▼ GEORGE GRYZENIA

Grand Rapids' Junior Wheelchair Basketball Team, the Junior Pacers, shows its intensity at practice. Mary Free Bed enthusiastically supports recreational and competitive wheelchair sports. Providing participation opportunities for athletic activities is an important component of the pediatric, brain injury, and spinal cord injury programs.

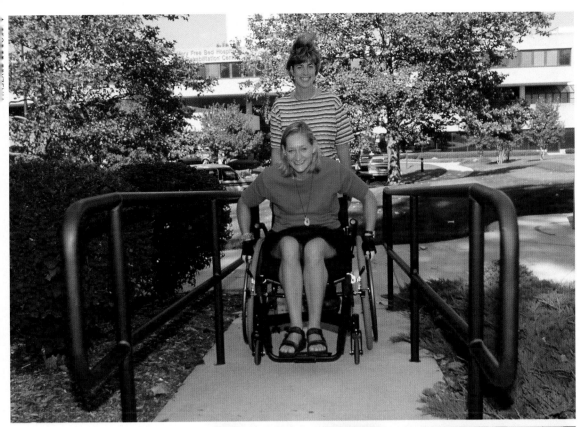

GEORGE GRYZENIA

NOT A TYPICAL REHABILITATION PROGRAM

Mary Free Bed has become a nationally recognized leader in developing unique programs and highly specialized services that are based on the needs of its patients—often developing programs that are not offered anywhere else. In addition to its inpatient care, Mary Free Bed offers many services through its outpatient facility.

Much of Mary Free Bed's history has involved helping children, and the same is true today. The highly trained staff of the hospital's Pediatric Program works with children in a number of specialized areas. These include mobility, communication, self-care, and psychosocial adaptations.

An important aspect of the children's program is the Area Child Amputee Center, the first such amputee clinic in the country. The clinic is nationally recognized as an innovative leader in its treatment of children with congenital and non-congenital amputations.

Other specialized programs at Mary Free Bed include the hospital's Brain Injury Program, a recovery process that occurs in stages and may continue for several years. The hospital's Stroke Program has helped patients since the 1960s, and

is designed to assist stroke patients in regaining independence in everyday activities. In addition, the Mary Free Bed Spinal Cord Injury Program helps patients adjust to their physical limitations and work toward maximum independence.

PREPARING FOR THE REAL WORLD

A life-altering illness or injury can present many difficult challenges, including the transition involved in the first few weeks or months of returning to one's home and community. To help bridge the gap, Mary Free Bed provides a realistic community environment within the hospital's own walls, called Independence Square™. The unique environment includes

a restaurant, a marketplace, a car and gas pump, an automatic teller machine, sidewalks, and stairs, all designed to help patients learn to manage real-life situations.

The driver rehabilitation program provides individuals with driver training and a complete assessment of their ability to safely return to the driver's seat following a major accident or illness.

Mary Free Bed Hospital and Rehabilitation Center offers an environment where patience and caring have no limits, and where fear and uncertainty are replaced with independence and hope. Above all, it is a place where people learn to believe in themselves and where they find the courage to face life again.

Clockwise from top: Therapeutic recreation therapist Mindy Whiteside assists Jocelyn Dettloff on the therapath course, a special area on Mary Free Bed's campus conceived by the Spinal Cord Team. It challenges patients in wheelchairs as they test different grades and materials, training them to maneuver on sand, ridged pavement, sidewalks, curbs, and gutters.

The Orthotics and Prosthetics division of Mary Free Bed shines as a fine example of the broad range of programs that provide outstanding service to patients and their families. Prosthetist John King works with Gladys Cebelak to ensure a comfortable fit as she walks with her new prostheses.

As therapy progresses, patients are encouraged to train for real-world activities in an exciting, realistic environment called Independence Square™. Kris Fowler, occupational therapist, encourages Elvis Saffell to select fruit from the grocery area, weigh his purchase, and prepare to pay at the checkout lane.

 N 1891, TALENTED CRAFTSMEN WHO WOULD SOON CREATE MANY OF the most enduring landmarks in downtown Grand Rapids—McKay Tower, Michigan National Bank, the YMCA, the Masonic Temple, and Welsh Auditorium—opened the doors of Hauser, Hayden, and Owen. In the decades that followed, the company filled out the

Grand Rapids skyline with prominent structures, such as the Old Kent Bank, Grand Center, Frederik Meijer Gardens, Grand Rapids City/Kent County Complex, and Van Andel Museum. Known today as Owen-Ames-Kimball Co., the firm is still building West Michigan, offering general contracting, construction management, and design/build services to the local marketplace.

SETTING THE PACE

Owen-Ames-Kimball's expertise in building educational, industrial, commercial, and health care facilities helped the company earn its current position as West Michigan's leading general contractor.

In fact, the company's general contracting, construction management, and design/build services offer distinct approaches to meeting each project's financial, environmental, and scheduling requirements. With a wealth of hard-earned construction experience, strategic alliances with key suppliers, and astute value-engineering capabilities, Owen-Ames-Kimball provides innovative solutions to the unique challenges of every project.

The company attributes much of its success to its focus on open dialogue between the company and its customers. "We know the importance of effective communication with our clients during all phases of the construction process," says John Keelean, vice president. "We need to keep the process running smoothly and up to customers' expectations." In order to accomplish this, face-to-face meetings to discuss design, schedule, and budget precede any construction activity. Periodic updates continue through all building phases and after completion.

With this attention to customer desires, Owen-Ames-Kimball continues to build relationships within the community, maintaining close contact with clients and resolving challenges through the creativity and ingenuity of its expert staff and extensive resources. These qualities, along with unparalleled financial strength, attract hundreds of clients, both large and small, throughout West Michigan. In fact, some current clients began their association with Owen-Ames-Kimball more than 40 years ago. Long-term clients include area giants such as Gerber, Herman Miller, Irwin Seating, Steelcase, General Motors, and Keebler.

Although Owen-Ames-Kimball still follows its original mission to provide the finest professional construction services to meet clients' needs, it continually adapts its business strategies to the changes in the industry—to set, not follow, the latest trends. Owen-Ames-Kimball has a history of leading the West Michigan construction marketplace, completing its first design/build project more than 30 years ago and providing construction management services since 1930.

Today, Owen-Ames-Kimball continues to keep a finger on the pulse of the industry. With a strong

Funding challenges left the McKay Tower at just four stories high in 1916, but Owen-Ames-Kimball brought it to its full, 15-story height a decade later when the building's funding was restored.

emphasis on employee training that promotes job skills, safety, quality, integrity, and willingness to step up to responsibility, Owen-Ames-Kimball is continually investing in its future and the future of its clients.

This successful, full-service approach to building and diverse project experience led Owen-Ames-Kimball to create two wholly owned subsidiaries: Owen-Ames-Kimball Company in Fort Myers and Muskegon Construction Company in Muskegon. The headquarters remains in the heart of Grand Rapids.

PREPARING FOR THE FUTURE
To ensure a qualified and educated workforce for the future, the company provides comprehensive train-ing and apprenticeship programs. Owen-Ames-Kimball also actively recruits new staff members through traditional and nontraditional sources to employ a group of men and women reflecting the diverse demographics of the surrounding community. As the first construction firm in West Michigan to hire a female project superintendent, Owen-Ames-Kimball is proud of its status as an equal opportunity employer.

Tom Healy, Owen-Ames-Kimball's sixth president in more than a century, sees a prosperous future for the firm. "Our strong physical and financial foundation provided by our founders and past employees gives us a strong base for a solid future," says Healy. "We must continue to train our employees and stay at the cutting edge of all new developments because of the increasing sophistication of the construction industry. Clients will expect more, so we will provide more, thus securing our status as the premier general contractor in the area."

Since the wave of immigration to West Michigan in the 1890s, Owen-Ames-Kimball has been building Grand Rapids and beyond. Through 100 years' worth of enduring landmarks and thousands of other projects, Owen-Ames-Kimball's quality, superb craftsmanship, and timeless appeal set the company's work apart from the rest. And with more than a century of experience, customers can continue to count on Owen-Ames-Kimball to build West Michigan tomorrow.

Clockwise from top:
Owen-Ames-Kimball built the Ford Museum in 1981, giving Grand Rapids yet another notable landmark that has drawn national attention and thousands of visitors yearly.

A 14-foot, cascading waterfall; five stories of glass windows; and 22-foot, concrete, treelike supports were included in the construction of the 15,000-square-foot Frederik Meijer Gardens conservatory, which showcases 16,000 exotic plants and trees.

Located in downtown Grand Rapids on the banks of the Grand River, the Van Andel Museum posed the challenge of building part of the structure over the water.

AINT MARY'S HOSPITAL WAS FOUNDED IN 1893 BY A TEAM OF FIVE Sisters of Mercy, and today it continues to serve the Grand Rapids community from the same site on which it began. The Saint Mary's of today, however, has grown far beyond the hospital walls to become a communitywide health care system. Saint

Mary's Health Services strives to be an organization known for highly effective and compassionate people, and high-quality health care services.

The Saint Mary's network includes the 250-bed Saint Mary's Hospital, as well as the hospital's regional Kidney Dialysis and Transplant Center. Saint Mary's is the only hospital in West Michigan that performs kidney transplants. Saint Mary's provides excellent primary care, as well as offering a range of specialty care that includes

the area's only thyroid center; gastroenterology and endoscopy services; obstetrics care; neonatal intensive care; spine care program; intensive care units staffed with board-certified intensive care physicians; extensive diagnostic and laboratory facilities; and a rapidly growing seniors program, Health Plus.

Advantage Health, a division of Saint Mary's Health Services, is Grand Rapids' largest physician group, offering family practice, gerontology, pediatrics, internal

medicine, and obstetrics at 18 locations throughout the Greater Grand Rapids area. Another part of Saint Mary's is Americare Home Healthcare, which offers not only nursing and personal care in the home, but also medical equipment sales. Saint Mary's Living Center, also part of the network, provides skilled nursing care for long-term care needs as well as a subacute unit for shorter-term needs. Saint Mary's also operates a variety of clinics and physician offices in underserved and special need areas—including Clinica Santa Maria, Browning Claytor Health Center, Catherines Care Center, Heartside Center, and McAuley Clinic—in keeping with its commitment to provide care outside the hospital walls and in the communities. Saint Mary's Health Services also includes a day care center, Giggle & Grow, and the Michigan Athletic Club (MAC), which is a full-service health and fitness club that offers members a full range of athletic and exercise options, plus wellness classes.

Saint Mary's is also developing a $16 million Health and Learning Center, which is scheduled for completion toward the end of 1998. The center will be the home base for Saint Mary's residency training, and has a revolutionary design that will facilitate interaction between physicians and other health providers. The patient will be considered part of the healing team, and the facility will provide most of the services a patient might need in one location.

For more than 100 years, Saint Mary's has been committed to the Grand Rapids community. And just as the founding sisters planned, the mission to provide compassionate, quality health care for all those who need it lives on at Saint Mary's.

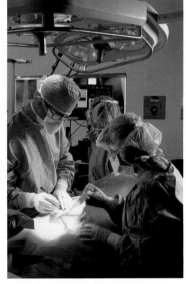

Saint Mary's Hospital offers a range of specialty care that includes the area's only thyroid center; gastroenterology and endoscopy services; obstetrics care; neonatal intensive care; spine care program; intensive care units staffed with board-certified intensive care physicians; extensive diagnostic and laboratory facilities; and a rapidly growing seniors program (left).

Saint Mary's Health Services strives to be an organization known for highly effective and compassionate people, and high-quality health care services (right).

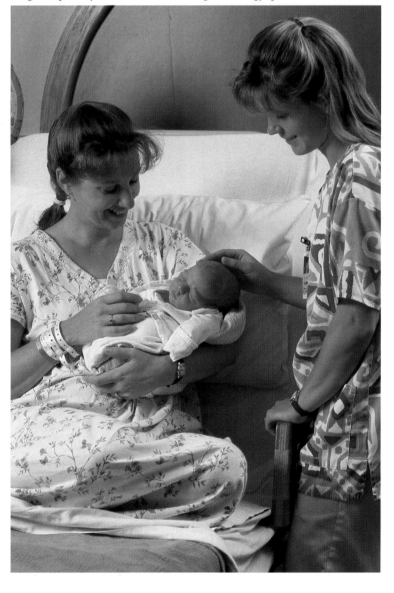

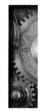

N 1912, Grand Rapids was aptly nicknamed the Furniture City, with nearly 60 furniture companies—working mostly with wood—located in the city. In the spring of that year, Metal Office Furniture Company was formed by a group of professionals with a firm belief that there was a market for metal office furniture and supplies. Nearly 90 years later,

the company, now known as Steelcase Inc., has grown from its original workforce of just 34 employees to become the leading designer and manufacturer of office furniture in the world. Today, the company, its subsidiaries, and its joint ventures employ 19,000 people worldwide.

GLOBAL PRESENCE

From a small company originally formed to build steel wastebaskets, safes, and desks, Steelcase has grown into an industry giant that serves countries all over the world. Its expansive product line now includes both metal and wood office furniture, systems furniture, seating, computer support furniture, office and lounge seating, desks, case goods and storage cabinets, task lighting, and accessories. Recently Steelcase unveiled Pathways®, a revolutionary design concept integrating furniture, work tools, technology products, and interior architecture. The company manufactures at 31 facilities in the United States, Canada, and Mexico, and, through international subsidiaries, joint ventures, and licensing arrangements, at 20 facilities throughout the rest of the world.

"Our objective is to help customers create working environments that support their corporate strategy and culture," says James P. Hackett, president and chief executive officer of Steelcase Inc. "It's not just furniture anymore. The name of the game is working environments that integrate furniture, work tools, technology products, and interior architecture. The Pathways concept serves as an example of how Steelcase has expanded its focus and capabilities beyond its core products, and subsequently will shape the indus-

try well into the 21st century. Today, we've taken to calling our portfolio of products and services 'spaceware,' to reflect the increasing amount of knowledge and technology we're building into them."

Focused on far more than just selling office furniture, Steelcase's strategy is to help people work more effectively by offering comprehensive, integrated work environments that support customers' strategic intent. The company leads the industry in product innovation, and since 1994 has won 24 design awards for new products and enhancements across its product lines. Nowhere is this innovation more evident than in the company's Corporate Development Center, an incredible, $111 million, pyramid-shaped edifice that is the most comprehensive research and development facility in the industry, complete with 11 testing laboratories.

INNOVATION FOR THE FUTURE

Steelcase is constantly keeping its eye on the future, studying the ways people work and developing products that will work smarter for the high-performance business. This vision of the future can be seen in Steelcase's own headquarters. The company's Leadership Community, conceived by Hackett, is an executive work environment that is anything but traditional. An interactive work area was designed to foster team interaction and decision making among executives. "This Leadership Community is a learning experience for us to understand how we can work smarter and also better serve our customers who are facing similar challenges," Hackett notes.

In the years ahead, Steelcase is poised to remain at the forefront of the industry, creating work environments that trans-

form the ways people work and help them work more effectively than they ever thought they could. "We invest heavily in research and technology, and are constantly making efforts to better understand work for individuals and teams," says Bob Black, Steelcase vice president, marketing. One of the most effective ways Steelcase has found to do this is to be students of the workplace. "We learn as much from our customers as they learn from us," Black says, "and we've made extensive efforts to develop the communications link with our customers. We're convinced that there's no better way to develop products that really work for the people who use them."

Steelcase Inc. is poised to remain at the forefront of the office furniture industry, creating work environments that transform the ways people work and help them work more effectively than they ever thought they could.

ERVICE. MOST BUSINESSES TALK ABOUT IT. FOR THE PAST 100 years, Gordon Food Service (GFS) has focused on it. That sets it apart from other businesses in the food service industry. If someone refers to the company as Gordon Foods, a quick correction will follow: "It's Gordon Food Service." Service is

foundational to the success of GFS. When combined with high standards in the quality of food it distributes, both service and quality work together to make it the largest independent food distributor in the country today.

IT STARTED WITH BUTTER AND EGGS

Back in 1897, 23-year-old Isaac Van Westenbrugge borrowed $300 from his older brother Martin to start a business delivering butter and eggs to Grand Rapids grocery stores in his horse-drawn wagon. His first "distribution center" was

the barn behind their home, where his wife, Cornelia, ladled butter from 50-pound tubs into one-pound earthen crocks and used candles to check each egg for freshness. In 1916, Van Westenbrugge hired Ben Gordon, a high school senior, to help during the afternoons and on Saturdays. In 1921, Gordon married Van Westenbrugge's daughter Ruth. And in 1933, he became a partner in what became known as the Gordon-Van Cheese Company.

Today, Gordon Food Service distributes food and food-related items to restaurants, hotels, hospi-

tals, schools, and camps. The company also operates cash-and-carry stores, called GFS Marketplace, that support customers and offer food for special events and parties of any size. GFS carries in excess of 15,000 items that fall into 11 product groups: groceries, meats, poultry, dairy, frozen foods, seafood, fresh produce, beverage systems, tabletop and supplies, clean power/sanitation systems, and disposables. The company headquarters is located in Grand Rapids, with three distribution centers in Michigan and one in Ohio. There are sales offices and GFS Marketplace stores in Michigan, Indiana, Illinois, Ohio, Kentucky, and Pennsylvania. Two distribution centers in Ontario and five in Quebec make up GFS Canada, where GFS has the distinction of being the second-largest food distribution service in Canada.

CORNERSTONE VALUES

The mission statement at Gordon Food Service is quite simple: "Our purpose is to serve our customers with the highest-quality food service products and services. We achieve this purpose through innovative systems and the spirit and integrity of our people." GFS further defines seven Cornerstone Values to which the company adheres: Customer is King; Networking Organization (through initiative, teamwork, and decision making); Everyone is Important; Rewards for Performance (including financial incentives and recognition); War Room Mentality (with an emphasis on results); Integrity (of customers, employees, and suppliers); and Philosophy of Sharing (ideas and profits).

Dedication to quality is evident in every aspect of the company. GFS' sales representatives pride themselves on the close relationships they develop and maintain

For the past 100 years, Gordon Food Service has focused on its service to customers (top).

Gordon Food Service (GFS) distributes food and food-related items to restaurants, hotels, hospitals, schools, and camps (bottom).

with their customers, and they know their customers' histories and menu formats inside and out. The sales representatives take orders on laptop computers, then transmit the orders immediately to the Grand Rapids data center, which in turn quickly forwards the order to the nearest distribution center.

While that's impressive in itself, it's only the beginning. Gordon Food Service has a goal of 99 percent in stock at all times, which means 99 percent of the items a customer orders are at the distribution center ready to be shipped. Then, there's the company's on-time departure goal of 99 percent, which means the sales-service people leave the distribution center according to schedule and arrive at the customer's site on time.

Gordon Food Service is not satisfied with simply just reaching quality goals. It takes the stance that there are many more quality steps just waiting to be discovered—steps that will improve service to customers. Quality is measured in terms of what each customer thinks. The company's emphasis on quality may seem obsessive to some, but GFS believes that it is very important to the customer, and, therefore, it is important to GFS.

Growing into the Future

GFS moves into its second century of business having experienced double-digit growth for many years. Entering the Canadian market just three years ago, GFS has become the second-largest food

service distributor in Canada, with more growth planned there and elsewhere. To put the growth of this $1.5 billion company into perspective, 10 percent annual growth means GFS has to ship 30,000 more cases today than the same day last year. Needless to say, Gordon Food Service is diligent about maintaining controlled, but permanent growth.

But company growth isn't the only growth on which GFS focuses.

The firm is very dedicated to the professional and personal growth of its people, which is evident in the attitudes of those who work there. GFS people could easily be picked out of a crowd because they're spirited and enthusiastic, less concerned about rules and policies, and more concerned with getting the job done. The employees feel that GFS is their company. This is supported through a meaningful profit sharing plan that rewards their efforts year after year. GFS also acknowledges outstanding employee performance through annual inductions into the Gold Club, as well as with various departmental recognition awards.

Between the people and the product, Gordon Food Service customers get all they could ever need from a food service distributor: the highest quality, the best selection, unparalleled service, and a caring concern for their success. It's no surprise that GFS has been quite successful throughout its history. And there's no doubt that by maintaining its philosophy and values, the company will grow and prosper for a second century of service.

The company operates cash-and-carry stores, called GFS Marketplace, that support customers and offer food for special events and parties of any size.

GFS carries in excess of 15,000 items that fall into 11 product groups: groceries, meats, poultry, dairy, frozen foods, seafood, fresh produce, beverage systems, tabletop and supplies, clean power/sanitation systems, and disposables.

BULMAN PRODUCTS, INC.

N THE FRONT SECTION OF A SMALL PAPERBACK BOOK TITLED *Origin and Development of Bulman Industries*, the first paragraph reads, "Elvah Orville Bulman had an idea for a product. He also had the rented loft of one not very large and not very new barn, $200.00 capital and a great deal of determination in the year 1905." His product

was the Gem Take-up Twine Holder, a dispenser that held a cone or ball of twine.

In the years that followed, Bulman's company grew rapidly, and his product line expanded to include roll paper holders, cutters, and store fixtures. After retirement, his son, Orville Elvah Bulman, carried on until 1970 when he sold the company, but the Bulman name lives on. Today, Bulman Products, Inc. is the country's leading manufacturer of metal dispensers and cutters for rolls of art paper, gift wrap, food service wrapping film, and various industrial rolled products such as air bubble cushioning, poly foams, and single-face, corrugated cardboard.

FROM DEFENSE TO DISPENSERS

Jack Kirkwood, Bulman's owner, president, and CEO (along with a number of other titles), is the first to admit that he never planned on buying a business. He originally worked as a defense contract administrator in Michigan and Florida, and opted to return to Grand Rapids, where he joined Rospatch Corporation (now Ameriwood)

in the sales and customer service departments. Kirkwood worked his way up to the position of sales manager at Rospatch, and in 1980, he was asked to transfer to Bulman Products, which Rospatch had purchased from Orville Bulman 10 years earlier.

Kirkwood took over as Bulman Products' general manager, and after a few years, he made the decision to invest his own personal funds—"signing his life away," as he puts it—to buy the company. "When I bought this business, I saw it as a challenging opportunity, and a chance to build and develop

the business. And I've never once been sorry. There's a tremendous amount of satisfaction in creating a product from scratch, and having a whole market out there that actually wants to buy it."

Bulman's product line includes a complete line of dispensers, cutters, racks, and packing/shipping tables that are sold through distributors located around the country. Kirkwood says his direct customers are really the 3,500 distributors located throughout the United States and Canada, but end users include large industrial companies, such as General Motors and Steelcase; schools; department stores; huge shipping companies, such as FedEx and UPS; and nearly every corner drugstore, grocery store, butcher shop, or other business where paper is used for decorating, cushioning, wrapping, or shipping.

THE BULMAN PROCESS

Kirkwood's facility has 26,000 square feet of production space, including a large packaging and shipping area. The manufacturing process starts with coiled steel

DAVE RACZKOWSKI/THE GRAND RAPIDS PRESS

Jack Kirkwood, Bulman Products' owner, president, and CEO, stands in the 26,000-square-foot production space, which includes a large packaging and shipping area (top).

Bulman has grown considerably since its humble beginnings in a small, old, rented barn in 1905 under the direction of Elvah Orville Bulman (bottom).

Bulman's popular line of racks and cutters used in schools and art supply centers are durable, versatile, and safe.

that is first formed and then cut or stamped into a variety of shapes, using roll formers and punch presses. The parts are welded, degreased to remove oil and impurities, and prepared for painting, which is done with a powder-coating process. The final step is baking the parts in a 40-foot, gas-fired oven that uses infrared lighting to help speed the finishing process, which liquefies the powder coating and bakes the finish to a hard gloss. Parts are then assembled into the finished product, which is packaged and sealed for shipment.

Kirkwood says that while most of Bulman's products have ordinary, off-the-shelf applications, the company has developed some custom products for customers. One such job was for a large plastics manufacturer in New Jersey, for which Bulman developed a special dispenser for a film material used in laboratories. "This film is used to seal the tops of beakers at the end of the day," he says, "and our customer needed a special unit to hold and dispense the roll of film. There wasn't anything like that on the market, so we produced one for them."

Another major customer in Minnesota had developed a special coated paper used in factories to deflect sparks and protect products

Bulman dispensers for gift wrap and ribbon are found in malls, department stores, and gift shops all over the United States and Canada.

during the welding process. The company needed a dispenser to promote this paper, so it selected one of Bulman's standard dispensers. Since then, the customer has purchased more than 30,000 of these roll dispensers, and has become one of Bulman's largest customers.

Bulman Products employs 24 production workers, and also sponsors an enclave of mentally and physically challenged workers from Hope Network for assembly of hardware and small parts, and other routine assignments. Kirkwood says that because the company is so small, his employees are a close-knit group of people who are committed to maintaining high levels

of quality and customer service. Employee turnover at the company is very low.

Through the years, sales at Kirkwood's company have grown steadily. In 1982, annual sales volume was about $800,000; today, it tops $4 million, and Kirkwood says he expects this growth to continue. "We have a niche product with a very large customer base," he says. "Our distributors know they can count on us for quality products and competitive pricing, and they also know we keep our promises to ship when we say we're going to ship. That level of commitment has gotten us where we are, and I'm convinced it will be the key to our success in the future."

THE BEST SEATS IN THE HOUSE AT SOME OF THE NATION'S major venues have been provided by Irwin Seating Company. Carnegie Hall in New York City; Bobby Vinton Blue Velvet Theatre in Branson, Missouri; Fenway Park in Boston; Kravitz Center for Performing Arts in West Palm Beach;

Arthur Ashe Stadium, the U.S. Tennis Center in Flushing; and Boston Museum of Fine Arts Auditorium, designed by I.M. Pei, all feature seating made by Irwin.

STILL FAMILY OWNED AFTER 90 YEARS

Irwin Seating was founded in 1907 by five investors, including three Irwin brothers: Earle, Eber, and Robert. The company began as a manufacturer of school furniture and auditorium seating. In the 1970s, when the demand for school furniture declined due to decreasing school enrollments, Irwin decided to concentrate its efforts on seating for theaters and indoor arenas. By 1982, the company's sales had reached $16 million,

and auditorium and arena seating had become its biggest seller. The company soon began to increase its market share, and by 1990, annual sales had risen dramatically, to more than $55 million. Today, annual sales exceed $106 million, with 80 percent of those sales in auditorium seating.

For the past 15 years, Irwin Seating has remained the number one manufacturer of public seating for indoor arenas, auditoriums, and performing arts venues, as well as schools, churches, corporate auditoriums, and movie theaters all over the United States. The company is still owned and operated by the Irwin family, and since 1984, Earle S. "Win" Irwin—grandson of

founder Earle Irwin—has been president and chairman.

"The major difference between our company and other seating manufacturers," says Win Irwin, "is that our specialty is indoor auditorium seating, and we sell more of it than anyone in the world. Customers come to us because they know we make high-quality, durable products, and we're experts in our field. We're focused, and we work very hard at understanding the different markets we serve and knowing what their individual needs are."

Irwin Seating has three separate production facilities located in Grand Rapids on Fruit Ridge Road: the Upholstery and Wood Fabrication Factory, the Classroom

Today, sales at Irwin Seating exceed $106 million, with 80 percent of those sales in auditorium seating.

For the past 15 years, Irwin Seating has remained the number one manufacturer of public seating for indoor arenas, auditoriums, and performing arts venues, as well as schools, churches, corporate auditoriums, and movie theaters all over the United States.

Focused Factory, and the Auditorium Metal Fabrication Focused Factory. Together, these operations have a total of 550,000 square feet of state-of-the-art manufacturing and warehousing, and each features cellular, just-in-time manufacturing techniques.

Irwin Seating's Canadian subsidiary is located in Etobicoke, Ontario, and produces most of the seating sold to the Canadian market. In addition, the Canadian operation features a 62,000-square-foot seating restoration facility that restores and renovates old and worn-out seating for customers all over North America. Some of the venues for which Irwin Seating has successfully done restorations—including elegant historical seating—are Carnegie Hall and the Ed Sullivan Theatre, both in New York City; Ravinia Festival in Chicago; Princess of Wales Theatre in Toronto; Henry Ford Museum in Dearborn; and Tiger Stadium in Detroit.

Irwin's other subsidiary, Folding Bleacher Company, is located in Altamont, Illinois. Acquired in 1991, the company specializes in telescopic bleachers and platforms—such as those found in high school gyms—that fold, or telescope, into the wall for storage.

THE CHANGING FACE OF MOVIE THEATERS

Irwin says his company's sales to the movie theater market have shown a consistent increase during recent years, largely due to changes in movie theaters. Gone are the local movie houses with crowded, uncomfortable seats and one movie screen showing a single feature presentation. Today, cities have multiple-screen movie complexes that feature superb sound and luxurious seating with plenty of legroom, higher backs, beverage cup holders built into the arms—which Irwin Seating was the first to introduce—and the newest feature: flip-up arms that remove barriers between seats, made for moviegoers who want to sit closer to each other, or who need extra room for themselves.

"Movies are immensely popular today," says Irwin, "but that really isn't the biggest change, because people in this country have always been moviegoers. The difference is, now theaters have to compete with your home, where the television and video equipment are often quite sophisticated. Their challenge is to provide a total entertainment package with pictures, sound, comfort, and ambience that motivates you to leave your home and go visit the theater."

VISION FOR THE FUTURE

Irwin says his company plans to increase its sales in the international market, which presently amount to about 10 percent of total sales. He says that one huge area of opportunity is in the movie theater market in Asia, Latin America, and Europe. "American films are extremely popular worldwide," he says. "And with today's technology, it's now possible for them to receive our films at the same time we receive them, so we expect this market—and the demand for our cinema seating—to grow rapidly." The company has established a joint venture in Port Klang, Malaysia, where a manufacturing operation will serve the company's markets in Southeast Asia.

Going forward, Irwin says his vision is for the company to continue to be a world leader in public seating. "People turn to Irwin Seating because of our excellent quality products, our values, our integrity, and our superior service," he says. "We want to be considered a world-class company. And after more than 90 years of continued success, we have every reason to believe in a very prosperous future."

THE AMWAY GRAND PLAZA HOTEL HAS BEEN CALLED ONE OF the most elegant establishments in the country. Located on the east bank of the Grand River, in the heart of the city's museum and entertainment district, this four-star hotel charms visitors with its lustrous Austrian crystal

chandeliers; domed ceilings delicately trimmed in gold leaf (the largest installation of gold leaf in North America); 17th-century, hand-carved Italian sunburst; and lovely antique furnishings. Well-traveled individuals accustomed to the best hotels in major cities around the world are pleasantly surprised by the Amway Grand Plaza's level of elegance, sophistication, and friendliness found in a midsize midwestern city.

A LEGACY OF ELEGANCE AND GRACE

The Amway Grand Plaza was formerly the Pantlind Hotel. Built in 1913, the Pantlind was fashioned after English Adams architecture by its designers Warren & Westmore of New York City, who also designed the lavish Grand Central Station and the Biltmore Hotel. By 1925, the Pantlind was considered one of the 10 finest hotels in America.

In 1978, the hotel was purchased by Rich DeVos and Jay Van Andel, cofounders of Amway Corporation, and renamed as the Amway Grand Plaza Hotel. Immediately, an extensive reconstruction of the hotel began to restore its history of grace and elegance. Its original section reopened in 1981, and the 29-story glass tower was completed two years later in 1983.

Today, the Amway Grand Plaza is West Michigan's largest and most complete hotel and convention complex. It features 682 designer-decorated guest rooms, including 40 spacious suites, all decorated in a rich, traditional style representative of Grand Rapids' fine furniture history.

The Grand Plaza offers a plethora of dining choices, including two restaurants specializing in fine dining. The graceful and charming 1913

Room has been recognized more than any other Grand Rapids-area restaurant for excellent service and exceptional cuisine. The incomparable Cygnus offers guests breathtaking views from the Grand Plaza's 29th floor, along with cutting-edge gourmet cuisine and dancing under the stars. The Grand Plaza's seven other restaurants and lounges are all uniquely different in atmosphere and specialty, and offer guests a choice of cuisine ranging from express gourmet sandwiches and traditional café favorites to lavish luncheon buffets. Guests may also find exciting entertainment in Tinseltown, a restaurant and bar designed to pay tribute to music and movies.

UNPARALLELED SERVICE

The genuine friendliness and caring attitude of the Amway Grand Plaza's staff is incomparable. For the Grand Plaza's attention to even the smallest details, it has earned the prestigious Mobil Four-Star Award. This award is only received by the top 2 percent of all lodging establishments rated by Mobil

in North America. This designation demonstrates the quality experience guests will receive when visiting.

Guests of the Grand Plaza often comment about the friendly attitude of the hotel staff, who pay attention to detail and are willing to handle requests quickly and with a smile—a caring attitude not found everywhere by the hotel's well-traveled guests.

This level of superior service also extends to convention and meeting visitors, representing about 60 percent of the Grand Plaza's business. For 12 consecutive years, the hotel has won the prestigious Pinnacle Award from *Successful Meetings* magazine, and has also earned *Meetings & Conventions* magazine's Gold Key Award and the Planner's Choice Award from *Meeting News* magazine's readers. All of these awards are presented for excellence in service and outstanding facilities.

Often called the convention planner's dream, the Amway Grand Plaza has 30 meeting and banquet rooms, each individually decorated, providing more than 40,000 square feet of function space. The hotel is linked by an enclosed skywalk to the Grand Center, offering an additional 120,000 square feet of exhibit space plus auditorium facilities seating 2,400 people. The skywalk also links the hotel to the Van Andel Arena, a sports and entertainment facility.

Many first-time guests are often surprised to find one of the country's finest hotels in the heart of downtown Grand Rapids. With its rich history and reputation for exceptional service, the Amway Grand Plaza Hotel is certain to have many repeat visitors and will keep on pleasantly surprising new ones.

The Amway Grand Plaza Hotel is West Michigan's largest and most complete hotel and convention complex. It features 682 designer-decorated guest rooms, including 40 spacious suites, all decorated in a rich, traditional style representative of Grand Rapids' fine furniture history (top).

Located on the east bank of the Grand River, in the heart of the city's museum and entertainment district, the four-star hotel charms visitors with its lustrous Austrian crystal chandeliers; domed ceilings delicately trimmed in gold leaf; 17th-century, hand-carved Italian sunburst; and lovely antique furnishings (bottom).

FOR MORE THAN 80 YEARS, THE NAME GUARDSMAN HAS BEEN A familiar one to those who know and appreciate fine wood furniture. Founded in 1915 as Grand Rapids Varnish Corporation, the company's original product was varnish for local wood furniture manufacturers. Through the years, the company—now

called Guardsman Consumer Products—has built a reputation as America's premium supplier of high-quality furniture care products, and has also expanded and diversified to offer a wide array of consumer specialty products.

SPECIALISTS IN NICHE MARKETING

One of the company's greatest strengths is its ability to seek out market niches. "We've never concentrated on being the biggest consumer products company," says Kip Vander Hyde, Guardsman's vice president and general manager. "Instead, we've concentrated our efforts on being successful at niche marketing for all divisions of our business. It's what we specialize in, and we see enormous potential for our company both in the United States and many other parts of the world."

Guardsman Products, which became a strategic business unit of Indianapolis-based Lilly Industries, Inc. in 1996, manufactures and distributes a wide variety of consumer products through four separate businesses: the Interior Care Division, the Consumer Products Division, the Specialty Products Division, and the WoodPro Division. All four divisions provide services or products that are marketed worldwide.

From offices in the United States, the United Kingdom, and Australia, the Interior Care Division provides fabric protection and furniture care products to consumers through furniture stores in the United States, Canada, Mexico, South Africa, and Europe. In fact, the Interior Care Division is the world's largest supplier of the retail-applied fabric protection known as Fabri-Coate.

The Consumer Products Division markets several well-known brand-name consumer specialty items, such as Guardsman Furniture Polish, Goof Off paint remover, One-Wipe dust cloth, and the well-known Chip Clip snack closures. Guardsman's third division, the Specialty Products Division, manufactures private-label automotive aftermarket products, such as brake part cleaner, fuel injector cleaner, and engine oil supplements.

CONTINUING TO DIVERSIFY

Vander Hyde says he sees continued growth and diversification for Guardsman in the future. "We've grown rapidly since 1990," he says. "In fact, we've more than tripled our sales and earnings in a highly competitive marketplace. I definitely see that growth continuing through our pursuit of niche markets."

Vander Hyde expects the company to become even more market driven and more innovative. "The very nature of our business is that we're different and complex," he says, "and we're very diverse for our size. If there's one thing that really sets us apart, it's that. We see unlimited opportunities for our company to find niche markets and to serve them. There's no doubt in my mind that we have a very bright future ahead of us."

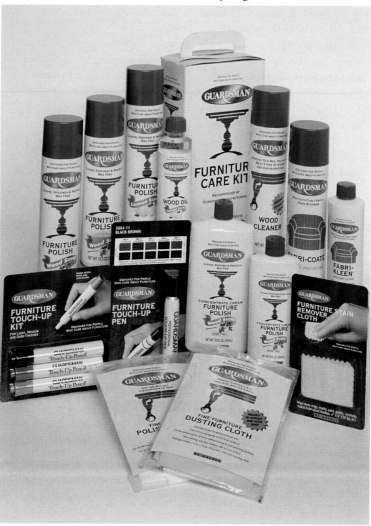

During its more than 80 years, Guardsman Consumer Products has built a reputation as America's premium supplier of high-quality furniture care products.

THOUSANDS OF PEOPLE CHOOSE GRAND RAPIDS COMMUNITY College (GRCC) each year. Whether pursuing an associate's degree, job training or retraining, lifelong learning, or simply discovering one's pursuit, GRCC offers diverse academic options for everyone. Like those who attend GRCC every year, thousands have discovered its value: credits transfer to four-year institutions; day, evening, weekend, and off-site classes are offered; it is affordable; classes are smaller; and there are more than 160 curricula from which to choose.

Regardless of the reason, all of these students have one thing in common: they seek knowledge, and Grand Rapids Community College provides an ideal academic environment for them to find it.

LIBERAL ARTS: THE HEART OF GRCC

Founded in 1914 as a liberal arts preparatory school for the University of Michigan, the school was originally called Grand Rapids Junior College and was the first two-year public community college in the state of Michigan. Initially, six faculty members taught courses in rhetoric and composition, mathematics, history, biology, physics, Latin, and German; the first graduating class totaled 49 students.

Today, GRCC's expansive campus covers a total of eight city blocks, and it is the fifth-largest community college in Michigan. There are nearly 14,000 students enrolled, studying more than 1,600 classes that range from anthropology to chemistry, criminal justice to computer programming, and economics to Spanish. In addition to traditional classroom environments, classes are also taught through community service offerings, seminars, workshops, training classes, and other educational activities.

GRCC's faculty is well known for including some of the finest professors in their respective fields. Some of its distinguished members are Walter Lockwood, a screenwriter who has written three CBS television movies in the past six years; Greg Forbes, a biology professor and internationally recognized expert on sea turtles; Jonathon Russell, a photographer whose photography program is known throughout the country; Nancy Clouse, a well-known artist and author; Mary Scanlon, a pianist, composer, and Fulbright scholar; and Duane Davis, whose vocal jazz ensemble has been recognized as the nation's best.

MEETING A WIDE VARIETY OF COMMUNITY NEEDS

Richard W. Calkins, president, says that GRCC is very clear on its niche in the community: "We're a two-year college, and that means our mission is very different from other schools. We know what our focus is, and we concentrate on it. Our task is to determine what this community wants and needs, and then determine how we can provide it." Calkins says one way GRCC listens to the community is by holding regular forums in which anyone interested can participate and offer input that will help guide the colleges planning for the future.

GRCC has traditionally been known as a two-year transfer college because it offers so many courses designed to prepare students for a four-year college or university. In fact, according to Kent County statistics, 33 of every 100 students begin their college careers at GRCC—including a large number of practicing attorneys and doctors. More than 60 occupational programs and approximately 80 preprofessional programs are offered through the school.

GRCC's instructional programs are organized into three schools, each of which includes liberal arts and occupational education programs. The School of Social Science and Humanities offers studies in social science, behavioral sciences, English, language and thought, visual and performing arts, and hospitality education. The School of Mathematics, Natural Science, Health and Wellness offers courses in mathematics, physical science, biological sciences, dentistry, nursing, occupational therapy, and radiological technology. And the School of Workforce Development includes studies in architecture, business, criminal justice, computer applications, drafting, engineering, electronics, energy management, fashion merchandising, interiors and furnishings, manufacturing, and technology, as well as appren-

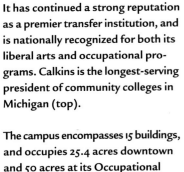

Since 1975, Richard W. Calkins has led Grand Rapids Community College. It has continued a strong reputation as a premier transfer institution, and is nationally recognized for both its liberal arts and occupational programs. Calkins is the longest-serving president of community colleges in Michigan (top).

The campus encompasses 15 buildings, and occupies 25.4 acres downtown and 50 acres at its Occupational Training Center. Classes are also offered at several off-site locations during the academic year (bottom).

JOHN CORRIVEAU

ticeship programs. A total of seven associate degrees are offered at GRCC in the areas of applied arts and sciences, arts, business, general studies, music, nursing, and science, as well as more than a dozen one-year program certificates.

The occupational training program at GRCC offers practical, short-term, noncredit training classes designed to place people in jobs in the shortest time possible. The GRCC Occupational Training Center—located at the corner of Leonard Street and Ball Avenue in northeast Grand Rapids—provides training and various certifications for people who wish to gain occupational skills and enhance their employment opportunities.

The college's Business and Technical Training program is dedicated to providing customized

training and services to the business community. The program annually serves more than 350 area businesses and industries, and offers workshops on 165 diverse topics—including team skills and problem solving, computer-aided design and computer-aided manufacturing (CAD/CAM) applications, and statistical process control, as well as many others—to employees from throughout West Michigan.

ADAPTING TO CHANGE

Calkins says GRCC has always been and will continue to be responsive to the changing needs of the community. "We're in the middle of immense change in education," he says, "and colleges will have to learn to adapt to students' changing lifestyles while still maintaining a tradition of

excellence. The word 'change' will be at the heart of successful institutions. And while that might be a new concept for some institutions, it's not for us. That's always been our way of thinking."

One of the most recent additions includes the development of the Community Learning Enterprise (CLE), which was established to promote and deliver products and services to continually improve learning systems throughout the community. The CLE is a network of educators and business and community leaders who are working collaboratively in the arena of individual, organizational, and community learning.

The college is currently finalizing a 20-year construction program, which included the complete renovation of the Spectrum Theatre; GRCC's Applied Technology Center, which was built in partnership with Ferris State University; a newly renovated music center; a second parking ramp; and a new, $30 million science building, which is scheduled for completion in 2000. In spite of these physical improvements, Calkins says the school's primary focus remains on teaching: "Buildings are important, but they're still just bricks and mortar to enhance instruction. The most vital element in GRCC's success is to create an environment where we can help students learn. That's always been our focus, and it always will be."

Clockwise from top:
Students from a baking and pastry class, one of GRCC's recent curriculum additions, watch Marcia Rango, hospitality education instructor, demonstrate the art of bread making. The internationally acclaimed hospitality education program includes transfer, associate degree, and certificate options.

Students at GRCC are among the 10 million nationwide who attend a community college. Along with its strong academic programs, GRCC provides many collegiate and community activities.

GRCC's long-standing liberal arts program includes several community partnerships within the theater program. The new, $6 million Spectrum Theater Building was completed in 1997. Students practice improvisation in a theater class seminar.

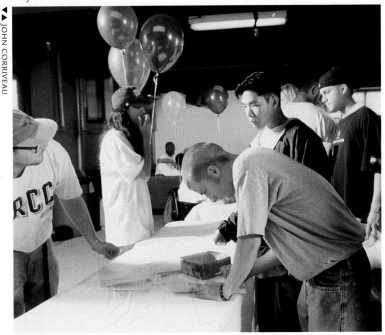

ACK IN 1917, COMPETITION FROM LARGE, NATIONAL CHAINS FORCED small, independent grocery stores to make a choice: either find a way to band together, or be forced out of business. So, during that year, 27 independent grocers officially joined together to form a cooperative organization called the Grand Rapids

Wholesale Grocery Company. And their strategy worked. Today, that organization has evolved into Spartan Stores, Inc., the ninth-largest grocery wholesaler in the United States. It has grown from the 27 original members to 450 independent supermarkets located in Michigan, Indiana, and Ohio. And from its first purchase of a boxcar load of sugar, Spartan Stores now distributes more than 40,000 products.

AMAZING SUCCESS STORY

During Spartan's first seven years of business, the company added 154 new members, and increased its capital and its overall efficiency. By the end of the 1920s, the future was looking rosy. Even during the Great Depression, the company continued to expand. In 1934, the company was strong and sales had surpassed the $1 million mark; by 1949, that sales figure had topped $10 million.

Clockwise from top right: Spartan Stores, Inc. distributes more than 40,000 national brand and private label products, and provides operational services to 450 supermarkets in Michigan, Indiana, and Ohio. Fifty-three of these stores are in the Greater Grand Rapids area.

Nearly 1,700 associates work at Spartan's 135-acre main complex in Byron Center, where each week 675 truckloads of product leave the gates.

More than 1,800 items make up the Spartan private label brand, which is one of the most widely distributed and recognized private labels in Michigan.

The 1950s brought several significant changes for the company, including the establishment of its first wholly owned subsidiary, the United Wholesale Grocery Company. During this time, the Spartan warrior was adopted as the official company symbol, to signify strength through unity. And in 1954, the first Spartan private label product—a bag of coffee—marked the beginning of a complete line of Spartan brand products. Today, the line has grown to more than 1,800 Spartan brand items, representing one of the most widely distributed and accepted private labels in Michigan.

The 1960s and 1970s brought continued growth for Spartan Stores, which began to add new areas of customer service such as in-store bakeries, delis, and general merchandise departments. In 1975, the company moved into its current, 1 million-square-foot warehouse and office complex on 76th Street, and by 1982, Spartan Stores had reached a landmark $1 billion in annual sales.

From 1985 through 1997, Patrick M. Quinn served as president and led the company through years of unprecedented growth. During this time, sales nearly doubled from $1.3 billion in 1984 to $2.54 billion in 1995. Quinn also initiated a Together We Serve corporate phi-

losophy to put the emphasis on service.

Today, Spartan Stores has seven subsidiaries, including J.F. Walker Company, Inc., which supplies products to 3,700 convenience retailers in seven states; L&L/Jiroch Distributing Company, which supplies products to convenience retailers, and confections, tobacco products, and specialty foods to retail grocers; Market Development Corporation, a real estate holding company with title to more than 1 million square feet of real estate in supermarkets and shopping centers; Shield Benefit Administrators, Inc., a third-party employee benefit administrator; Shield Insurance Services, Inc. and Spartan Insurance Company, Ltd., both insurance providers for Spartan Stores' retail customers; and United Wholesale Grocery Company, a cash-and-carry wholesaler serving 4,700 convenience stores from 13 locations in Michigan and Ohio.

Focused on the Customer

From its headquarters in Grand Rapids and a second warehouse in Plymouth, Michigan, Spartan Stores buys, receives, warehouses, and distributes products to its independent retail customers. The Grand Rapids grocery warehouse is nearly 600,000 square feet and holds more than 2.3 million cases of product; the perishable warehouse covers more than 300,000 square feet; and the general merchandise warehouse includes more than 280,000 square feet.

According to Gary Evey, Spartan Stores' communications manager, the company's focus is on helping its retailers gain a competitive market advantage to become more successful. "Our 450 independent retail supermarkets enjoy the flexibility of having individual identities," says Evey, "yet they're able to work together with us to benefit from our company's buying power, support, and marketing opportunities—much like a chain. We often use the phrase 'buying together, selling together, maintaining independence,' and that, along with our company motto, is indicative of our strong commitment to our customers."

Spartan Stores also offers its retailers a wide array of services that extend far beyond the supply and delivery of product. The company provides more than 150 business-related services ranging from helping retailers purchase land for a new store to designing and printing grand opening promotional materials.

A Good Corporate Citizen

Through its Spartan Brand Cash for Labels program, Spartan Stores contributes in excess of $150,000 annually to more than 5,000 community organizations. The company also donates more than 2 million pounds of food every year to Second Harvest state food banks, International Aid, American Red Cross, and local soup kitchens and organizations.

Since 1985, Spartan Stores has been an exclusive sponsor of the Michigan Special Olympics Summer Games, and is also a major contributor to the Special Olympics held in Ohio and Indiana. In the last 12 years, the company has contributed more than $4 million to Special Olympics. Spartan Stores also regularly sponsors the Walter Hagen Golf Classic to benefit the American Cancer Society of Kent County, as well as supporting many local colleges, United Way, Junior Achievement, the arts, emergency relief for victims of national disasters, and other community programs.

In 1995, Spartan Stores, Inc. was honored as the top grocery industry company in the country with *Supermarket Business* magazine's annual Award of Excellence. And in 1996, the company was included in the Fortune 500 list of America's largest industrial and service companies. "We've always measured our success in terms of our customers' success," says Evey, "and we will continue to do that in the

years ahead. Our goal is to help our retailers stay strong and independent, and to support them with the finest quality products and services. This has worked for us for more than 80 years, and it will be at the heart of our continued success in the future."

Among its many community involvement efforts, Spartan Stores, Inc. has been the exclusive sponsor of the Michigan Special Olympics Summer Games since 1985, annually contributing nearly $300,000 and providing 800 volunteers (top).

Spartan is an efficient, low-cost distributor focused on a simple objective: getting to its customers the right product at the right price at the right time (bottom).

WITH ENORMOUS TANKS OF SUGAR, FLOUR, AND LIQUID coatings, the environment at Holland American Wafer is like something out of *Willy Wonka and the Chocolate Factory*. Specially designed mixers whip giant-sized batches of fluffy fillings, and continu-

ous streams of liquid dough are pumped directly to massive ovens. There are enormous quantities of vanilla, chocolate, and strawberry sugar wafers and other confections, all waiting to be cut or packaged. But instead of a movie set, this is part of a typical day at Holland American Wafer Company.

A SWEET ADDITION TO GRAND RAPIDS

In 1919, G. Adrian Heyboer started the business he called Holland American Wafer. Initially operating

Holland American Wafer Company's chocolate enrobing machine covers wafers with chocolate.

out of his home, Heyboer produced a small variety of Dutch Twins treats, including sugar wafers, chocolate sticks, and caramel-coated wafers, which he would then deliver to grocery stores in tin boxes that he picked up and refilled later. Through the years, as the demand for Heyboer's tasty products continued to grow, the company also grew, adding associates, increasing the variety of products offered, and expanding several times at its South Division location. In 1978, the company moved, this time to a 135,000-square-foot facility on Roger B. Chaffee Memorial Drive, where it is located today.

NOT JUST WAFERS ANYMORE

Through the years, Holland American Wafer not only has grown larger, but also has diversified. According to Stu Vander Heide, the founder's grandson and current president, the company continues to expand into many new product areas. "Some people still think of us as a company that's limited to making old-fashioned sugar wafers," he says. "But the truth is, we make a wide variety of not only sugar, chocolate, and

caramel wafer cookies, but also granola, granola bars, and marshmallow crisped rice treats. Our presence in the cookie, cereal, and cereal bar markets is really quite large."

Holland American Wafer distributes its products through three different channels. The company has contract manufacturing arrangements and partnerships with major food manufacturers, for whom it produces and packages granola, granola bars, and cereal bars. It also makes a variety of store brand products for large retail grocers, convenience stores, and consumer buying clubs; and it markets its own Dutch Twins brand wafer cookies, chocolate caramel cookies, and cereal bars through retail channels.

A DIFFERENT WAY OF BAKING

In addition to delicious and well-guarded family recipes, Holland American Wafer uses state-of-the-art baking technology to ensure the high quality of its products. In the 1950s, the company invested in European band ovens, which were designed to bake two layers of wafers in continuous sheets, rather than in individual sheets; the result is greater consistency in the quality and color of the wafers. Today, these ovens are still in use, and the company is one of only two places in the world that uses this high-volume method of baking, a method Vander Heide says is far superior to any other.

"We continuously have visitors from major food corporations," he says, "who actually come here to see how we can do things for them. They're interested in our baking systems, our computer systems, and our bar-coding and inventory processes. We're constantly on the lookout for new and better technology to help us work more efficiently, make our processes run

In addition to delicious and well-guarded family recipes, Holland American Wafer uses state-of-the-art baking technology to ensure the high quality of its products.

more smoothly, and ensure the finest-quality products."

When it comes to making decisions about new investments in equipment or technology, the company is committed to all levels of associates being involved in decision making. "We believe in being a learning organization," says Vander Heide, "and that means we learn from each other. Our people are continuously encouraged to express their opinions and ideas about how we can work better, what processes we should use, and what technology and equipment can help us work more efficiently." Vander Heide says that over the last five years, the company's investments in technology and equipment have tripled.

According to Vander Heide, the 325 associates at Holland American Wafer are an extremely dedicated

and loyal group of people. The company uses cross-functional teams to help with decision making, gives out regular bonuses based on productivity and company profitability, and also gives incentives to associates for perfect attendance.

"Our company philosophy is based on the simple truth that people are valuable, and they deserve to be treated that way," Vander Heide says. "Our turnover rate is very low, and I believe it's because our associates are happy here. They're in an environment of respect where they feel appreciated. Because of that, they're willing to go the extra mile for us and for our customers." The company encourages associates to regularly rotate jobs within the manufacturing facility to break the monotony of doing the same tasks repeatedly;

it also has an overtime policy that is completely voluntary.

In terms of growth, Holland American Wafer has doubled the size of its workforce since 1992, and an additional 85,000-square-foot facility was purchased to increase the company's manufacturing and warehousing space. Vander Heide says his vision is to stay ahead of the game. "Vince Lombardi said that there's no such thing as luck, but rather, opportunity meets preparedness," says Vander Heide, "and I sincerely believe that. If we're ready for the future, there's loads of opportunity. The world is constantly changing, and those changes present continued opportunities for success. The right things have happened for us, and I believe they'll continue to happen. How we prepare ourselves is key."

In terms of growth, Holland American Wafer has doubled the size of its workforce since 1992, and an additional 85,000-square-foot facility was purchased to increase the company's manufacturing and warehousing space (left).

An employee performs research and quality analysis in the company's Quality Assurance laboratory (right).

Enormous quantities of wafers, granola bars, and many other confections wait to be packaged by the wrapping machine or cut by the treats slitter.

KENDALL COLLEGE OF ART & DESIGN IS A SCHOOL WHERE creativity is a part of everyday life and where students are encouraged to explore their artistic vision to its fullest. Known for being innovative and for providing the absolute finest in art and design education, Kendall offers programs

in fine arts, illustration, industrial design, interior design, furniture design, visual communications, and art history. But Kendall does more than just teach students how to create art; it also prepares them for professional careers in art and design.

Originally founded in 1928 as a living memorial to one of the country's most prominent furniture designers, David Wolcott Kendall, the school officially opened its doors in 1931 with 35 students. Over the years, Kendall grew steadily, changing its name to the Kendall School of Design, and then to the Kendall College of Art & Design. Today, with a student population of approximately 600 and as one of only two

art and design schools in the state of Michigan, Kendall has evolved into a highly respected and nationally recognized four-year college specializing in art and design.

A UNIQUE ENVIRONMENT

According to Dr. Oliver H. Evans, Kendall's president, students who attend Kendall are part of an environment that's competitive enough to challenge, supportive enough to nurture, and attractive enough to inspire. "Kendall students are encouraged to fully develop their talents by professors who are themselves working artists," says Evans. "Many of them have earned national recognition for their talents in art and design, and they're eager

to share their skills and insight with students."

Kendall's classes are small, allowing students to receive personalized attention. The curriculum is specialized and intensive, with bachelor's degree programs offered in fine arts, furniture design, illustration, industrial design, interior design, visual communications, and art history. Kendall students have access to superb resources, such as a comprehensive arts library, a fully equipped model and wood shop, a photography studio and darkroom, computer labs featuring state-of-the-art technology, and an impressive art gallery, which regularly exhibits a wide variety of work by both national and international artists.

Kendall's campus is in the heart of downtown Grand Rapids near the historic Heritage Hill district. Because of the school's close proximity to art galleries, museums, theaters, concert halls, restaurants, and coffeehouses, culture and entertainment are always within walking distance.

DIVERSE STUDENTS, DIVERSE CHOICES

Kendall has a history of introducing students of varied ages and

Clockwise from top:
Known for being innovative and for providing the absolute finest in art and design education, Kendall College of Art & Design offers programs in fine arts, illustration, industrial design, interior design, furniture design, visual communications, and art history.

"We provide an environment that allows students to take their talents and run with them. When they graduate from Kendall, they've gained a greater appreciation for art and design. But they've also gained the ability to pursue professional lives as artists and designers," says Dr. Oliver H. Evans, Kendall's president.

Kendall works on a continuing basis with local school teachers and administrators to create a greater awareness of art and to help keep it alive in the schools.

backgrounds to career possibilities they may never have imagined before. While many of Kendall's students are of traditional college age, there are also many adult students who have returned to college, and who may have family and job responsibilities in addition to school. Kendall makes it a priority to be sensitive to the demands of these students' busy lives, helping them get the most out of their education and preparing them for art and design careers when they graduate.

The school also offers a wide variety of continuing studies classes. Each year, more than 2,000 students enroll in approximately 150 courses designed for children, youth, and adults. Subjects are diverse, covering such areas as photography, fashion design, watercolor and oil painting, computer design, and basic drawing.

STRONG FURNITURE TIES

When Kendall was originally founded, its specialty was furniture design, and the school is still closely connected to the furniture industry. "It's difficult to find a furniture company anywhere that isn't touched by Kendall graduates in some way," says Evans, adding that Kendall is known throughout the country for its excellent furniture design programs. West Michigan is widely regarded as the office furniture capital of the world, and many students who specialize in furniture design often go on to work as designers for local office furniture companies. Many others move to North Carolina, which is now the home of most residential furniture companies.

TIES TO THE COMMUNITY

From the very beginning, many Grand Rapids citizens and businesses have generously supported Kendall with gifts and donations, and Kendall is highly committed to giving back to the community. Each year the college provides support to the Arts Festival by making its facility available for exhibits, performances, and participatory activities. Kendall also regularly

sponsors programs such as the Regional Scholastics Arts Awards competition, which attracts more than 500 pieces of artwork from area junior and senior high schools. And the college works on a continuing basis with local school teachers and administrators to create a greater awareness of art and to help keep it alive in the schools.

AN EXCITING FUTURE BECKONS

In 1996, Kendall entered into an alliance with Ferris State University, and the merger between the two schools will be complete by 2000. As part of the merger plan, Kendall will expand its facility by 44,000 square feet, including new classrooms, a student center, and

student studio space. For students, this affiliation means additional facilities, resources, and programs, as well as expanded learning opportunities in both art and technology.

According to Evans, Kendall will continue to grow, but the school will always remain small enough to provide students with the kind of focused education it's known for. "We provide an environment that allows students to take their talents and run with them," he says. "When they graduate from Kendall, they've gained a greater appreciation for art and design. But they've also gained the ability to pursue professional lives as artists and designers."

Kendall students have access to superb resources, such as a comprehensive arts library, a fully equipped model and wood shop, a photography studio and darkroom, computer labs featuring state-of-the-art technology, and an impressive art gallery, which regularly exhibits a wide variety of work by both national and international artists (top).

Kendall's classes are small, allowing students to receive personalized attention. The curriculum is specialized and intensive, with bachelor's degree programs offered in fine arts, furniture design, illustration, industrial design, interior design, visual communications, and art history (bottom).

When Tom Peters wrote *In Search of Excellence*, he profiled exemplary companies that were successful because of their attitudes about quality, attention to detail, loyalty to customers, and commitment to employees. If Peters had encountered Betz

Industries, he would surely have included it as an example of such excellence. As a maker of metal castings for the automotive and machine tool industries, the company has all the qualities necessary to be rated as world class: an unparalleled attitude toward quality, a high concern about protecting the environment, a strong sense of commitment to its employees, and a true determination to provide customers with the absolute best products and services.

A Craft Learned in Europe

Metal casting—the making of objects by pouring molten metal into a cavity mold—has played a significant role in history. Cast-bronze cannons, railroad wheels, cooking kettles, and cast-iron bridges were all created through this process. When Karl Betz Sr. was living in his native Germany, he learned that a trade was an important part of one's education. He spent countless hours training with the best craftsmen in the foundry industry. At the

age of 21, Betz left Germany for the United States to work in a foundry. It was here that he met Marie Geiger, also an emigrant from Germany. They were married in Grand Rapids, and six years later built a 40- by 40-foot building and established Betz Foundry.

Beginning the business in 1933 at the height of the Great Depression, Betz realized the only way his business could survive was if he, Marie, and their few employees took immense pride in their work and focused on customers' needs. An entrepreneur from the start, Betz saw an opportunity to make new cast-iron firepots for home owners to replace worn-out parts for coal and wood-burning furnaces. His business eventually branched out into producing machine tool castings, and then expanded further into serving major automobile makers like General Motors, Ford, and Chrysler.

Another Generation

Betz' sons, Karl Jr. and Ken, joined their father in the family business after college. Karl Sr. had explained that in Europe, his trade was considered one of the most challenging and respected. He considered his craft an art form, creating structure from concept, and he took great pride in the quality and precision of his work. In 1984, the elder Betz died; however, the passion he had for his craft and for serving customers lives on.

Both brothers agree on the legacy left by their father. "Even though he's no longer with us," says Karl Jr., "his philosophy and the pride he took in the metal casting industry are still present in our business today. Those qualities will always be a part of Betz Industries."

Ken Betz (left), vice president, and Karl Betz Jr., president, are the second-generation leaders of Betz Industries.

Through the years, Betz Industries has expanded extensively. What started out as a 1,600-square-foot foundry has grown into a 300,000-square-foot, state-of-the-art manufacturing firm.

Betz Industries utilizes and aids in engineering the latest handling, molding, melting, and blasting equipment. Capacity has expanded to the production of castings ranging from 40 to 40,000 pounds. The company's largest customers are still General Motors, Ford, and Chrysler, but Betz Industries has also become the primary casting source for Toyota and Honda of North America. "Given the quality standards for the automotive industry, we are proud of our reputation and relationship with each of them," says Karl Jr. Machine tool castings also remain a large and important part of the company's business. Diversity in their customer base allows Betz Industries to survive during normal industry downturns.

THE PRECISION CRAFT OF PATTERN MAKING

In the past, die casting patterns were typically made of wood, which was expensive and often cumbersome. Today, the castings produced by Betz Industries are most often made of evaporative styrofoam patterns, a revolutionary pattern-making method that originated in Germany. First developed in the 1960s, the styrofoam method was viewed as a labor saver, but the surface defects originally associated with this process, such as residues caused by entrapment of gases, made it a less than perfect casting method. Betz immediately saw the potential quality and cost advantages of the styrofoam patterns. The people at Betz Industries have worked for years to perfect the technology that makes the lost-foam process, which uses styrofoam patterns and is more desirable than cavity mold making, which utilizes wood patterns.

One of the quality controls that allows Betz Industries to produce such high-precision castings is having its own pattern shop. The quality of the pattern is an extremely important aspect in producing high-quality castings. "Pattern making is also an art," Ken says, "and it's a difficult, highly skilled process. In our pattern shop, we have precision pattern makers who have trained for up to eight years in their trade. They're the best at what they do, and their high levels of skill—including CAD/CAM design and CNC solid model cutting—help us ensure the very best precision castings for our customers." An apprenticeship program was established in 1994 at Betz Pattern to ensure a highly skilled staff for the future.

Today, Betz Industries uses styrofoam patterns about 75 percent of the time. Ken continues, "What we've found is that we can control the gases that are created

Betz Industries' corporate office is located in the northwest Grand Rapids area.

by controlling the density of the styrofoam, so we've established strict guidelines for the styrofoam we buy for our patterns." This allows pattern making to be more accurate at a significantly lower cost. Betz Industries is one of only a few companies in the world to specialize in both the production of styrofoam patterns and the use of those patterns to manufacture iron castings.

MORE THAN A FOUNDRY

Karl Jr. explains, "Our customers are demanding more complete services: patterns, castings, heat treating, and machining. Betz is preparing to be a turnkey outlet for its customers." As a result, the corporate name was changed from Betz Foundry to Betz Industries.

Its strikingly beautiful corporate headquarters, located on Grand Rapids' northwest side, also reinforces Betz Industries' positive image. The front of the building features natural landscaping, and prominently displayed is a cast-iron sculpture of the corporate logo, custom-made by Betz artisans. The main staircase railings also incorporate the cast-iron logo to indicate the pride so evident throughout this organization. Inside the building, a spacious, sun-filled lobby surrounded by floor-to-ceiling windows welcomes visitors.

As for the Betz Casting Center, it could not contrast more from the foundries of yesterday. It is an ultramodern facility that features highly sophisticated technology, including computerized statistical process controls (SPC) that are used to guide every stage of the casting process. It is here that the actual casting process takes place. The process begins by covering a styrofoam pattern with a refractory ceramic coating, drying it, burying it in a sand mold, and putting a gating system on to allow the metal to travel into the casting. Next, the molten iron is poured into the mold, which vaporizes the styrofoam pattern. Once it has cooled, the casting is

Betz Industries team members produce a sand mold by tucking sand over and around the pattern surface.

A Betz team member pours molten iron into a sand mold.

extracted from the mold. The last step involves shot blasting and cleaning the casting.

Karl Jr. states, "Today, things have changed dramatically in our industry. We realize that in order to attract and keep skilled workers, we must constantly strive to improve the workplace environment.

At our company, we've installed high-energy dust collection systems, as well as fresh air make-up units that collect the air and filter it. Advancements in sand handling techniques have also improved working conditions, along with everyone's sharing the responsibility for keeping work areas neat and tidy."

Where the Company Is Headed

Betz Industries has continued to enjoy significant growth, and new opportunities for growth and prosperity are anticipated in the years ahead. In 1993 the company had 75 employees, a number that today has reached 100. The facility currently produces 2,000 tons of product per month, and it is expected that production will reach 3,000 tons per month by the turn of the century.

The Betz brothers are continually exploring new technology that will allow even more precision in pattern making and that will improve the quality of the company's products. Another expansion, presently in progress, will increase the size of the facility to nearly 400,000 square feet in 1998.

Karl and Ken encourage regular exchanges of ideas and technology improvements with businesses located in other countries around the world. "We participate in round-table discussions on a regular basis with both Japan and Germany. These interactions have contributed significantly to perfecting the styrofoam pattern-making processes, and we believe there's tremendous knowledge and expertise to be gained from participating in the forum."

As for the company's growth, Ken notes, "We don't have a large sales staff. We've grown because of customers who know of our reputation for quality and service. With the support of our engineering and development staff, we'll continue to be aggressive and keep looking for better ways to make our product."

Ken and Karl Betz attribute their growth and success to the values imbued in them by their father and mother: integrity, fairness to others, good work ethics, and setting goals and completing them.

Today, a third generation and a strong support team is prepared to continue the growth and successes of Betz Industries.

Betz Industries uses induction melting to produce gray iron and ductile iron castings. Iron is tapped from the furnace into ladles below. Overhead cranes take the ladles to the mold pouring area.

A 15,000-pound casting after shot blasting

A True Team Effort

Both Karl and Ken Betz believe that strong relationships with employees, as well as continuous communication, are essential in the continued success of their company. "Customers come to visit us and often comment on not only the quality of our facility, but also the productivity of our employees," says Ken. "Our employees know we expect a lot of them, as we do of ourselves. They work very hard and have a tremendous amount of pride in the work they do. We think of them as the key to our success. We're close to our people, making us a very strong team."

N 1933, EARL BECKERING SR. FOUNDED HIS OWN BUSINESS AND CALLED IT Beckering Construction Company. Originally from the Netherlands, Beckering had worked his way over to the United States as a carpenter on a ship, and finally settled in Grand Rapids. From the very start of his business, Beckering established a reputation for a strong work ethic,

During the 1970s, Pioneer Incorporated established a relationship with Foremost Insurance Company, and handled millions of square feet of construction in Foremost Industrial Park. In addition, Pioneer also constructed one of the most elegant buildings in West Michigan: the new Foremost Insurance world headquarters, located in a wooded setting in Caledonia (top).

Some of West Michigan's most prominent and impressive buildings, including Bridgewater Place, are products of Pioneer Incorporated (bottom).

personal service, quality craftsmanship, and a hands-on management approach, and through the years these qualities have continued to be his company's trademark. In 1962, under the leadership of Beckering's son, Earl Beckering Jr., the company's name was changed to Pioneer Construction, reflecting the innovative attitude and expanding services of the rapidly growing firm.

The company today is called Pioneer Incorporated, and it has grown into the largest full-service general contracting firm in West Michigan and one of the largest in the nation. Pioneer has a multitalented workforce of more than 325 employees—in fact, it's the largest construction employer in West Michigan—and many employees have worked with the company more than 15 years.

According to Tom Beckering, the founder's grandson and Pioneer Incorporated's president, his company owes its growth and success to its employees, who are some of

the finest skilled tradesmen in the industry today. "Our people have done more for the reputation and growth of this company than anything else," he says. "Because of that, along with the trust we've built with our customers through the years, Pioneer has been a very successful company." Beckering joined Pioneer in 1971, when sales were slightly more than $5 million annually. In 1975, he became president, and in 1979, he purchased the company from his father. Today, Pioneer

Incorporated's sales have grown beyond $100 million annually.

A COMPLETE LINE OF SERVICES
Pioneer is a full-service general contracting firm that excels in a broad range of services. The company's design/build program offers customers the advantage of flexibility, creativity, and personal involvement. During the design/build process, a Pioneer representative, the architect, and the future building owner all work together as a concept team—with each member contributing individual ideas, knowledge, and expertise to achieve the right final concept. Through this innovative team approach, customers establish strong working relationships with Pioneer, and achieve a high-quality, cost-effective building that's been custom designed around their needs, time constraints, and budget considerations.

Tailored Building Systems, a division of Pioneer, addresses the needs of small businesses requiring post frame and metal building construction. The division ensures that Pioneer's scope of projects covers the full spectrum of sizes.

Pioneer Incorporated also offers customers the advantages of construction management. The company's construction management philosophy is simple: putting the

right people in the right places at the right time. To maintain its high standards, Pioneer seeks out and retains some of the top supervisors in the industry, and keeps customers up to date with ongoing, on-site access to project superintendents and key personnel. Through the company's construction management services, customers are assured of outstanding quality, lower interim finance costs, on-time completion, and peace of mind.

COMMUNITY VISIBILITY

When it comes to Pioneer's construction services and the projects the company has completed, it would be easier to list those the firm hasn't worked on. Some of West Michigan's most prominent and impressive buildings are products of Pioneer Incorporated, including Bridgewater Place, Hope College, Patterson Ice Arena, Holland American Wafer, First of America, Grand Valley State University,

Steelcase, Aquinas College, Calvin College, Grand Rapids Community College, and Cascade Engineering, just to name a few.

During the 1970s, the company established a relationship with Foremost Insurance Company, and handled millions of square feet of construction in Foremost Industrial Park, including the Marriott Hotel (now the Crowne Plaza), and the IBM building. In addition, Pioneer also constructed one of the most elegant buildings in West Michigan: the new Foremost Insurance world headquarters, located in a wooded setting in Caledonia.

Beckering says although Pioneer has completed many large, high-profile construction jobs, the scope of its projects often varies. "We do all kinds of jobs for our customers," he says, "and we're set up to handle all sizes and shapes. The way we look at it, it's the small job that eventually becomes the big job, and we want to continue to handle

all of them." In addition to handling construction for its own jobs, the company also often acts as a subcontractor for some of its competitors, doing carpentry, steel, and concrete work on a project-by-project basis.

There are now some fourth-generation Beckerings who have joined Pioneer Incorporated's ranks: Tom's son and son-in-law are now part of the business, and Beckering says he's very optimistic about the future. "I foresee strong growth for us, especially in the general contracting area," he says. "And I definitely think the future is bright for West Michigan. With increased outgrowth and expansion going south toward Kalamazoo, and west toward Lake Michigan, we're fast becoming a large, metropolitan area. And although our company does jobs all over the country, we'd prefer to work right here. This is our community and we're excited about being a part of its growth."

Pioneer constructed the Grand Valley State University Natural Science Building (top left and right).

The headquarters building of Structural Concepts Inc. is another Pioneer project (bottom left and right).

I N 1934, A CHEMICAL ENGINEER NAMED J.B. HAVILAND FOUNDED A LABORA-tory and chemical supply company in Grand Rapids. He may not have known it at the time, but he was building the foundation of one of the largest privately held chemical distribution companies in the United States. And what started out as a small research and testing lab is

today Haviland Enterprises, Inc., a major corporation with two separate divisions, 150 employees, 400,000 square feet of manufacturing space, more than $50 million in annual sales, International Organization for Standardization (ISO) 9002 certification, and a reputation for being one of the country's foremost experts on chemicals, quality control, workplace safety, and environmental protection.

TWO MAJOR MARKETS

Perhaps without knowing it, almost everyone has purchased Haviland's products at one time or another. Each year, the company ships more than 250 million pounds of chemicals and compounds for industrial, commercial, and consumer use throughout the United States and to other parts of the world. Haviland Enterprises has two separate divisions: Haviland Products Company and Haviland Consumer Products Company.

Haviland Products Company serves the industrial market with specialty blending, packaging, and distribution of a wide variety of chemical products, including industrial cleaners, specialty products for anodizing aluminum, electroplating specialty products, and basic chemicals for making pharmaceuticals, foods, furniture, automobiles, and most other manufactured products.

Haviland Consumer Products Company formulates, blends, packages, and distributes more than 75 different swimming pool products for more than 50 different private label customers, serving some of the country's largest mass marketers of private label products. Major customers include dealers and distributors of swimming pool chemicals; carpet cleaning supplies; household cleaning supplies, such as window cleaners, spot removers, and floor cleaners; and a wide variety of flexible plastic hoses used

for such products as swimming pool vacuums, farm planting equipment, carpet sweepers and cleaning machines, and machines that blow insulation into attics.

SCIENTIFIC ACUMEN

According to E. Bernard Haviland, president of Haviland Products and Haviland Consumer Products, the company is different from most chemical distribution businesses in several ways. "For one thing, we make it a practice to hire people who are trained in chemistry, and who can do more than just deliver chemical products," he says. "Approximately 15 percent of our employees have degrees in a scientific field, so we're able to provide customers with greater technical competence and experience in multiple business situations."

Haviland's on-site testing laboratory houses modern analytical and testing equipment to ensure

What started out as a small research and testing lab is today Haviland Enterprises, Inc., a major corporation with two separate divisions, 150 employees, 400,000 square feet of manufacturing space, more than $50 million in annual sales, International Organization for Standardization (ISO) 9002 certification, and a reputation for being one of the country's foremost experts on chemicals, quality control, workplace safety, and environmental protection.

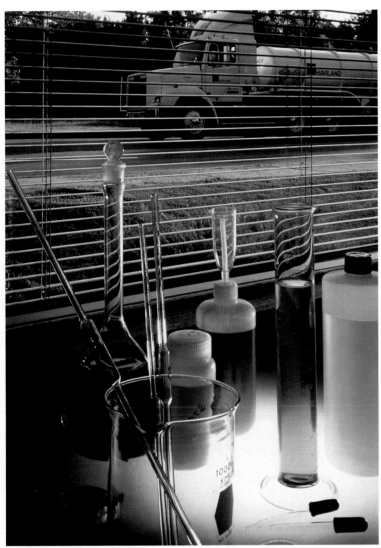

the quality of products received, as well as those being shipped. "We test the integrity of every load of material that comes into our company, as well as every load that we send out," says Haviland. "We use our lab for extensive quality control efforts, helping to meet the specific requirements of our customers."

Because of the skill and expertise of Haviland's staff, the company is able to provide technical consultation to customers, who often ask for advice on storage and transportation issues, as well as the use, handling, and disposal of chemicals. Haviland staff members often spend time consulting with customers in their own plants to provide on-site advice and guidance.

SETTING A SHINING EXAMPLE

Since its beginning, Haviland has been instrumental in helping industry meet its environmental responsibilities. Joe Haviland, the founder's brother, was a chemical engineer who was active in developing the first waste treatment equipment sold to metal finishers in Grand Rapids, and was seen as one of the foremost experts on environmental quality issues.

"When the Environmental Protection Agency started citing businesses for violations in the 1960s and 1970s, Joe Haviland was the resource they turned to," Bernard Haviland says. "He played a leading role in developing effluent purification processes that drastically cut down on pollution and helped eliminate pollution from manufacturing plants. Joe Haviland was truly committed to protecting and preserving the environment, and his beliefs are deeply ingrained in our company today."

Haviland Enterprises is equally dedicated to safety issues, and it is viewed as an industry leader in personal and environmental safety education and training. "Chemicals are an essential part of our everyday lives," says Haviland, "but of-

ten, the very mention of the word 'chemicals' gives people a negative impression. That's largely because the industry has done a poor job of informing the public of its extensive efforts to ensure safety in the use of chemicals. At our company, we make it a priority to educate people about the importance of chemicals, and how to use them safely."

Haviland has a full-time safety director who is available to customers and others in the community for consultation and guidance. The company's safety department has a library of more than 100 videos with titles like *Flammables*, *Chemicals and You*, and *Chemical Safety*, all of which are available to customers, schools, and governmental institutions.

Haviland says after four years of record growth and profit, he's extremely optimistic about the future. One major change is the company's employee stock ownership program, which will mean that for the first time in history, Haviland Enterprises will not be solely family owned. "We have a group of talented, dedicated people in this company," says Haviland. "They are dedicated to quality and to exceptional customer service, and they've played a pivotal role in helping us get where we are today. It's exciting to see them become part owners and reap the rewards of their efforts. And as we continue to grow and prosper, we'll work as a team to improve our business and serve our customers."

Each year, the company ships more than 250 million pounds of chemicals and compounds for industrial, commercial, and consumer use throughout the United States and to other parts of the world (top).

Haviland Consumer Products Company formulates, blends, packages, and distributes more than 75 different swimming pool products for more than 50 different private label customers, serving some of the country's largest mass marketers of private label products (bottom).

LMOST ANY CONSTRUCTION COMPANY CAN BUILD BUILDINGS, but when it comes to building houses for fish, mammals, birds, amphibians, reptiles, arachnids, and invertebrates, a special kind of construction company is needed that isn't afraid to tackle tough challenges. For Wolverine

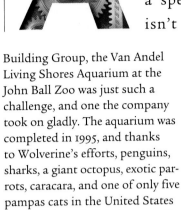

Building Group, the Van Andel Living Shores Aquarium at the John Ball Zoo was just such a challenge, and one the company took on gladly. The aquarium was completed in 1995, and thanks to Wolverine's efforts, penguins, sharks, a giant octopus, exotic parrots, caracara, and one of only five pampas cats in the United States all have a wonderful place to call home. It's no surprise that the project captured national recognition for Wolverine, earning the company a National Excellence in Construction Award from the Associated Builders and Contractors.

Wolverine Building Group currently employs about 150 people, and is one of the three largest construction employers in West Michigan.

STRENGTH IN NUMBERS

Wolverine has combined the strengths and resources of three separate companies—Wolverine Building, Wolverine Construction Management, and Fryling Construction—under the umbrella of Wolverine Building Group to form a business that is truly full service. This arrangement offers a tremendous advantage to customers, who are able to reap the benefits of Wolverine's diverse variety of construction talents, combined years of experience, seasoned employees, and expansive equipment.

For more than 55 years, Wolverine Building has specialized in conventional and pre-engineered design/build packages, working with industrial, commercial, and recreational clients. The company has a team of specialists who have made it one of the largest design/build, full-service general contracting firms in West Michigan.

Wolverine Construction Management treats planning, design, and construction as integrated tasks within the building process. An experienced Wolverine construction manager can bring these tasks together from the beginning of the project to help balance cost, quality, and schedule; significantly

improve coordination; and help avoid potential problems and conflicts.

Fryling Construction has more than 50 years' experience in the construction of offices, retail establishments, churches, hotels, and multiple-housing projects. The company has long been known for its highly skilled workers, as well as for its excellent workmanship and competitive pricing.

By combining the specialized skills and expertise of these three companies, Wolverine Building Group can offer customers many years of experience, as well as the unique ability to custom-tailor solutions for virtually any project anywhere.

HIGH-PROFILE PROJECTS

If the Living Shores Aquarium project is indicative of Wolverine's ability to handle challenging projects, then building Old Kent Park—sometimes referred to as Whitecaps Stadium—is definitely another example. Wolverine built the original stadium, which had 6,000 fixed seats and lawn seating for an additional 2,000 fans, prior to the Whitecaps' 1994 inaugural season.

After breaking all-time attendance records two years in a row, the team was ready for a larger home, and again turned to Wolverine.

Wolverine completed the Van Andel Living Shores Aquarium in 1995. Thanks to the firm's efforts, penguins, sharks, a giant octopus, exotic parrots, caracara, and one of only five pampas cats in the United States all have a wonderful place to call home.

The expansion added 1,000 new permanent seats and four new skyboxes, as well as concessions, a first aid station, and a souvenir shop. And like the aquarium, the Old Kent Park project earned Wolverine another prestigious Associated Builders and Contractors award.

Butterworth Hospital selected Wolverine Building Group for its Butterworth South Health Pavilion, a $14 million outpatient center located in Cutlerville. The building includes a sun-filled atrium area and a total of 110,000 square feet of space devoted to outpatient health care services. The project—which took only 395 days to build—was completed on time and within budget. Butterworth was pleased with the final result, and recently selected Wolverine Construction Management to provide all of their construction services through the end of 1999.

A TEAM OF CONSTRUCTION PROFESSIONALS

Wolverine Building Group has been immensely successful, and Stan Cheff, the company's president, wastes no time in saying that the credit belongs to the firm's team of highly talented and experienced employees. "We can't stress enough how much we value our people," he says. "The number of seasoned construction workers has been shrinking over the years, so it's more important than ever for our company to attract and keep the best workers. Our turnover rate is extremely low. Our employees stay because they're happy with us, and they know we're committed to them." Wolverine currently employs about 150 people, and is one of the three largest construction employers in West Michigan.

A major part of Wolverine's commitment to its employees is its emphasis on education and training, particularly job site safety. The company has won several national, state, and local safety awards in recent years, and continues to make safety one of its highest priorities. An example of this is its safety harness system, similar to those worn by mountain climbers, which Wolverine requires its workers to wear for construction of all steel erection above the ground.

BUILDING THE FUTURE

Wolverine Building Group's combined sales are fast approaching the $100 million mark, and are likely to surpass that figure by the end of 1998. "By combining the three companies' resources and people at our new headquarters building on Barden in Kentwood," Cheff says, "Wolverine has positioned itself for future growth. We are now able to serve our customers' needs with the widest possible breadth of experience, resources, and expertise from a single location, and at lower costs."

Cheff is clear about the direction in which Wolverine will continue in the future: "We have been, and will continue to be, totally customer focused—which is why 70 percent of our business is from repeat customers. It's our desire to do more than just build buildings. We want to focus on building relationships."

Butterworth Hospital selected Wolverine Building Group for its Butterworth South Health Pavilion, a $14 million outpatient center located in Cutlerville. The building includes a sun-filled atrium area and a total of 110,000 square feet of space devoted to outpatient health care services.

Wolverine built the original stadium at Old Kent Park, but after the Whitecaps broke all-time attendance records two years in a row, the team was ready for a larger home, and again turned to Wolverine. The expansion added 1,000 new permanent seats and four new skyboxes, as well as concessions, a first aid station, and a souvenir shop.

WHEN A MAJOR METROPOLITAN AIRPORT WORTH SEVERAL billion dollars is paralyzed because one of its key systems isn't functioning, it's nothing short of a disaster. But Denver International Airport found itself in this exact situation. Because of a non-

operating baggage-handling system, the airport remained closed for a year and a half past the scheduled opening date. At that point, the City of Denver approached Rapistan Systems, and within six months, the company had built and installed a brand-new, state-of-the-art baggage-handling system that worked, allowing the airport to finally open.

As North America's largest material-handling systems company, Rapistan Systems builds and implements hundreds of automated systems every year, generating more than $5 billion in sales during the past 20 years. The company's superior skills in material-handling technologies have helped major clients in a variety of industries, such as wholesale and retail distribution, parcel and freight handling, printing and publishing, apparel, pharmaceuticals, food and beverage, automotive manufacturing, electronics, air cargo, and, of course, airport baggage handling.

THE COMPANY'S ROOTS AND GROWTH

Rapistan Systems got its start in 1939 as Rapids Standard Company, a business that designed and manufactured large industrial casters for the Detroit automotive indus-

try. Shortly afterward, the owners were asked to make conveyers to transport fruit crates for apple and cherry orchards all over West Michigan. During World War II, the Rapids Standard Company expanded into handling defense products for the military. Within the following years, the company continued to expand the conveyer aspect of the business, particularly in distribution centers for major retailers, such as Sears and Wal-Mart. In 1966, the company name was shortened to Rapistan. After several more changes in ownership, Rapistan was acquired in 1992 by Mannesmann Dematic A.G., the world's largest material-handling corporation; the company is now known as Rapistan Systems.

The acquisition by Mannesmann Dematic brought Rapistan additional advanced material-handling technologies, which allowed the company to greatly expand its business and its ability to serve customers. Today, Rapistan Systems has a seven-building campus in Grand Rapids, including three manufacturing plants, a new two-story technology center, and a schoolhouse used for customer education programs. The company employs more than 2,300 people, of whom nearly 700 are engineers, and it has an ongoing commitment to continuously invest in capital equipment and advanced technology. Rapistan Systems has manufacturing plants in Marietta, Oklahoma; Santa Rosa; Toronto; Mexico City; and São

Clockwise from top:
Rapistan Systems employs more than 2,300 people, of whom nearly 700 are engineers, and it has an ongoing commitment to continuously invest in capital equipment and advanced technology.

A spiral conveyor belt is an efficient use of space in a distribution center without a lot of extra room.

As the largest conveyor manufacturer in the world, Rapistan Systems offers advanced package-handling conveyor systems, including conveyors for high-speed package distribution.

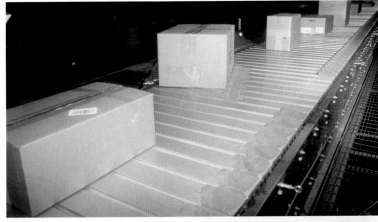

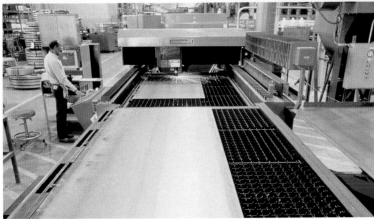

Paulo, as well as 18 distributors throughout North America. Since the acquisition, the company's sales have soared. In 1990, sales were slightly more than $160 million, and by 1997, this number had increased to a whopping $620 million.

A Variety of Solutions

Rapistan Systems' flawless handling of the Denver International Airport crisis is indicative of its ability to pinpoint a customer's problems and develop precisely the right solution, no matter how complicated. The company has a comprehensive range of products, and it is well known for superior technology and engineering, as well as for the talent and ability to develop systems that meet customers' individual requirements. According to John Raab, Rapistan Systems' vice president of marketing, no two customers are alike: "We serve many different markets, and each market presents its own unique challenges. It's our job to analyze those challenges and provide the very best solutions."

As the largest conveyor manufacturer in the world, Rapistan Systems offers advanced package-

handling conveyor systems, including conveyors for high-speed package distribution. These highly technical systems include distribution conveyors, sorters, and trailer loaders used by major merchandise distribution giants, such as Wal-Mart, Sears, JCPenney, The Limited, Lands' End, Walgreen Co., and Amway.

The company also develops advanced product-sorting systems, such as one used by a giant Toys R Us distribution facility located in Flanders, New Jersey. Each year, more than 10 million toys are received, labeled, sorted, and shipped at this operation using the unique Rapistan system, which keeps millions of toys moving to stores in New Jersey, New York, and Connecticut, and helps Toys R Us cope with growing storage demands and shrinking lead times. The system also allows fully automated material handling from the point of receiving to the point of shipping.

Rapistan Systems' platform conveyor systems serve major automobile manufacturers, such as Mercedes, Saturn, and General Motors. These systems—which include platform conveyors, verti-

cal lifts, and custom-designed products—are oriented specifically for large product-assembly plants. Platform systems allow workers to travel together with the product, which creates a more ergonomic work environment.

In addition to baggage-handling systems, Rapistan Systems' product line also includes advanced air cargo systems designed to provide accurate movement of cargo through air terminals. Lufthansa Cargo, a leading carrier in the air freight industry, uses a Rapistan flexible freight-handling system at its Chicago cargo terminal at O'Hare International Airport. The Lufthansa system includes a suspended electrified monorail, which helps conserve space and move box bins efficiently and quickly, and an automated storage/retrieval system that makes maximum use of space within the terminal.

Another Rapistan Systems product is the Automatic Guided Vehicle (AGV), a unique technology that was invented by the company in 1953. These innovative systems—which feature the same technology used by the Department of Defense in its guidance of tanks and jet fighters—are used for loading and towing components within manufacturing plants. These driverless vehicles are computer programmed to travel within a plant according to a customer's designated

Clockwise from top left: Packages are diverted by a high-speed sorter at the rate of 200 cartons per minute.

The Automatic Guided Vehicle (AGV) is used for loading and towing components within manufacturing plants, such as a 50,000-pound steel coil. These driverless vehicles are computer programmed to travel within a plant according to a customer's designated routes, and use no wires or in-floor mechanisms.

State-of-the-art equipment such as this laser cutting center keep Rapistan Systems at the forefront of its industry.

routes, and use no wires or in-floor mechanisms. AGVs can be used for either short- or long-distance moves within a plant. They are ideal for fast response time and material movement situations where there is a need to remove and supply loads upon demand. They also are beneficial in tight manufacturing areas, where aisles need to be safely shared by workers, forklift trucks, and AGVs.

MOVING PRODUCTS AND INFORMATION TOGETHER

Successful automated material-handling systems require products that are designed in tandem with the software controls that precisely support them. According to Raab, this is one of the most essential elements in the material-handling process, and one in which Rapistan Systems excels. "In most environments, information must travel simultaneously along with the product," he says, "because this is actually what makes up the complete system."

Raab points out that a conveyor developed for a major cargo company, such as Federal Express or UPS, wouldn't be complete without corresponding computerized information that can flawlessly track packages throughout the routing process. He continues: "A baggage-handling system developed for United Airlines must include not only the conveyor to move the luggage, but also computerized information to coordinate it with passengers' flight numbers, to ensure that they arrive at the destination together." Rapistan develops fully integrated systems that ensure precise coordination between information and products.

THE YEARS AHEAD

Today, Rapistan Systems is structured to address any type of material-handling requirement, no matter how simple or how complicated. Customers expect the company to provide leading-edge products and superior technology, and to offer high levels of engineering expertise and support.

In the future, Raab says, there will be greater challenges to keep up with technology, as well as environmental and ergonomic challenges. "Machines will need to become more adaptable to human beings," he says, "and safer and more friendly to the people who operate them." Committed to addressing these challenges, Raab indicates that Rapistan Systems is poised for continued growth and expansion: "Our company has a history of paying close attention to the needs of the market and constantly remaining on top of changes in technology. And we will make every effort to continue that in the future."

An elevating transfer vehicle handles a 30,000-pound air cargo container (top).

A 747 aircraft unloads a 30,000-pound air cargo container (bottom).

VAN'S DELIVERY SERVICE IS A COMPANY WITH A RATHER UNUSUAL marketing story. It does not have a sales force, it does little advertising, it has never done a direct-mail campaign, and it is just now working on a corporate brochure. Yet new business keeps rolling in, and the company's overall growth is astounding. Phil VanZytveld, whose father started the company, shares his secret to success. "Word of mouth," he says. "Come to think of it, if we ever did hire a sales force, I'm not sure we could keep up."

Bob VanZytveld started Van's Delivery Service in 1925 with one truck, one customer, and three deliveries a day to area hardware stores. His office was the family dining room, his desk the dining room table. His wife kept the company books and answered the phone. From the very beginning, he was completely devoted to his customers; in fact, his motto was "courtesy and promptness assured." Today, the business is still family-owned—now in its fourth generation—and has grown into a thriving company of more than 100 people.

DIVERSIFIED SERVICES

Today, the company serves more than 750 customers, providing them with full-service logistics. Van's Delivery Service has a staff of highly trained and skilled drivers who are known for being dependable and flexible, and are constantly in demand by major West Michigan companies. Ron VanZytveld, grandson of the founder and current president, says this demand is due to the company's high-caliber drivers and ability to make the process seamless for customers.

"We handle all the headaches," he says, "and that's something our customers appreciate. We can furnish a driver and a vehicle, or furnish our driver to use a customer's vehicle. We'll truck 65,000 pounds of steel across the state, or deliver one small skid of product across town. Basically, whatever our customers need, they know they can count on us to do the job right."

CONTINUOUS GROWTH

To meet increasing customer needs, Van's Delivery Service has continued to expand, adding trucks and services as the market demands. The company currently has 48 trucks, including 45 18-wheelers, used for longer hauls, and a specialized trailer that stretches out to 65 feet (a normal trailer is 48 to 53 feet long). Van's Delivery Service also uses a revolutionary new accordion-like tarping system for flatbed trailers called the Conestoga, which saves tremendous amounts of loading and unloading time for drivers making multiple deliveries.

The company has also continued to expand its warehousing services. Customers can ship products via rail, and Van's Delivery Service will unload the railroad cars, store the

products in the company's warehouse, take inventory of the products, and deliver them as needed for just-in-time manufacturing. As with the trucking side of the business, Van's Delivery Service expects to see increased demand for this type of warehousing, and the company now has more than 420,000 square feet of warehouse space.

Van's Delivery Service has seen so much growth since Bob VanZytveld started the business in 1925, he would barely recognize it today. But some things haven't changed: The company is still providing customers with exceptional service. And even after all these years, their motto is still "courtesy and promptness assured."

Clockwise from top:
Currently, Van's Delivery Service serves more than 750 customers, providing them with full-service logistics. The company has a staff of highly trained and skilled drivers who are known for being dependable and flexible, and are constantly in demand by major West Michigan companies.

Phil VanZytveld, whose father founded the company, served as president until he retired in 1995.

Van's Delivery Service currently has 48 trucks, including 45 18-wheelers, used for longer hauls, and a specialized trailer that stretches out to 65 feet.

1940 - 1969

WHEN BUSINESSES IN THE GRAND RAPIDS AREA HEAR the name Hungerford, Aldrin, Nichols & Carter, P.C., they likely think of long-lasting working relationships and a level of trust that extends far beyond the traditional definition of a certified public accounting firm. As it has since 1941, Hungerford, Aldrin, Nichols & Carter, P.C. specializes in serving closely owned, entrepreneurial companies that value the excellent service and personalized attention for which the firm is known.

A WEALTH OF EXPERIENCE

Owning and operating a business can be a daunting task, one that requires careful planning, a regular review of operating performance, and sound financial decision making—all in addition to the full-time responsibility of normal, day-to-day business activities. The professionals at Hungerford, Aldrin, Nichols & Carter, P.C. have years of experience and knowledge in financial and operational accounting; computer-related services; management issues, such as developing business plans; mergers and acquisitions; ownership transition; family business issues, such as children or spouses entering the business; and a host of other areas, including employee benefit plans, retirement planning, and tax planning. The firm provides these services through tailor-made solutions to each client's needs, rather than through a cookie-cutter, one-size-fits-all approach.

According to Jerry Nichols, Hungerford's president, concentrating on the issues that face closely owned businesses is a specialty that sets his firm apart from the large accounting firms. "This firm has always specialized in closely owned businesses," he says. "In fact, a significant number of the clients who were with our firm when it began are still with us today. We focus on closely owned businesses and enjoy working with them because we like working with creative, entrepreneurial companies. Through the years, we've developed many long-lasting relationships with clients whom we have helped prosper and become successful. Through this commitment, we have grown and our clients have grown, resulting in a stronger team."

The ever growing employee team at Hungerford, Aldrin, Nichols & Carter, P.C.—currently at around 50—is highly qualified to work with almost any type of business. The firm specializes in several distinct industries, including manufacturing companies of all types; wholesale distribution companies; the broadcast industry (both radio and television); real estate developers and construction contractors; professional service companies, such as law firms, finance companies, and medical and dental offices; and local governmental units, such as cities, townships, and school districts.

A TEAM APPROACH

One of Hungerford's greatest strengths is its people, and the personal interest they take in their clients. "We're genuinely interested in the business owner—not just the business," Nichols says, "and that's obvious to all our clients. We're a team of people who work well together and who make our clients feel comfortable working with us. They know our focus is always on them. And we let them know that we're in this business to help them realize their goals and dreams."

Many accounting firms experience frequent staff turnover. Quite the opposite is true at Hungerford, Aldrin, Nichols & Carter, P.C., and this makes the firm somewhat unique among its peers. "There's been a great deal of continuity between us and our clients over the years," says Nichols, "and that really adds to the efficiency and trust factors. It's conceivable for us to have the same staff person assigned to an account for more than 10 years, which means we have an opportunity to develop long-lasting client relationships and we get to know the client well."

The shareholders of Hungerford, Aldrin, Nichols & Carter, P.C. are (from left) Clifford A. Aldrin, Phillip W. Saurman, Daniel L. Carter, Peggy A. Murphy, Richard A. Hungerford, Jerry W. Nichols, John G. Clark, and Richard L. Chrisman.

The consulting services offered by Hungerford, Aldrin, Nichols & Carter, P.C. help the Grand Rapids Metropolitan YMCA with its effort to maintain state-of-the-art fitness centers, child care facilities, and camps. (From left) Ron Nelson, president and CEO of the recently upgraded downtown YMCA facility, and Annette Danigelis, controller, review budget and fund drive expectations with Rick Chrisman and Sheri Wert of Hungerford.

Hungerford is a firm that can do as much or as little as clients require, based on individual need. Since most closely owned businesses do not have a chief financial officer on staff, it's a natural role for the Hungerford team to step in and serve as an outside consultant, and assist with financial analysis and other finance-related matters. The team can either process its clients' general ledgers and payroll on the Hungerford computer system or work with clients to set up and operate their own system. Each year, Hungerford schedules a meeting with clients to implement strategic plans to effectively and efficiently operate their businesses. In other words, the firm presents clients with tax-saving ideas and proactive business recommendations for the coming year.

WHAT THE FUTURE HOLDS

Not content to rest on its reputation as a customer-focused accounting firm, Hungerford is helping to move its clients into a world market by offering them a presence on the Internet. A new division at the firm was started in 1996 with Hungerford's own Web site development. This division offers Web site "hosting"— storage space on its server for client Web sites set up and designed by Hungerford. The new division began as an extension of the firm's existing client services,

but today, of the more than 50 companies drawn to the firm's service, half are newcomers attracted by Hungerford's Web site expertise.

Internet clients include a mortgage company whose Web site allows the calculation of mortgages online, car dealerships that have reported numerous sales through their sites, and nonprofit organizations. In addition to design and host services, Hungerford offers file transfer protocol, guest books where site visitors can leave information about themselves, and the ability to register client sites with specialized search engines.

While adding this new technology to its service base, Hungerford's main strategy for its future success will be to keep doing what it has been so good at for almost 60 years: providing its clients with personal, imaginative, and timely service on a team-oriented basis. "It's our goal to help our clients to be successful," says Nichols. "Because, after all, our success goes hand in hand with theirs."

Grand Rapids' family-owned businesses like Lacks Industries rely on the financial, tax, and managerial expertise that Hungerford, Aldrin, Nichols & Carter, P.C. offers. Officers of the company (from left) Kurt Lacks and Richard Lacks Jr. consult with Jerry Nichols.

HEALTH AND CARE ARE TWO WORDS THAT DESCRIBE THE philosophy of Metro Health, a network of 140 area physicians, and Metropolitan Hospital. The caregivers in the network believe health care must be as compassionate as it is comprehensive. Metro Health believes in delivering care in a healing environment that allows for personal attention as well as for quality health care.

Metro Health believes modern medicine and technology are at their best when offered in the most patient-friendly environment. That balance is evident at Metro Health's Metropolitan Hospital. It's a small, intimate hospital—a place where procedures for arranging care are quick and efficient, where the highest level of teamwork with physicians is possible, and where the environment itself breeds personalized care.

An Alternative to "Big" Medicine

From the start, Metropolitan Hospital has offered an alternative. It was founded in 1941 by a group of osteopathic physicians who had a dream of building a hospital of their own, dedicated to the principles of holistic and patient-centered care. It has grown explosively since, but has not lost sight of those founding principles.

With 238 beds, Metropolitan is a medium-sized hospital that is smaller than the others in Grand Rapids by design. It offers all the sophisticated services of a modern, full-service community hospital, from intensive care to childbirth to emergency to rehabilitation, but in a less hectic, more personal environment. Metropolitan takes pride in illustrating that bigger doesn't always mean better.

The compact and recently renovated campus is tucked into a suburban neighborhood with free parking right outside the entrances. Most inpatients have single rooms; babies are born in a private, home-like setting; there is a separate center for outpatients; and most patients in the new Emergency Center wait no more than 10 minutes to be seen. There is a mood and tempo at Metropolitan that its patients and visitors notice immediately.

Stellar Ratings

Metropolitan Hospital can truthfully say it's been voted the best-liked hospital in town. Metropolitan came out on top in a survey that asked patients from each of the Grand Rapids hospitals to rate their hospital. Metropolitan was rated a full 20 percent above average. Its highest scores were for the "neighborhood feel" of its campus and its caring, personalized treatment of patients.

Metropolitan also participates in an ongoing patient satisfaction study at 700 hospitals nationwide. The results support the findings of the community study. Metropolitan consistently rates above average, and in the case of its Emergency Center, scores among the best in the nation.

The secret to these stellar ratings is contained in yet another survey—the employee satisfaction survey. Results show Metropolitan's employees take great pride in the organization, feel empowered, and have an overall positive attitude about their work. The committed veteran staff of Metropolitan understands the importance of personalized care and it shows.

Metro Health's Southwest Plaza building offers many traditional hospital services in a neighborhood setting, in addition to an urgent care center and the offices of more than a dozen physicians.

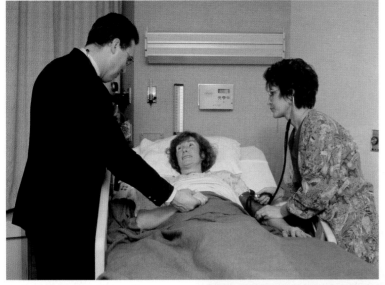

A COMMITMENT THAT GOES BEYOND HOSPITAL WALLS

The millions of dollars in annual charity care by Metro are matched by a personal commitment to the community by the organization's physicians and employees. At Oakdale Elementary School in Grand Rapids, they volunteer their time offering students guidance and tutoring. They even pair up with students as pen pals. During the holiday season, employees adopt families of Oakdale for gift giving.

Metro Health's 2-HEALTH community education program provides free health screenings and education. One example is the Hunter's Health Screening, where more than 500 hunters receive a free checkup each fall. Other large-scale screenings are offered for cancer, cholesterol, diabetes, and high blood pressure. The community education commitment also includes support groups, frequent free physician lectures, and a physician referral service.

The services of 2-HEALTH are made possible in part by the support of the Metropolitan Foundation. Additionally, the charitable organization supports the medical research and medical education activities of Metro Health.

Metro Health has an impressive commitment to medical education. It is a major teaching center for the Michigan State University College of Osteopathic Medicine, with more than 100 interns and residents in training at all times.

PHYSICIAN/HOSPITAL TEAMWORK MAKES THE DIFFERENCE

In 1995, the same patient-centered care vision that inspired Metropolitan Hospital's physician founders led to the formation of Metro Health, an organization that integrates hospital and physician care. The hospital and more than 100 area physicians now have a single organization that can arrange for any service needed to treat any illness. This seamless delivery system simplifies care for patients and improves access.

By forming this coalition, Metro Health physicians regained some control of patient care decisions from insurers. They are also more able to provide preventive services. Both improvements significantly benefit patients.

A NEW ERA IN NEIGHBORHOOD HEALTH CARE

The same close hospital/physician relationship that made Metro

Health possible has also made it possible to build a series of Metro Health Plazas around Grand Rapids. The most frequently used outpatient hospital services are now available in three neighborhood plazas that are also the site of physician offices. Southwest Plaza in Wyoming is the largest. It operates seven days a week and has room for 20 physicians. Metro Health plans to build numerous new plazas to supplement its two dozen other family practice sites.

HEALTH CARE IS A RELATIONSHIP

Connecting at a personal level, not just treating illness, is what Metro Health holds sacred. From building trusting partnerships with the largest health care organizations in the region to the private physician/patient conversations in exam rooms, the approach is the same. Metro Health understands that health care is a relationship, not a commodity.

Clockwise from top left:
The majority of patients at Metropolitan Hospital stay in private rooms.

Metropolitan Hospital employees tutor children each week at Oakdale Elementary, the hospital's partnership school in Grand Rapids.

The aquatherapy pool at Metro Health's Southwest Plaza enables patients to participate in state-of-the-art physical therapy.

THROUGHOUT ITS HISTORY, SMITHS INDUSTRIES AEROSPACE has played an essential role in the evolution of the aviation industry. The company's own development has demonstrated its ability to adapt to constant changes in aviation throughout the second half of the 20th century. ■ In 1943,

in the midst of World War II, the company—then known as Lear Avia—first came to Grand Rapids to manufacture radio, navigation, and electromechanical actuating aircraft equipment for the U.S. military; a year later the company's name changed to Lear,

LABAKK STUDIO

Voice and Data Recorder (VADR®) markets continue to expand for Smiths Industries Aerospace, with business in all of the U.S. armed forces and in many foreign military and commercial aircraft operations (top).

Grand Rapids, through Smiths Industries, has been a long-standing crossroads in advanced flight management systems for both military and civil aircraft (bottom).

Inc. Although the end of the war brought decreased demand from the military, there was an increase in demand from civilian customers, and soon Lear was producing aircraft instruments and automatic flight control systems for civilian aircraft.

In 1962, Lear merged with Siegler Corporation, and became Lear Siegler for the next 25 years. Then, in 1987, the company was acquired by the British aerospace leader Smiths Industries, resulting in a new, stronger company.

DEFENSE SYSTEMS NORTH AMERICA

In 1994, the company's facilities in Grand Rapids, Clearwater, and Florham Park, New Jersey, were combined to consolidate and restructure Smiths Industries' North American aerospace opera-

tions. The new division was called Defense Systems North America (DSNA) and was headquartered in Grand Rapids. According to Robert Ehr, DSNA president, approximately 75 percent of the division's sales are to the military, and the other 25 percent are civil related. "We have a broad range of aerospace products," Ehr says, "ranging from very sophisticated flight management systems for the military and for Boeing 737 jets, to flight data recorders—often referred to as black boxes—used in both commercial and military applications."

The Grand Rapids facility is primarily an engineering division and serves as the major engineering site for DSNA; it employs approximately 900 people, half of whom are engineers. The Clearwater plant is a manufacturing facility that enlists approximately 300 people, and the Florham Park plant is a combined engineering, design, and development operation with approximately 200 employees.

Smiths Industries manufactures highly technical and sophisticated products, such as stores management and weapon control systems for the Navy's primary attack fighter plane, the F/A-18, as well as for the Marine Corps' "jump jet," a one-person aircraft that can fly vertically, stop in midair, go almost anywhere, and land anywhere; it is like no other plane in existence.

In addition to avionics equipment, Smiths Industries manufactures position navigation equipment for the primary tank used by the U.S. Army: the M1A2 tank produced by General Dynamics. In addition, Smiths Industries has an agreement with Saudi Arabia, which also uses this tank, to design the equipment in Grand Rapids and then coproduce it at the country's plant. The company also has an agreement with Japan, for whom

LABAKK STUDIO

it supplies flight data recorders and other products used on Japanese aircraft.

A COMPANY WITH A CLEAR FOCUS

The company—which now has approximately $250 million in annual sales—has grown steadily every year since DSNA was formed, and DSNA is projected to grow to more than $300 million by the end of the century. Smiths Industries' profitability has increased dramatically. "We were a marginally profitable operation in the past," Ehr says, "and now we're among the top performers. One major reason for that is because we're very focused—we have a clear idea of where we're going, and we know how we're going to get there."

Smiths Industries concentrates only on products and technologies where it can either be number one or number two. Major customers include the U.S. government, which is DSNA's largest customer; Boeing-McDonnell Douglas, for whom Smiths Industries is a silver-level preferred supplier; Boeing-Seattle; and Lockheed-Martin.

EXTRAORDINARY GROWTH, ENORMOUS POTENTIAL

Since 1996, Smiths Industries' DSNA has won every key strategic program it has pursued. A major coup occurred when the company decided to expand its operations by tapping into the United Kingdom's market for health and usage monitoring systems (HUMS), which are used for monitoring

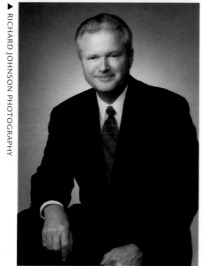

an aircraft to gauge its health and performance. Smiths Industries was successful in this venture, winning the first major HUMS award for military helicopters given by the United Kingdom's Ministry of Defence—a major step in DSNA's entry in the global market.

"Even though we're a British-owned company," Ehr says, "we are still DSNA, and are perceived as a U.S. operation. By winning this, we've not only won a huge production contract for a brand-new high-tech product, we've also now established a presence in the United Kingdom." Smiths Industries' DSNA was also awarded two contracts from another United Kingdom customer, British Aerospace, for the Nimrod program, a project valued at approximately $30 million.

A significant area of DSNA's growth has been in the production of flight management computers developed for Boeing's $30 million

737 passenger jets, the fastest-growing commercial passenger jet. In 1996, the company was producing approximately five of these highly technical systems per month, an amount equal to the number of planes being built. As the number of planes continues to grow, so does the demand for Smiths Industries' products: By the end of 1998, the company expects to produce up to 40 of them per month.

Smiths Industries is excited about the future and sees huge opportunities. "The market will change, and we'll continue to change with it," Ehr says. "And more than before, our focus will remain on customer satisfaction."

Clockwise from top left: The U.S. Army and foreign governments are customers to Smiths' Industries' land navigation systems.

Avionics provided by Smiths Industries can be found throughout civil and military aircraft.

Employees are highly skilled and trained in electronics for the company's advanced technologies.

"The aerospace market will change," says Smiths Industries President Robert F. Ehr, "and we will continue to change with it. And more than ever before, our focus will remain on customer satisfaction."

COUNTRY FRESH WAS CREATED IN 1946 BY A GROUP OF 70 INDEPENdent grocers who envisioned a cost-effective dairy cooperative as a way of competing with the major national grocery chains that were beginning to dominate the market after World War II. True to its initial function, the fledgling company was

founded as the Grocer's Cooperative Dairy. The products were marketed in member stores under the Country Fresh brand name.

Beginning in a single, modest plant on Garden Street in Grand Rapids, the young dairy had few employees, but an unshakable dedication to quality and service that has never wavered. It was a success from its very inception, and has since gone through three major stages of growth and expansion.

THE EARLY DAYS

The initial stage was one of technological development. With the early customer base clearly defined as independent grocers, dairy management was free to emphasize production over marketing, and was an industry leader in such bold innovations as packaging milk by the gallon, introducing plastic containers, delivering on wheeled carts called bossies, and eventually instituting computer controlled production systems. During this initial growing period, the Country Fresh product line was focused on traditional dairy items like milk, ice cream, cottage cheese, half-and-half, and sour cream.

By 1958, a little more than 10 years since its inception, the dairy had outgrown its Garden Street beginnings and moved to a much larger and more modern plant on Buchanan Avenue, where it remains today in spite of undergoing many phases of physical expansion. By the 1980s, the name was changed to Country Fresh, Inc. to more closely align its corporate identity with that of its highly successful product brand name.

A NEW DIRECTION

Country Fresh's second stage of growth began a few years after the name change. This period also coincided with a significant change

in management. George Cope, the dairy's first president, and a production-oriented dairyman, retired in 1982. His successor was Delton Parks, who brought with him not only a broad-based history of dairy management and operation, but a keen sense of marketing as well. This latter talent would be vital to the changing role of the dairy, as product lines expanded to include other than traditional dairy staples and competition became more broadly based.

Under Parks and an aggressively active board of successful food retailers, the second stage of growth was one of acquisition and line expansion. From the early 1980s to

Clockwise from top:
Country Fresh's Grand Rapids plant and offices have been located on Buchanan Avenue since 1958. An additional, 70,000-square-foot freezer has been recently added.

Country Fresh maintains a fleet of more than 100 trucks and refrigerated trailers that carry the strong brand identification throughout the state.

The Country Fresh guarantee of customer satisfaction was formalized in 1986 into the CARE line, where calls to the toll-free number get prompt attention and are logged into the quality control system for statistical tracking.

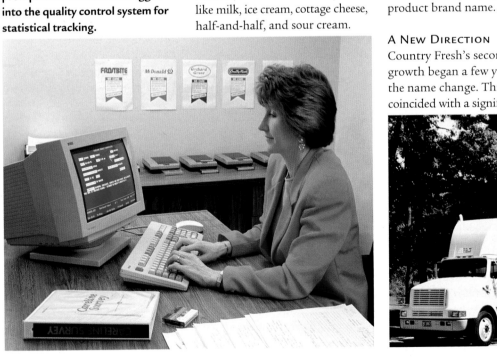

the company's 50th anniversary in 1996, Country Fresh, Inc. added McDonald Dairy in Flint; Burger Dairy in New Paris, Indiana; Embest Dairy in Livonia; and the Frostbite novelty production in Toledo, Ohio, to its corporate family. Other facilities including Country Fresh, Ohio, and a juice bottling plant called Southeastern Juice in Chattanooga were added.

One of the most significant aspects of this second-stage growth was the expansion of the Country Fresh customer base. The original concept of serving only independent retailers who were members of the co-op had a theoretical limit to it.

On the other hand, the total market for dairy and related food and beverage products is virtually unlimited. Therfore, the second-stage growth combined product line expansion of such items as water, ice, juices, beverages, and novelties, with marketing expansion into convenience stores, institutions, schools, and food service companies—especially in the beverage and novelty fields.

By the late 1990s, all divisions of the company were busy not only selling their own brands regionally, but also producing products for other divisions and for other customers outside the Country Fresh family.

Throughout this extremely active second stage, the original founding commitment to quality and service was never forgotten. On the technical side, constant investments were being made in plant expansion, equipment upgrades, computerized control, and new techniques in long-shelf-life milk processing.

On the service side, Country Fresh has always been sensitive to the needs and changes of social issues. In the 1980s, the company formalized the founders' original guarantee of satisfaction into a printed promise on every container, along with a toll-free number to a dedicated CARE line, where customers could communicate directly with the corporate office.

Quality control was greatly aided by the use of sophisticated laser jet code printing on every pack-

age, so individual products could be traced back to the exact time of production. Tamper-evident packaging was introduced throughout the varied product lines, and local environmental concerns were dealt with promptly. At the Grand Rapids plant, a whey storage facility, capable of holding 180,000 gallons, eliminates this liquid byproduct from the sewer system and transfers it to a feed facility for farm animals. Other commitments to waste management have been equally effective.

TODAY'S COMPANY

The company's third stage of growth and expansion, begun in September 1997, is built around a merger with the Suiza Foods Corporation of Dallas. This move made Country Fresh part of a publicly held company with expanded resources for additional growth and acquisition. Still operated independently as a Grand Rapids-based corporation, Country Fresh is entering an era of dairy consolidation and resource pooling in a strategically strengthened position. What began as a dream of a few local grocers has since become a reality for thousands of area employees, retailers, farmers, and suppliers who have

contributed to, and shared in, this remarkable success story.

At the time of the Country Fresh 50th anniversary, the Grand Rapids plant employed more than 330 people who processed an excess of 1.5 million pounds of milk every day. The total Country Fresh family employs more than 1,500 people in 12 plants and branches, and produces more than 4,000 different products, some of which are distributed throughout the Midwest, as well as all the way to the East Coast.

Country Fresh is the classic American success story come true in Grand Rapids, where a handful of independent businessmen had an idea whose time had come—and whose future looks brighter than ever.

**Clockwise from top left:
Products manufactured at the Grand Rapids plant include fluid milk, water, orange juice, cottage cheese, sour cream, dips, cream cheese, and yogurt.**

Testing for fat content in milk is one of many quality control procedures performed daily by lab technicians in the Grand Rapids plant.

Country Fresh brand ice cream is distributed by all Country Fresh divisions. The complete line includes more than 100 regular and feature flavors in a variety of square half-gallon and premium Pride round half-gallon containers.

MANY BUSINESSES AND INDIVIDUALS DEPEND DAILY ON LARGE, heavy-duty, diesel-powered equipment, such as locomotives, semitrailer trucks, buses, drilling rigs, tugboats, and power generators. And it is quite likely that the fuel injectors powering the engines that keep this equipment

running have been manufactured by an enterprise called Diesel Technology Company (DTC).

Diesel Technology is the world's largest manufacturer of electronically controlled unit fuel injectors and pumps used in industrial engines ranging in size from 100 to 40,000 horsepower. The company was originally formed in 1947 as a division of General Motors to supply fuel injectors to other GM organizations. In 1988, Penske Transportation and Detroit Diesel Corporation copurchased the assets from General Motors, and renamed the company Diesel Technology Corporation. For its first four years, the company's major customers were Detroit Diesel (the sister company) and Electromotive, General Motors' locomotive division.

In 1992, Penske Transportation formed a partnership with Robert Bosch Corporation, Europe's preeminent supplier of fuel injection systems, to form a new partnership, owning and operating DTC. This move created important opportunities for Diesel Technology in the European market, where emission standards were demanding new engine fuel systems. Today, the company's sales are fairly well divided between the United States and Europe.

A SUPERIOR PRODUCT

Diesel Technology's vision is to be the preeminent heavy-duty fuel system supplier in the world. As engine producers move to meet stricter worldwide emission standards, the role of fuel systems

has become especially critical, and DTC has positioned itself to provide assistance to its customers in meeting their regulatory and performance requirements.

Diesel Technology developed the world's first electronic unit injector in 1985, and has since worked to perfect the system and its capabilities. Electronic fuel systems use advanced computer technology, so they're exceedingly accurate and far superior to mechanical systems. Unlike the old-style mechanical fuel pump systems, electronic systems use computers to control the amount of fuel pressure. This means they're extremely precise down to the millisecond, which results in increased energy efficiency and a dramatic decrease in emissions.

Diesel Technology manufactures more than 150 different models. Since its inception, the company has built more than 25 million precision fuel injectors, typically selling 75,000 units per month.

IT DOESN'T SEEM LIKE A FACTORY

To those having preconceived notions of what a factory should look like, Diesel Technology offers a refreshing surprise. The immense plant has more than 900,000 square

Diesel Technology is the world's largest manufacturer of electronically controlled unit fuel injectors and pumps used in industrial engines.

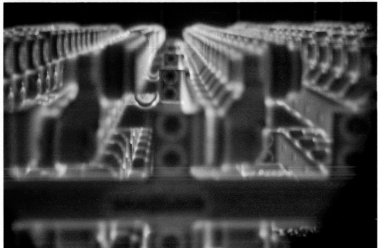

feet of floor space, and features plenty of open spaces, high ceilings, and natural lighting. Everything—from the floors to the massive machinery—is clean, free of clutter, and maintained in top operating condition. The vision is of a truly world-class workplace in action.

Glass casing surrounds many of the machines to cut down on noise and dirt, and special coolants are used throughout the process to reduce heat buildup. The air is kept clean by a mist collection system that filters particles out of the air. DTC's people philosophies are demonstrated by plant freezers full of free popsicles distributed in hot weather, by children's Halloween and Christmas parties, and by various employee sports tournaments and activities.

The equipment at DTC is state of the art. Since 1990, the company has invested more than $55 million in new technology and machinery. Areas within the facility are divided into separate business units based on customers, and include Pump (Mack, DaimlerBenz), PDE (Volvo, Iveco, Scania), North American

Operations (Detroit Diesel, EMD), and Heat Treat. Employees work in business teams and are responsible for their own quality, delivery, and cost.

A Place Where People Want to Work

Diesel Technology is very committed to its employees, and thus has an extremely low turnover rate. The company is growing fast: Of the 1,500 employees, more than 60 percent have been hired within the last five years. Continued growth is predicted.

The company wants to attract and keep employees who are reliable, enthusiastic, motivated to learn, and interested in being team players. Because of this, the hiring process is involved, lasting about two months. Interested applicants go through a process involving in-person interviews, aptitude tests, and 100 hours of training in work-related courses at Diesel Tech University. It is DTC's experience that this extensive hiring process provides the company with team-oriented people who

have basic knowledge, are trainable, and are committed to the goals and objectives of the company. All employees know and understand the company's values of customer focus, quality, teamwork, development of people, and entrepreneurship.

The Road Ahead

In addition to the growing fuel injection business in the United States, there is tremendous potential in the European market, as well as in Asia and Eastern Europe. There may be future opportunities to expand outside the heavy engine market as the needs of customers dictate.

DTC believes that the real future of the company is in the hands of its employees. It's a progressive company, young in thought and totally focused on customers. An outstanding group of employees who are motivated, talented, and dedicated to the highest levels of quality are Diesel Technology's greatest asset. And they're also without a doubt the key to the company's success in the future.

The equipment at DTC is state of the art. Since 1990, the company has invested more than $55 million in new technology and machinery.

EEDY MANUFACTURING CO. WAS FOUNDED IN 1947 BY HAROLD Leedy Sr. in a four-stall garage on Hall Street. The company was initially a job shop doing subcontract work for a variety of local manufacturers. Daniel Klein joined the company in 1951, and became a partner shortly thereafter. ■ Leedy Manufacturing

began making products in 1954 for Big Dutchman of Zeeland, Michigan, a firm that had pioneered the automation of commercial egg production and controlled more than 90 percent of the market for feeding, watering, ventilation, confinement, and egg collection equipment. In the late 1970s, Leedy, along with a Georgia investor, Daniel Speicher, purchased all Big Dutchman equipment lines associated with the production of chicken and turkey for meat, and Cyclone International was formed in Holland, Michigan.

In 1978, both Leedy and Klein, who was then president of the company, died of cancer, and Harold "Buzz" Leedy Jr., who had become involved in the company in 1972, began the purchase of both of their interests from their estates.

During the 1980s, consumption of chicken and turkey rose dramatically, leading to prosperity for both Leedy Manufacturing and Cyclone. Leedy continued to supply parts to Big Dutchman, which had concentrated most of its efforts on egg production equipment and had relocated to Pennsylvania by way of Atlanta. Leedy also began to expand its base into other industries such as material handling, machine tool, meat processing, recreation, and automotive.

In 1989, after Big Dutchman had changed owners several times, Leedy helped negotiate a merger

Leedy Manufacturing officers (from left) Gerald Suttorp, vice president manufacturing; Harold "Buzz" Leedy, president; Thomas Brooks, vice president sales; and Donald Freehafer, vice president engineering, make up a portion of the company's customer-oriented team.

of Big Dutchman and Cyclone, forming a new company that took the Big Dutchman name. Leedy, Speicher, and Josef Meerpohl, a resident of Germany, are the major shareholders of the company, with Warren Stuk holding a minority position. Today, the company has 225 employees with plants in Holland, Michigan; Kentucky; and Alabama—totaling 275,000 square feet—and with sales offices in South Carolina; St. Petersburg, Florida; and Kuala Lumpur, Malaysia. Big Dutchman produces more than 16,000 active items—with 58 percent of its sales in North America—and its equipment supplies as much as 25 percent of the U.S. chicken production of 145 million birds per week, as well as 50 percent of the

U.S. egg production of 1.4 billion eggs per week. Forty-two percent of the company's sales is concentrated in the Far East, Latin America, Africa, and the rest of the world.

Leedy Manufacturing, which continues under the ownership of Buzz Leedy, has 120 employees and two plants that total 85,000 square feet. The company has three primary product lines—gear reducers, winches, and pulleys—and, in addition, provides a wide variety of manufacturing services ranging from CNC machining and gear cutting to fabrication and welding. Leedy currently produces more than 4,000 active items for its customers on an ongoing basis. Leedy's customer base is 75 percent agricultural, and, together with Big

Leedy Manufacturing has 120 employees and two plants that total 85,000 square feet.

Buzz Leedy, Daniel Speicher, and Josef Meerpohl are the major shareholders of Big Dutchman, which produces more than 16,000 active items—with 58 percent of its sales in North America—and its equipment supplies as much as 25 percent of the U.S. chicken production of 145 million birds per week, as well as 50 percent of the U.S. egg production of 1.4 billion eggs per week.

Dutchman, the two companies have combined annual sales of more than $75 million.

According to Leedy, his company is known for its versatility, and its ability to handle the needs of customers quickly and efficiently. "At Leedy Manufacturing, we keep our systems simple, so we can make changes easily and be as flexible as possible," says Leedy. "Our customers know they can depend on us to provide them with whatever they need, and turn things around quickly. In fact, we're probably about as versatile as any company in the Midwest." Leedy credits his employees for his company's ability to service customers in this way. "Our workforce is made up of a team of loyal, customer-oriented people," he adds. "We're a small company and we have a family-type atmosphere. We seem to attract people who like that type of environment."

A disaster occurred in 1987 that tested the company's ability to act as a team: A major fire destroyed one of the two Leedy plants, and the loss was devastating. "We lost everything in the fire," says Leedy, "including our building, inventory, and equipment. And what made it worse was that it happened during one of the busiest times in our history. Because of an incredible team effort on the part of our employees, along with the help of outside contractors, we were able to rebuild and equip a new building on the same site and were back in full production in only 12 weeks. And thanks to our employees, during the whole construction process, we never missed a delivery."

As the company moves into the future, it will continue to invest in advanced manufacturing methods and state-of-the-art equipment, and also concentrate on its strengths of versatility and flex-

ibility in order to serve a growing variety of customer requirements. The company's international business is expected to grow rapidly.

"Because chicken and egg consumption are continuing to escalate," explains Leedy, "the domestic outlook is very strong for our business. But there has been a huge increase in our international business, as well. In 1989, our sales outside of North America were less than 15 percent of total sales, and today that figure has risen to more than 40 percent. As markets continue to open and people in other areas of the world gain more disposable income, a higher priority will be placed on an improved diet. That means the potential for poultry and egg production worldwide is virtually endless." And Leedy Manufacturing and Big Dutchman are poised to continue their leadership in the growing industry, as they have for more than 50 years.

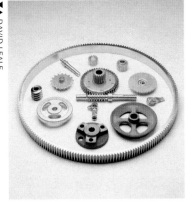

Gear reducers and winches are two key Leedy product lines (left).

A sampling of Leedy products and components includes specialty gears and shafts (right).

THE YEAR WAS 1947. WORLD WAR II WAS OVER, THE BOYS WERE home, materials shortages were commonplace, and pent-up consumer demand was rising. In that year, a fledgling aluminum extruder—Light Metals Corporation—was founded on Madison Street in Grand Rapids. ■ Because of war-related

shortages, Light Metals first had to find aluminum raw material, and then had to seek peacetime products and markets that fit its capabilities. Using an improvised extrusion press with a capacity of only three-inch billets, workers fabricated products such as watch bands and pipe stems for a small group of manufacturers and distributors.

THE GROWTH BEGINS

Over the following years, Light Metals outgrew its first plant, and, during the Korean War, moved to larger quarters at Leonard Street and Monroe Avenue. In that period, the company also began to serve a larger number and a wider range of West Michigan customers, making such products as extruded

aluminum jukebox trim, refrigerator door hardware, desk drawer pulls, glass channels, and mirror frames.

A real breakthrough occurred in 1958, when Light Metals gained orders for a new heat sink design from Delco Remy, and for decorative bumper parts for the Cadillac Division of General Motors—marking an entry into selling automotive parts. These parts were the first of many new components that forced another move in 1961—this time to the site of the current, 200,000-square-foot facility located on Grand Rapids' southwest side.

What was once a small company of 10 employees has now grown to become an industry powerhouse, employing more than 200 engineers, support staff, and highly skilled UAW-member shop workers. Today, Light Metals Corporation is a full-service supplier of fabricated aluminum extrusions. These products are used extensively in industries as diverse as electronics, automotive, appliance, and contract furnishings. With customers across the nation, the facility has grown to utilize state-of-the-art techniques and equipment in keeping with the demands of those customers. Complete design services and prototyping round out the firm's offerings.

As a full-service fabricator, Light Metals not only extrudes the shapes for its parts (now formed from billets weighing 80 pounds), but is responsible for further processing such as piercing, notching, bending, anodizing, and buffing. Those components are then mated with other elements into a subassembly, which is included in the customer's end product. The company is known for development and delivery of parts requiring very tight tolerances, and high-quality standards.

As a leader in the field, Light Metals was an innovator in the use of computer-aided design and statistical process control. To demonstrate the company's technical expertise and to meet the growing demand for certified compliance with quality standards, in 1997, Light Metals' processes became certified under the internationally recognized ISO 9002 standards, as well as the automotive industry's QS 9000 program.

Light Metals' products have come a long way from the pipe stems produced back in 1947. With the company's impressive history of growth and tradition of quality, Light Metals' subassemblies will continue to be an important part of many different products for years to come.

Light Metals Corporation is a full-service supplier of fabricated aluminum extrusions. With customers across the nation, the facility has grown to utilize state-of-the-art techniques and equipment in keeping with the demands of those customers.

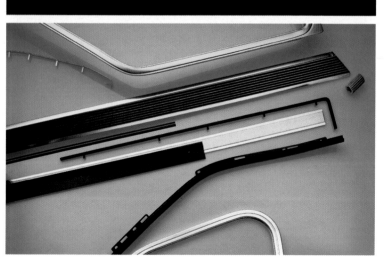

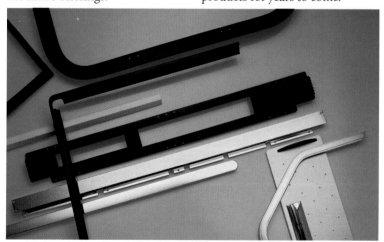

THE TERM "INTELLECTUAL PROPERTY" HAS A GREAT DEAL OF meaning in today's technologically competitive world. By way of definition, it reflects the products of the human mind—artistry, innovation, and creativity—that are immensely valuable and well worth protecting. For more than

40 years, the law firm of Price, Heneveld, Cooper, DeWitt & Litton has specialized in preserving and shielding intellectual properties through patents, copyrights, and trademarks.

COMBINING LAW AND SCIENCE

Price, Heneveld, Cooper, DeWitt & Litton has a staff of attorneys trained in either science or engineering, as well as law. Often combining multiple degrees in chemistry or biology with an extensive legal education, these attorneys are required to pass not only the standard bar exam, but a second bar exam that covers federal patent practices.

Such breadth of knowledge is essential for those specializing in protection of intellectual property. "Today's technology is unbelievably sophisticated, and getting more so all the time," explains Dick Cooper, a partner of the firm. "We're dealing with patents on new pharmaceutical compositions, scientific developments, highly sophisticated devices—and it's essential that we fully understand these things in order to adequately protect them." Because of the firm's extensive experience and commitment to continued learning, its attorneys have the expertise to successfully obtain, enforce, or defend their clients' intellectual property rights anywhere in the world.

SUCCESS FUELED BY CLIENT GROWTH

Lloyd Heneveld, one of the firm's original founders, recalls how, prior to the 1950s, there were very few firms in Grand Rapids that specialized in intellectual property work. "I formed a partnership with Peter Price in 1955," says Heneveld, "and at that time, most of the Grand Rapids companies were

going to Chicago and Detroit for their patent, trademark, and copyright work. We were able to capture many of these Grand Rapids-area clients like Steelcase, Prince Corporation, and Grand Haven Stamped Products, and because of their growth, our firm also grew. Plus, those who had previously turned to firms in bigger cities found out they could get better service, and equally competent service, right here at home."

Price, Heneveld's clients are often highly technical companies that develop an amazing array of innovations. Clients such as Eveready (home of the Energizer), Brunswick, and Perrigo are examples. One client, Cannon-Muskegon, makes sophisticated superalloys for high-speed military defense airplane engines; for Dow Chemical, the firm has worked to protect

polymer technology related to exciting new materials; Price, Heneveld's work with a major pharmaceutical client has helped secure patents for drugs used in the treatment of AIDS and cancer, as well as cholesterol-lowering drugs; and for Millennium Dynamics, a Cincinnati-based company, the firm has worked to patent software that enables computers to recognize 2000 as a valid date.

Price, Heneveld, Cooper, DeWitt & Litton serves more than 300 clients both nationally and internationally through its worldwide network of associate law firms. As protecting intellectual property becomes ever more important, the firm is poised to be on the leading edge of this specialty. Now the largest intellectual property law firm in West Michigan, Price, Heneveld plans to continue to be a leader in its field into the 21st century.

For more than 40 years, the law firm of Price, Heneveld, Cooper, DeWitt & Litton has specialized in preserving and shielding intellectual properties through patents, copyrights, and trademarks.

W HEN MOST PEOPLE THINK ABOUT A CAR'S EXHAUST system, they are likely to consider such things as the muffler, tailpipe, or manifold. It's doubtful that the word "flange" would come to mind first, but flanges are essential to a properly functioning

vehicle because without them, the entire exhaust system would fall apart. Grand Rapids-based Pridgeon & Clay has specialized in manufacturing exhaust system flanges for more than 50 years, and today it is the largest North American supplier of these vital automobile components.

Starting Out in a Garage

In 1948, John S. Pridgeon and Donald V. Clay founded the company in a small, converted garage on Grandville Avenue. Originally started as a tool and die business, Pridgeon & Clay's earliest products included speakers for radios (and later for televisions) and wrought iron furniture legs marketed to small furniture manufacturers and do-it-yourselfers. Today, the metal stamping company has grown to more than 550 permanent and 150 temporary employees, and manufactures more than 2,000 different automotive parts, including exhaust-system-related compo-

Pridgeon & Clay, Inc., founded by John S. Pridgeon and Donald V. Clay in 1948, began in a small, converted garage. The company now occupies 450,000 square feet of manufacturing and office space in two locations, as well as a 40,000-square-foot plant in central Indiana.

nents, support brackets for motor mounts, heat shields, transmissions, instrument panel brackets, and basically anything else that holds things together under a vehicle's hood or dashboard.

The company now occupies 450,000 square feet of manufacturing and office space in two locations, as well as a 40,000-square-foot plant in central Indiana that handles light manufacturing. This site also serves as a distribution center for

exhaust system customers in the Indiana area.

Bob Clay, the cofounder's brother and current Pridgeon & Clay president, says the company has three separate markets for its products: "We're considered a tier-one supplier to the major automobile makers—primarily General Motors and Ford—for brackets and flanges," he says. "Another important market for us is other tier-one suppliers, who also buy

With more than 70 presses ranging in size from 40 to 1,250 tons, Pridgeon & Clay has the capacity to meet the demands for a wide range of stampings.

The training center educates, tests, and certifies Pridgeon & Clay's staff members, supporting the corporate philosophy of employee empowerment and ongoing training.

their brackets and flanges from us. And we sell to the aftermarket, or large exhaust system manufacturers who install replacement systems on used cars." In one form or another, the automobile industry represents 99 percent of Pridgeon & Clay's business.

FULL-SERVICE SUPPLIER

Because of its superior research and development capabilities, Pridgeon & Clay is often involved with customers through entire projects. With a cutting-edge research and development center, certified laboratory, and highly qualified technical staff using the latest computer-aided design/computer-aided manufacturing (CAD/CAM) systems, the company is able to provide customers with a full range of highly specialized services, which include building prototypes, testing, and mass-producing the products.

Pridgeon & Clay has grown to its current position in the industry through its ability to build tooling and parts, and then to supply customers with these products. Tooling is a very expensive part of the whole process, and Pridgeon & Clay builds and owns much of its tooling. By doing this, the company is able to amortize the cost over many projects, which in turn saves the customer money.

QUALITY ATTITUDE, QUALITY RECOGNITION

Pridgeon & Clay's customers value their relationships because of the high levels of quality, service, and expertise the company provides. The customers know they can always count on superior service and exceptional quality for which Pridgeon & Clay has repeatedly been recognized.

The company has won many awards and distinctions, including General Motors' Targets for Excellence, which is the automaker's official stamp of approval for top-quality parts and service, and Ford's Q-1 Award, also for superior quality and service. In addition to being ISO-9001 certified by the International Organization for Standardization, the company is QS-9000 certified, again for overall quality and service excellence.

Pridgeon & Clay's manufacturing facilities are state of the art, with more than 70 presses ranging in size from 40 to 1,250 tons. The company is always on the lookout for the newest, most up-to-date technology and equipment. It was one of the first companies in Grand Rapids to use high-speed transfer presses, and also one of the first to use CAD/CAM technology. Bob Clay says, "It's important in our industry to stay current, and we're committed to continuously

doing that." The company has eight high-speed transfer presses, quick-change presses, automatic presses, fine blanking machines, precision milling machines, robotic and spot welding equipment, and epoxy tooling capabilities used primarily for patterns and fixtures.

A VALUABLE TEAM

The staff of Pridgeon & Clay is a loyal team of people whom the company values immensely. In spite of the unavoidable changes that happen whenever a business experiences rapid growth, the company's turnover rate is low, with many employees having 10 or more years' seniority. The manufacturing facility is clean and orderly. The offices are connected by a long, white hallway, where employee photography is prominently framed and displayed on the walls along with each employee/photographer's name.

Pridgeon & Clay plans to continue with what it does best. "We intend to maintain steady growth each year," says Clay. "And we'll do this by sticking to what we know best, continuing to provide customers with the levels of service and quality they expect, and also by being responsive to what's changing in our market. This has worked for us for 50 years. We believe it will continue working for us far into the future."

N AUGUST 14, 1949, THE FIRST TELEVISION STATION IN WEST Michigan—WOOD TV8, then known as WLAV TV—made its historic debut. ■ Broadcasting from a small part of what is now McKay Tower in Grand Rapids, WOOD TV8 laid the groundwork for its reputation as an innovator

in its industry by becoming the first station to service the West Michigan community. Many other firsts would follow, each strengthening the critical bond with viewers that has made WOOD TV8 West Michigan's leading source for news and information.

INNOVATION

Since its inception, WOOD TV8's vision and foresight have kept it in the forefront of technological advances, securing a loyal audience. Scott Blumenthal, WOOD TV8 president and general manager, is proud of his company's record. "Our station has a history of staying out in front, ahead of the in-

dustry in terms of cutting-edge technology. It's something we've been known for since the very beginning, and it's something we're committed to continuing," he says.

Indeed, WOOD TV8's legacy of innovation only began when it hit the airwaves. On New Year's Day 1954, the station introduced color television to West Michigan with its broadcast of the Tournament of Roses parade. That same year, it became the strongest station in the United States when it boosted its signal from 100,000 to 316,000 watts of power. Later, WOOD TV8 would become the first station in West Michigan to offer live, local programs, and it

would revolutionize the local news scene by becoming the first in the area to utilize 24-hour news coverage, the first to use satellite and electronic news gathering, and the first to transmit remote live news. WOOD TV8 also has the first fully operating computerized newsroom, and has recently unveiled Chopper 8, the area's first and only news helicopter. Truly, WOOD TV8 has continuously proved its commitment to evolving to meet the increasingly sophisticated needs of viewers.

INFORMATION

Viewers have come to rely upon WOOD TV8 for the latest, most accurate, and most timely information possible. Its high-tech newsroom, bolstered by a fleet of mobile units, a satellite truck, and Chopper 8, is easily mobilized to cover any breaking news stories, live from anywhere. The vehicles are also supported by a series of Skycams located throughout West Michigan. Remotely controlled from the 24-Hour News 8 Satellite Center, these high-powered cameras are strategically mounted atop buildings in Grand Rapids, Muskegon, Lansing, Kalamazoo, and Battle Creek. These Skycams give viewers instant access to video of changing weather conditions, traffic accidents, community events, and breaking news long before the competition.

For the most up-to-the-minute weather information, viewers tune into 24-Hour News 8's Storm Team 8. Its Live Doppler Plus, a powerful radar system, uses a high-resolution beam that reaches out and tracks changing weather conditions, providing West Michigan the highest level of accuracy and the earliest warnings possible. Storm Team 8 is also responsible for the Local Weather Station (LWS), a 24-hour, live broadcast of radar imaging,

The news team for 24-Hour News 8's 6 p.m. broadcast consists of (from left) Chief Meteorologist Craig James, anchors Suzanne Geha and Tom Van Howe, and Sports Director Jack Doles.

Producing more local news on a weekly basis than any station in the state of Michigan, WOOD TV8 has the largest staff of any Michigan station outside of Detroit .

in-depth forecasts, and weather updates that many in the unpredictable climate of Michigan find invaluable.

WOOD TV8's Internet site, woodtv.com, is another important tool made available to viewers. It offers live Doppler radar imaging, Storm Team 8 forecasts, and frequently updated local news stories to those whose schedules do not allow the conveniences of newscasts at 5 a.m., noon, 5, 6, and 11 p.m. In addition, woodtv.com has secured a partnership with MSNBC, and provides links to sites that detail regional, national, and international events, as well as the latest in sports, entertainment, business, and commentary.

Not surprisingly, WOOD TV8 has a long history of winning awards and accolades from its industry. In particular, 1997 was a banner year. The station won six Associated Press awards, seven first-place awards from the Michigan Association of Broadcasters (MAB), and the MAB's highest honor, Station of the Year. Also, both the National Education Association and the Michigan Education Association recognized WOOD TV8 for its outstanding efforts in educational programming. In addition, the station took home a Gracie Award in recognition of outstanding contributions by professional women. And according to A.C. Nielsen Company ratings, WOOD TV8 continued to rank as the most watched station in West Michigan.

INSPIRATION

As the leading television station in the West Michigan community, WOOD TV8 is committed to giving something back to its viewers.

"We produce more local news on a weekly basis than any station in the state of Michigan," says Blumenthal, "and we have the largest staff of any Michigan station outside of Detroit. This means that we have a tremendous number of resources enabling us to provide an extraordinary amount of time to community service projects."

WOOD TV8's community outreach program Arts Are Cool in School encourages grade school students to broaden their horizons by developing an understanding and appreciation of the arts. Let's Write Off Prejudice, a diversity awareness program, invites children from West Michigan elementary schools to submit creative work, such as essays, poetry, or artwork, that represents the benefits of diversity in race, religion, or physical limitation. The highly successful Angel Tree project supplies more than 22,000 gifts for needy West Michigan children during the holiday season. The Children's Miracle Network Champions Broadcast, which the station has sponsored since 1990, now raises more than $1 million each year to benefit sick children in West Michigan. Plus WOOD TV8's highly acclaimed Education First programming emphasizes the positive aspects of education by spotlighting creative programs, award-winning teachers, and innovative curricula.

WOOD TV8 is committed to providing more than just entertainment. Through community outreach and responsible programming, it hopes to help those in need and to positively impact the future.

ILLUMINATION

In the coming years, WOOD TV8 will continue to excel and lead, blazing new trails in search of quality enhancements for viewers. Already, the station is planning a complete digital conversion by 1999, a full seven years ahead of the industry's 2006 deadline. Once again stepping to the forefront, WOOD TV8's digital transmission will provide viewers a much higher quality signal and crystal clear reception. According to Blumenthal, the changing landscape of television will not diminish its influence on the future. "TV will certainly play a vital part in the overall communications environment," he says, "but when it comes to how it will be delivered and what will be included, that's still undetermined. There is one thing we do know for sure: WOOD TV8 will continue to maintain its tradition to stay out in front of the rest, and provide viewers with the very best news, information, and entertainment. We consider that a responsibility that's ours to fulfill."

Clockwise from top left: WOOD TV8 has the first fully operating computerized newsroom, and has recently unveiled Chopper 8, the area's first and only news helicopter.

Its high-tech newsroom, bolstered by a fleet of mobile units, a satellite truck, and Chopper 8, are easily mobilized to cover any breaking news stories, live from anywhere.

For the most up-to-the-minute weather information, viewers tune into 24-Hour News 8's Storm Team 8.

RESTORING OUR PAST—BUILDING OUR FUTURE." THIS PHRASE IS an official motto at DeVries Companies, but more than that, it's also a sincere commitment to the community. As one of Grand Rapids' leading real estate developers, DeVries offers many types of building expertise and dedicates its efforts to

preserving the community's history, as well as specializing in new developments that enhance Grand Rapids' growth.

William DeVries Sr. started out building barns in Portland, Michigan, during the 1920s, which led to work in commercial construction and remodeling. In 1950, DeVries moved his wife and five sons to Grand Rapids and started his own company, William DeVries and Sons Construction. Among his first projects were several schools, churches, industrial buildings, and the very first Meijer Thrifty Acres, which DeVries built in 1962, on Kalamazoo Avenue and 28th Street.

PRESERVING YESTERDAY, BUILDING TOMORROW

All five of William DeVries' sons—Charlie, Bill Jr., Ken, Ed, and Bob—have been involved with the company at one time or another. In 1970, Bob and Ed went out on their own to form DeVries Development, which is a real estate land developer, building developer, and building management company with properties and land all over the West Michigan area. Initially, Bob and Ed concentrated on developing and leasing buildings, and eventually moved into construction work on the buildings they leased.

In 1975, Bob and Ed formed two additional divisions: DeVries Construction, Ltd. and Ed DeVries Properties. Today, the three divisions are collectively known as DeVries Companies, and together they offer Grand Rapids an unparalleled combination of diverse experience and expertise.

Ed DeVries Properties is a full-service real estate brokerage firm that primarily concentrates on handling industrial and commercial properties. DeVries Construc-

tion is a full-service design/build general contractor that specializes in both renovating and preserving historic buildings, as well as constructing new commercial and industrial buildings.

As for the company's expertise in working with old, historic buildings, Ed DeVries says his father was the inspiration behind it. "We

grew up watching our dad do all sorts of remodeling projects," he says. "Because he had lived through the depression, he had learned to reuse anything and everything he could. He never threw anything away—even pulled old nails out of lumber to reuse them. And he gave us an appreciation for different architectural styles, as well as

DeVries Companies offer Grand Rapids an unparalleled combination of diverse experience and expertise.

the character and intrinsic value of historic buildings."

In addition to a 19th-century fire station, a railroad freight depot, and one of Grand Rapids' original furniture factories, one of DeVries' most challenging and visible restoration projects was Aldrich Place, located on the corner of Ottawa Avenue and Monroe Center. The building is actually on the site of the Old Stone Catholic Church, which burned down in 1850 and was replaced in 1874 with a new structure built in an Italian Renaissance style. Over the years, the building had deteriorated, and in 1997, DeVries completed a major renovation of Aldrich Place—including

duplication of the Italian Renaissance scrollwork along the roof—and unveiled the building to the public.

DeVries specializes not only in building renovation and preservation, but also in the construction of new buildings. Projects have included four industrial parks, Cross Creek West and numerous other condominium projects, Coopers Landing, the C.E. Stehouwer building, and RBC Ministries.

PERSONALIZED SERVICE
The people at DeVries Companies make it a priority to develop a close working relationship with customers, meeting with them to discuss business plans, as well as

identifying and understanding their businesses inside and out. "With our experience and expertise, along with our three separate companies," says Ed DeVries, "we can work with our customers to determine if their needs are best met by leasing space, expanding their businesses, selling their property, or purchasing property to construct a new facility."

DeVries Companies welcomes opportunities to work with both large and small companies. When Ed DeVries received a call from two women whose home-based pottery business was ready to expand, he says the company went to work looking for the right solutions. "Their business was small but growing, and they needed help deciding what to do," he says. "We started by looking at old buildings, and when we didn't find anything that worked, we began to look for property, and consulted with them on what kind of new building would work best for them. In many ways, we acted as their business consultant: We sold them the property, designed and built their building, and helped them with financing. Later, as they continued to grow, we helped them acquire additional property and also did some remodeling for them. Developing this type of relationship with small businesses, working closely with them and watching them grow, is very rewarding and is something we enjoy doing very much."

Bob DeVries says he's excited about the future, and anticipates a tremendous amount of growth ahead. "One of the best things about Grand Rapids," he says, "is that there's so much integrity here. Everyone is looking out for the good of the community, and there's a lot of optimism here. I see this area continuing to grow and flourish in the years to come, and our role will be to continue supporting the community by renovating and preserving what's old, and continuing to build the new. We're proud and excited to be a part of it all, and we plan to play a major part in this community's growth."

SOUTHEAST OF GRAND RAPIDS LIES THE QUIET TOWNSHIP OF Caledonia, where rich farmland stretches for miles and the air is crisp and clean. Tucked away in the countryside, not far from the intersection of 68th Street and Kraft Avenue, there's a small lake. A nearby driveway winds through acres of woods and leads

to a rather unexpected discovery: the headquarters of Foremost Corporation of America, located in one of the most stunning buildings in all of West Michigan.

PROVIDING A SPECIALTY PRODUCT

Founded in 1952, Foremost was originally headquartered in the red brick Federal Square Building on the corner of Pearl Street and Ionia Avenue in downtown Grand Rapids. The company began with just three employees and one account, Union Bank. Starting out as a single-specialty insurance company, Foremost was the first in the country to offer insurance designed especially for mobile homes. Over the years, the company expanded its product offering to include insurance for motor homes and travel trailers, and has since rounded out its product line by adding policies for automobiles and site-built homes. Today, the company insures more than 1 million policyholders and sells insurance in every U.S. state except Hawaii.

Foremost has traditionally provided insurance through insurance agents, mobile home and recre-

ational vehicle dealer agents, and agents affiliated with lenders, as well as through direct contact with customers. In 1989, the company was selected by the Washington, D.C.-based American Association of Retired Persons (AARP) as the preferred company to offer mobile home insurance to its members. Foremost was chosen by the AARP because of the quality of its product, its commitment to superior customer service, and its willingness to offer AARP customers reasonable prices.

NEW OPPORTUNITIES LEAD TO NEW PRODUCTS

Foremost's affiliation with the AARP provided the company with experience that led to other direct

marketing efforts. In 1996, the company began a homeowners and auto insurance program that it markets to companies and organizations. By aligning itself with these groups, Foremost obtains introduction and access to their employees or customers. This allows the company to succeed with its innovative direct sales approach to offering high-quality, competitive auto and homeowners insurance.

Agreements to market insurance through these relationships open up new, large markets to Foremost, according to President, Chief Executive Officer, and Chairman of the Board Richard L. Antonini. "We've found that a relationship is crucial if direct

From its headquarters in Caledonia, Foremost Corporation of America offers customers a range of insurance programs, including auto insurance coverage begun in 1996.

marketing is going to be efficient and cost effective," Antonini says. "People who are affiliated with a business or organization are often open to opportunities endorsed by that organization. We can offer them a streamlined way to take care of their home and auto insurance needs, and we make it easy for them."

AN ORGANIZATION FOCUSED ON ITS EMPLOYEES AND CUSTOMERS

Credit for Foremost's continued success and growth can be attributed solely to its people. "It takes more than capital to succeed," Antonini says. "Our employees are the heart of our organization; they make things happen. They're dynamic and they welcome challenges. That's how we continually provide high-quality insurance products and superb service to customers and prospective customers." Another vital part of Foremost's success is the caring attitude of its employees toward customers and toward each other. "As far as I'm concerned, that attitude contributes more than anything to our outstanding results," Antonini says.

As a company, Foremost is progressive in its attitude toward providing employees with flexible schedules that work comfortably within their lives. A significant number of the company's employees work at home, connected to the company via computers and modems. Many other employees based at the corporate headquarters are on flextime schedules—working schedules that suit their family demands—yet working dur-

ing core business hours. According to Don Collins, Foremost's vice president of human resources, the company's focus is on getting the work done, rather than on telling people how and when to do it. "We've experimented for a long time with things like flextime and work-at-home," he says. "What we've found is that productivity is much higher when people are allowed to be more independent and have more control of their time in order to attend to their personal needs—like attending critical school events for their children and scheduling doctor and dentist appointments."

AN ORGANIZATION POISED FOR GROWTH

Foremost Corporation is financially sound, and according to Antonini, "carefully nurtured for growth." One major sign of the company's financial strength is the A+ rating it received from A.M. Best Company, the independent rater of insurance companies.

Best's Ratings ranked Foremost among top industry leaders in both financial soundness and ability to pay claims. Foremost also has been rated a Ward's 50 company for several years, placing it among the top 50 property and casualty insurance companies in the nation for financial strength.

As for the future, the company will continue to look for opportunities to grow, paying attention both to its well-established independent agency base and to direct marketing opportunities. "As we look to the next century, we plan to continue being progressive in our thinking, providing additional products and services that customers demand," says Antonini. "Our first priority is and always will be to satisfy the insurance needs of our target customers, and to provide them with good value, superior products, and the financial security that insurance is intended to provide. With that as our focus, our future is extremely exciting."

Foremost got its start in 1952 as a specialty insurer offering coverage designed for mobile homes. Since then, it has added homeowners policies to its list of services.

E DWARD TWOHEY, THE SENIOR PARTNER AND FOUNDER OF Twohey Maggini, PLC, is a man with an interesting and unique background. Twohey came to Grand Rapids and began practicing law in 1949, first working at Legal Aid. He had attended Notre Dame Law School and left Grand Rapids in 1951 to serve

in Korea with the U.S. Navy. However, few people—including former classmates—know that Twohey's birth name was actually Flanagan, and he is the nephew of the famous and much loved Father Flanagan of Boys Town. In fact, when Twohey was in high school, he lived at Father Flanagan's Boys Town for several years, eventually becoming the mayor of Boys Town. Twohey later went off to college, naval service in World War II, and then law school, where the mayor became a lawyer, and the rest became history.

In 1953, when Twohey returned to Grand Rapids from the navy, he specialized first in general practice, and later developed a specialty in real estate and corporate law. Today, Twohey Maggini is a full-service law firm, and in addition to medium and large corporations, the firm also works with credit unions and banks, real estate brokerage firms and agents, general contractors, and both small and large retail establishments, as

Edward Twohey, the senior partner and founder of Twohey Maggini, PLC, came to Grand Rapids and began practicing law in 1949.

well as a host of other clients. The attorneys at Twohey Maggini also regularly work with private clients who need representation and counseling in such diverse areas as real estate, estate planning, bankruptcy, and major personal injury cases, as well as criminal law.

STRONG RELATIONSHIPS
The firm totals 12 individuals, including seven attorneys, one paralegal, two legal secretaries, and three full-time administrative support people. Kent Mudie, one of the firm's partners, says a major strength of Twohey Maggini is the strong relationships that exist between the people who work there.

"We're all friends here, and I believe that's very important," says Mudie. "It's something that sets us apart. We all know each other,

One major strength of Twohey Maggini is the strong relationships that exist between the people who work there. Members of the firm include (front, from left) Patrick M. Muldoon, Edward L. Twohey, (back, from left) Kent W. Mudie, David Schoolenberg, Cathryn M. Keating, John A. Potter, Anthony J. Valentine, and Todd R. Knecht.

we trust each other's judgment, and we can fill in for each other whenever there is a need. Each of us has different qualities and strengths, and we complement each other. And every one of us is involved in making sure our clients are taken care of. That's not only valuable to each of us, it's of tremendous value to our clients."

Mudie says that through the years, Twohey Maggini has been a sort of "training ground" for distinguished legal careers, as four partners of the firm have left to become judges, and one left to become a U.S. attorney.

STRONG COMMUNITY COMMITMENT
As a longtime member of the Grand Rapids community, Twohey Maggini is strongly committed to serving and improving the legal profession, as well as to taking an active part in community organizations and affairs. The firm's attorneys contribute at many levels, all regularly volunteering with various charitable, civic, professional, and political organizations.

Twohey was one of the first Legal Aid attorneys—eventually serving as president of the society in the Grand Rapids area—and has continued to be actively involved with the Legal Aid Board. Twohey also did much of the legal work to create the Chamber Foundation, which is the fund-raising arm of the Grand Rapids Chamber of Commerce, where he served as president for a number of years.

Twohey continues to be involved with the Chamber itself.

Other Twohey Maggini attorneys have served as officers, directors, board members, and trustees for such environmental and community organizations as the Jaycees, YMCA and various YMCA camps, Michigan Audubon Society, Trout Unlimited, and American Civil Liberties Union, as well as various environmental agencies, senior citizen homes, and city and township boards. In addition, several Twohey Maggini attorneys have served as legal instructors at colleges, such as Aquinas, Seidman Graduate School, and the University of Detroit.

BUILDING A SOLID FUTURE IN WEST MICHIGAN
Mudie says that in the years ahead, Twohey Maggini will grow large

enough to provide clients with the diverse services they need, but will remain small enough to provide the personalized, hands-on service the firm has long been known for. Today, most of Twohey Maggini's business is either repeat business or comes to the firm via referral from existing clients.

"It's a fact that clients talk to each other," says Mudie. "Our firm's clients trust us, and they have confidence in us. That's the very best testimony to the quality of legal services we provide. People come to us because they hear about our knowledge, our experience, and how committed we are to serving our clients," he says. "That's how we've built this firm through the years, and we'll continue to build on that for all the years ahead."

John Potter and his fellow attorneys at Twohey Maggini regularly work with private clients who need representation and counseling in such diverse areas as real estate, estate planning, bankruptcy, and major personal injury cases, as well as criminal law (left).

Twohey Maggini is a full-service law firm, and in addition to medium and large corporations, the firm also works with credit unions and banks, real estate brokerage firms and agents, general contractors, and both small and large retail establishments, as well as a host of other clients. Among those guiding the firm's activities are Cathryn Keating and David Schoolenberg (right).

Kent Mudie (right), one of the firm's partners, with Anthony J. Valentine, says, "We're all friends here, and I believe that's very important. It's something that sets us apart. We all know each other, we trust each other's judgment, and we can fill in for each other whenever there is a need."

OB WOOD, CHAIRMAN AND CHIEF EXECUTIVE OF G&T INDUSTRIES, Inc., is always on the lookout for new opportunities and new ways for his company to expand. Consequently, G&T has become a widely diversified company, employing 500 people in divisions that range in focus from supplying engineered

foam products for an almost inconceivable variety of applications to pursuing international marketing partnerships on behalf of its clients. According to Wood, the company will always maintain its focus on seeking better ways to meet the ever changing needs of its customers. "We're a totally market-driven company," he says. "That means whatever we do, we do it on behalf of our customers, to better serve their needs and add to their success."

Founded in Grand Rapids in 1954 by Robert Greiner and Kenneth Tarbell, G&T Industries began as a regional foam fabrication business, then called G&T Distributors. Initially supplying fabricated latex foam rubber cushions to the many residential furniture manufacturers in the Grand Rapids area, G&T eventually began to broaden its customer base and pursue other markets. In 1975, the company name was changed to G&T Industries to reflect its growing diversification.

CORE BUSINESSES

Today, G&T Industries is one of the largest privately owned fabricators of foam products in the country, serving a wide variety of industries, including residential, business, and contract furniture; automotive; industrial; military; medical; electronics; consumer products; recreational vehicles; marine; aircraft; and packaging. The company has six foam fabrication facilities located in Michigan, Pennsylvania (two), Indiana, Ohio, and Georgia, and has plans for two additional plants before the turn of the century.

G&T's Decorative Products Group supplies value-added, soft-surface materials to many of the same markets and customers served by the G&T Foam Group. Of particular emphasis and success has been its work with original equipment manufacturers in the marine, recreational, and aircraft industries. For example, the division's Marine Specialties Group (MSG)

is the largest supplier of interior and exterior materials to original equipment boat manufacturers in the country. MSG has warehouses, showrooms, and sales offices in Florida, Tennessee, Indiana, and Michigan. Patrick Arnold, a G&T veteran of 32 years and the firm's senior vice president, established the company's customer-driven watchwords: "If it's important to you, it's important to us."

The commercial wallcovering market is another core business for G&T with two companies—DSI (Diversified Sales, Inc.) and Decorative Surfaces, Inc. covering a seven-state area in the East and Midwest for the country's number one commercial vinyl wallcovering manufacturer, RJF International. The G&T/DSI 40-year wallcovering program may well be the best example of partnership, loyalty, and relationship in the entire history of G&T. Richard Truex has been DSI's general manager for most of these years and, during this time, DSI and Decorative Surfaces have become RJF's largest distributor. The two companies specify and sell Vicrtex/Koroseal commercial wallcovering and Korogard wall protection products through the architect/design, contractor, and facility manager community. DSI/Decorative Sur-

Clockwise from top:
The personal, one-to-one relationship G&T Industries establishes with its customers is the company's greatest asset.

G&T Industries Chairman and Chief Executive Bob Wood

G&T Industries is a multifaceted company specializing in the design, development, and engineering of foam and decorative products.

faces was selected as Distributor of the Year in 1988, 1995, and 1996 from among more than 25 RJF distributors worldwide. "We are continuing to grow and expand our partnership with RJF," states G&T President Chuck Kaiser.

FURTHER DIVERSIFICATION

As a diversified company, G&T Industries has expanded far beyond its original core of specialized foam and fabric enterprises. G&T's New Business Opportunity Group has a variety of highly specialized entities with world marketing and distribution objectives.

World Resource Partnership (WRP), under Rol Grit's leadership, is a global resourcing and logistics company that became a G&T subsidiary in 1995. This group searches for overseas resourcing partners for a number of different markets including contract furniture and marine industries, helping to match customers with needed products and services available around the world.

International Market Strategies is a global distribution organization focused on marketing e-business software for IBM AS/400 worldwide sales and marketing channels. IMS, under Evan Harter's leadership, is dedicated to delivering best-of-breed intranet, Internet, and GroupWare solutions to its partners. Worldwide agreements—with state-of-the-art e-business vendors, such as IBM, Netscape, I/Net, and a variety of best-of-breed application tool developers—provide a leadership role in the e-commerce arena. International Marketing Strategies' new Application Mall

can be reached on the Internet at http://www.appsmall.com.

GTW, The More Space Place®, is committed to helping meet an ever growing market need for space in today's world. Featuring the renowned Murphy bed and including pocket offices and closet organizers, these systems enable home, condo, and apartment owners as well as hotels and motels to create distinctive, multipurpose rooms such as home offices, dens, guest rooms, and meeting rooms. Currently, The More Space Place products are sold through a growing, 15-franchise store system in Florida and the Midwest. Clark Williams, formerly a vice president with La-Z-Boy, is currently the chief operating officer for this new business opportunity group.

WHERE EMPOWERMENT IS A WAY OF LIFE

Wood and Kaiser are quick to credit G&T employees for the company's growth and success. "There are very special people here," Wood says. "We have a talented, motivated group that continuously gives 100 percent on behalf of our company and our customers." G&T is known for its family atmosphere and low turnover. Each year, the company holds its Employee Appreciation and Awards Banquet to honor its employees. To Kaiser, it's the best evening of the year due to the people, loyalties, and warm feelings that are evident in all who attend.

One philosophy at G&T involves letting each group govern itself as an independent unit, with its own

goals and objectives. "We prefer to empower the division heads to run their own areas, so they feel a sense of ownership," says Jim Knapp, G&T's CFO. "Before we undertake any sort of new venture, we make sure we have a champion who can run with it." G&T's management team seems to have an innate ability to spot talent, and it finds a tremendous amount of satisfaction in watching its employees grow and develop in their careers.

As for what's ahead, Wood says, "We'll keep looking for new ways to diversify and expand, always with an eye on the customers' needs. In the next five years, we envision G&T's growth will double, and this will happen by continuously looking for new products, new markets, new people, and new ways of doing business that add value and better meet our customers' needs. We're excited about where we are today, and we're even more excited about the future."

Clockwise from top: Hemisphere, a division of G&T's Decorative Products Group, supplies a wide range of diversified and integrated products to the aircraft industry.

G&T foams are used in seating for offices, restaurants, hospitals, and theaters.

Major marine manufacturers specify G&T foams, vinyls, and other decorative products to enhance interior styling and comfort.

F GRAND RAPIDS IS FAMOUS FOR ITS STRONG WORK ETHIC, THEN companies like Rapid Die & Engineering have certainly played a major part in helping it earn this reputation. Originally located in Detroit and called Lenco Die & Mold, the company was founded in 1946 by George H. Leonard. In 1955, Lenco Die & Mold moved to Grand Rapids

and changed its name to Rapid Die & Engineering.

Jim Jones, president of Rapid Die, says the reason for the company's move was Grand Rapids' favorable labor market. "Grand Rapids has always been known as a place where people are willing to work hard, and care about making quality things," he says. "Plus, this is a city known for being dependable and stable, and having strong work ethics. So moving here was the logical choice."

CHANGING WITH THE TIMES

Rapid Die & Engineering's original business was building die-cast dies for suppliers to the automotive industry. Some of the company's original customers, all manufac-

turers of zinc die castings, are no longer in business today, edged out by the industry trend toward plastics.

In the mid-1960s, Rapid Die & Engineering, seeing this definite shift toward plastics, gradually started focusing more on plastics and less on traditional zinc dies. By 1980, some 90 percent of Rapid Die's production was plastic molds. And today, Jones says the company builds plastic molds exclusively, and hasn't built a zinc die for more than five years.

Rapid Die's current customers manufacture plastic parts, such as grilles, housings for lamps, and interior trim for the automotive industry. These customers include Grand Rapids-based Lacks Indus-

tries, ADAC Plastics, Lescoa, and Lowell Engineering Corp., as well as Lear Corporation in Virginia and Kamco Industries, Inc. in Ohio.

FAMILY TIES

Rapid Die & Engineering has a history of attracting many talented employees and keeping them, as well as their families, for the long term. Jones points out that he was happy when the company moved to Grand Rapids. "My wife and I liked it here immediately," he says. "It's a beautiful area, and so much nicer than my native Detroit. It's where we chose to settle down and raise our family. I started out here as a mold maker, but my first real job was sweeping floors at a four-man shop in Hazel

From its headquarters in Grand Rapids, Rapid Die & Engineering has grown from 15 people in 1956 to 115 employees today.

Park. Since I'm president today, I guess you could say I worked my way up."

Jones' son Chris also started out like his father, sweeping floors at age 15. After graduating from school, the younger Jones eventually moved into a specialized company training program, and later followed in his father's footsteps and became a mold maker. He was named the company's general manager in 1994.

The Joneses aren't the only employees to stay with the company for a long period of time. In fact, Rapid Die employees usually start out young and work their way up the ladder, giving testament to the time and attention that Rapid Die puts into its employees. Overall, the turnover rate at Rapid Die is quite low, and about 10 percent of the company's employees have celebrated more than 25 years of employment with the company.

In addition to the Jones team, other Rapid Die & Engineering family ties have included eight father and son teams, one father and daughter team, one mother and son team, three grandfather and grandson teams, and 11 sets of brothers, all working as product designers, mold designers, machinists, or mold makers.

FOCUS ON THE FUTURE

Rapid Die & Engineering has grown from 15 people in 1956 to 115 employees today, and Jim Jones says the company will continue to grow and evolve as the industry demands it. "We use the most advanced technology available to develop our custom molds," he says, "and we will continue to look into more sophisticated programming as the need arises." But no matter how much the industry changes, or how much his company has to evolve to meet those changes, Jones says one thing will never change: "I still believe in the old-fashioned notion of values and hard work. That's what earned Grand Rapids the reputation it has today, and that's what brought this company to Grand Rapids in the first place. It's something we can all be very proud of."

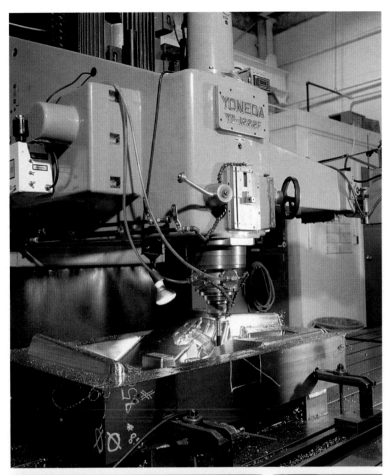

By 1980, some 90 percent of Rapid Die's production was plastic molds. And today, Jones says the company builds plastic molds exclusively.

BUTTERBALL FARMS, INC.

LEO PETERS WAS ALWAYS FASCINATED WITH THE FANCY DESIGNS HE saw on Whitman's chocolate candies. He also admired the cookie companies who embossed their tasty products with special holiday patterns or designs; the way Jell-O could be shaped by using special molds; and the fancy, embossed designs he sometimes saw on pats of butter. In fact, Peters was so intrigued with the idea of fancy butter designs that he started researching possibilities for mass producing the process. In 1956, after spending several years in Chicago, Peters returned to his native Grand Rapids to found Butterball Farms, Inc. Today, the company he founded is the world's leading producer of elegantly embossed butter and margarine.

A FAMILIAR HOUSEHOLD NAME

The name Butterball is most commonly associated with turkeys, and the Butterball turkey was another Leo Peters creation. Peters was well known for his ingenious genetic research that led to the development of turkeys with plumper, white-meat breasts, which he aptly named Butterballs. He later sold the patent and licensing rights for Butterball turkeys to Swift & Company, but negotiated the rights to license the Butterball name for his company's embossed butter products.

Peters' first customers for his butter were major airlines and hotels, but his company's biggest break came in the early 1970s with the fast-food giant McDonald's. According to Mark Peters, Leo Peters' son and current company president, it was the legendary Ray Kroc who actually made the decision to go with Butterball Farms.

"What really helped our company take off was the addition of breakfast to the McDonald's menu," Peters says. "At that time, they were contacting everyone who packaged butter, and they kept coming back to my father with additional requirements and package specifications. Kroc was very involved in the process, and was impressed with my father's willingness and ability to do whatever McDonald's needed. Kroc said our products would 'add a touch of class' to their breakfast menu." Kroc himself made the decision to choose Butterball Farms as McDonald's main supplier of butter, and today the company supplies butter for McDonald's restaurants located all over the United States, as well as in Far Eastern countries such as Singapore and Hong Kong.

A PLETHORA OF DESIGNS

Mark Peters, who took over as president after his father's death in 1995, says Leo Peters' legacy to the company he founded was the highest quality standards and a problem-solving mentality. "Dad had an incredible can-do attitude," Peters says. "No matter what the problem was, he was determined to solve it, and he'd do just about anything for a customer. He's gone now, but the values he instilled in this company are the same. If a customer comes to us with something we've never done before, we just figure out a way to get it done." According to Peters, Butterball designs and builds all its own equipment, so when new designs are needed or new challenges are faced, the company sets out to develop whatever machines it needs to handle the customer's requirements.

Butterball Farms remains at its original location on Buchanan Avenue near Hall Street.

Butterball Farms' customer list is indeed an impressive one, and is indicative of the company's talents and creativity. Butterball Farms has created seven different custom butter designs for Walt Disney World, as well as company logos and special butter creations for Hyatt, Sheraton, Westin, Hilton, and other major hotels around the country. Other clients are the famed Rainbow Room in Rockefeller Center; Scottsdale Conference Center and Resort; and Cygnus, the 1913 Room, and every other restaurant and banquet service within Grand Rapids' elegant Amway Grand Plaza Hotel.

Peters says Butterball's products are unique in the industry because of the high quality and intricacy of the designs. "Almost all companies who do what we do use stamping processes," he says, "which involves imprinting or depressing a design into the butter. Our process is embossing, which raises the image off the butter's surface, and enables more detail and a better rendering of the design."

MAKING EMBOSSED BUTTER

Development of each specialty butter design starts with the customer, who either provides camera-ready art or some idea of what kind of design is needed. A local wood-carver is then commissioned, who makes a sketch and transfers it to a woodblock, carving the wood to create an original die. From the wood, two more dies are created, which are used to actually mold the butter.

Butterball Farms is the largest single plant purchaser of butter from Michigan Milk Producers. Peters says the process of molding, freezing, and packaging butter is extremely labor-intensive, with 160 of the company's 200 employees involved in the packaging process. Butterball runs two full shifts a day, with a third-shift sanitation crew that completely cleans and sanitizes the 120,000-square-foot plant each night in preparation for the next morning's shift.

As for what's ahead, currently Butterball Farms' sales are about $15 million a year, and Peters says

he sees growth in the company's future. "We see a lot of potential, particularly in international markets," he says. "We have a unique product that is in high demand, and with our quality standards and problem-solving mentality, it's hard for the competition to even come close. We'll continue to pursue new markets and new opportunities in the future, but we'll continue to live by the principles that my father instilled in this company years ago, because they're the real reason we've achieved the success we have today."

Butterball Farms is the world's leading producer of elegantly embossed butter and margarine.

Butterball Farms' customer list is indeed an impressive one, and is indicative of the company's talents and creativity. Butterball Farms has created seven different custom butter designs for Walt Disney World, as well as company logos and special butter creations for Hyatt, Sheraton, Westin, Hilton, and other major hotels around the country.

MOORE & BRUGGINK, INC. IS A LEADING MUNICIPAL CIVIL engineering firm in Grand Rapids. Founded in 1956 by two former Grand Rapids city engineers, the company provides civil engineering, surveying, and municipal consulting services to state, city, county, village,

township, and private clients in the Grand Rapids area and throughout Michigan. The firm's unique specialty is to provide designs of function and beauty for the people who live, work, and play in the communities it serves.

WIDE BREADTH OF EXPERIENCE

Moore & Bruggink is experienced in the entire spectrum of civil engineering works. The firm's team of 14 highly skilled and licensed engineers provides planning, surveying, design, and construction engineering services for streets, highways, storm and sanitary sewers, water mains, land development, bridges, sidewalks, downtown renovation, parks, recreation, and landscaping. The firm also has extensive experience in wastewater treatment plants and water supply and treatment.

In conjunction with its engineering and consulting services,

Moore & Bruggink is licensed by the State of Michigan to practice surveying and is considered one of the major surveying firms in West Michigan. Moore & Bruggink has six professional surveyors on staff and seven survey crews, and its survey department is fully equipped

with computer-aided design (CAD) systems and the most sophisticated computerized surveying equipment.

SMALL-COMMUNITY NICHE

One of the more visible examples of Moore & Bruggink's talent for creating functional engineered beauty is the Standale Business District in Walker. In 1991, the firm was commissioned by the City of Walker to revitalize the area, which was dominated by an undivided four-lane highway that made the adjacent business areas difficult to access.

After careful analysis and planning, Moore & Bruggink redesigned the district, maintaining its beauty and villagelike charm while greatly improving the accessibility to area businesses. A center turn lane was added to M-45, allowing easier entrance into parking areas, and stores and offices were sheltered from the street by the addition of tree-lined grass medians. Moore & Bruggink's on-staff landscape architect softened and beautified the entire area by planting a variety of colorful flowers and maple trees to ensure three full seasons of color.

Moore & Bruggink has served many other communities as well, including Grand Rapids, Grandville, Kentwood, Zeeland, Holland, East Grand Rapids, Portage, Plainwell, Ferrysburg, Sparta, Ada, and Pentwater. In 1996, the firm was involved in building the first paved road on Beaver Island—a challenging project that required, first, a financing miracle, and then a construction project where all concrete, asphalt, limestone, and construction equipment had to be transported to the island via barge.

According to Bob Bruggink, vice president and partner, Moore & Bruggink is well known for its extensive knowledge and experience,

The Gus Lot represents a return to downtown Grand Rapids as the heart of a vibrant community. Moore & Bruggink, Inc. has had 42 years of partnering with public and private ventures to build the city (top).

Moore & Bruggink has been faithful to its Grand Rapids roots during the city's heyday in the 1950s and 1960s, its decline during the flight to the suburbs, and now its revitalization as the heart of the Metro Area. The renovation of Monroe Center is one of Moore & Bruggink's success stories (bottom).

and especially for its specialty in working with smaller communities. "We're known for our expertise and knowledge in all facets of engineering, but we're also known for our willingness to tackle the most complicated projects," Bruggink says. "And while we can and do handle projects of all sizes, we often work with communities that are too small to have their own engineering staff. We're well versed in all the laws, rules, and regulations that can easily intimidate a small community, and they can tap into our entire network of professional services. We know exactly what to do, who to talk to, and how to get the job financed, designed, and completed."

HELPING TO REVITALIZE GRAND RAPIDS

One of Moore & Bruggink's highest-profile projects has been its work on Monroe Center in downtown Grand Rapids. Previously a pedestrian mall, city planners recommended reopening the street to traffic as part of the revitalization of downtown, and Moore & Bruggink was hired as part of the city's team of professionals. "We teamed up with a local architectural firm to bring the city planners' dreams to fruition," says Gary Voogt, Moore & Bruggink's president, "and we've been involved in designing the road structure, utilities systems, and basically everything below the street, including the snowmelt system. We've also worked with the landscape architects on surface materials—such as brick for the streets, curbing, and sidewalks— and we're involved in construction inspection, scheduling, and surveying on the entire, unique project. On time and under budget," says Voogt.

Moore & Bruggink also has co-engineered the replacement for the city's historic North Park Bridge, an aged, narrow steel girder bridge that was constantly in need of repair and no longer able to meet the needs of modern traffic. Because the bridge was an official historic site, and also because of its sentimental value to the citizens of the area, there was controversy over

whether it should be repaired or replaced. Moore & Bruggink was commissioned to evaluate all the options, but finally recommended a new bridge for safety reasons. The firm codesigned a new, $6 million, four-lane concrete structure complete with arched facades, antique lighting, and wrought iron handrails to keep its authentic historical look while providing safety and capacity. Voogt says, "It's the prettiest of all the Grand Rapids bridges."

A SOLID PAST, A SOLID FUTURE

Most of Moore & Bruggink's business is with repeat clients, many of whom have been with the firm since its founding. Voogt says

he anticipates continued growth and stability in the coming years. "We were one of the first consulting civil engineering firms in the city of Grand Rapids," he says, "and we're the oldest, as well as the largest. We have an excellent reputation, we're a comfortable size, and we're able to provide high levels of service and expertise necessary to satisfy our clients. We've been blessed with good staff, good clients, and good friends in the communities in which we practice. This community is a great place to live and work, and there's every indication that it will continue to grow and prosper. And we intend to stay fresh and keep growing right along with it."

After designing all the utility pipes underground, Moore & Bruggink put the beauty back on top. The Standale project in Walker built a nice neighborhood on a state trunk line, and people are back on the sidewalks (top).

The North Park Bridge serves as a vital and beautiful link between the downtown city and its sister communities. The Grand River holds the same attraction today as yesteryear, when the city was founded by the rapids on the river (bottom).

HEN IT COMES TO GIVING SOMEONE CREDIT FOR HIS company's success, there's no question in Gary Proos' mind that it belongs to his employees. The president and owner of Plastic Mold Technology credits his team for their talents, their creativity, and their dedication to serving customers, and he's quick to say how valuable his employees are. "I've always said that my most important function in this company is to put together a team of people who can make us successful," he says, "and that's certainly the case here. Our employees are highly skilled and talented people, and it's our philosophy to let them use their talents and let them do their jobs. They know we don't need to look over their shoulders; we trust them to take the ball and run with it. And I believe the continued success of this company is a direct result of their efforts."

A Reputation for Tackling Challenges

Plastic Mold Technology was originally a machinery sales company called Woldring and Associates. Founded in 1958 by Adrian Woldring, the company specialized in electrical discharge machines, which were used to generate sparks to erode metal for the tool and die industry. In the process of demonstrating machinery to mold makers, Woldring became involved in mold making himself, and hired Proos as his apprentice in 1964.

In 1973, after leaving for a brief time to further his education, Proos purchased the company from Woldring along with a partner, Bill DeJonge, who retired in 1983. From the very beginning, Proos says he was aggressive about taking on new challenges. "I guess I got a reputation for having a can-do attitude," he says, "because there were lots of jobs I'd tackle that other shops just wouldn't. And that's still the attitude around here today. We're known for doing whatever it takes to serve the customer." Today, Plastic Mold Technology develops and manufactures plastic injection molds primarily for the automotive industry, serving auto manufacturers directly, as well as tier-one and tier-two suppliers. The company also serves customers in the appliance and furniture industries.

Once the molds are manufactured, Plastic Mold invites customers to the plant for "mold tryouts." The molds run on Plastic Mold's machines—which are duplicates of the machines in the customer's facility—in a process that saves the client downtime and money.

Plastic Mold Technology's 125 employees operate in teams and informal groups, rather than having strict lines of authority and significant management supervision. Proos says the company operates on the premise that everyone's opinion is important, everyone matters, and solutions are agreed on collaboratively by team members. Customers are each assigned both a project manager and a back-up project manager so the customers' needs and questions can

Injection molds built at Plastic Mold Technology are used to manufacture interior trim parts of automobiles, including instrument panels, hood meters, steering column covers, and air-conditioning bezels.

The company develops and manufactures plastic injection molds primarily for the automotive industry, serving auto manufacturers directly, as well as tier-one and tier-two suppliers.

always be handled quickly and efficiently.

INCOMPARABLE COMMITMENT TO CUSTOMERS

Plastic Mold's relationships with its customers are long-term and ongoing, and Proos says that some customers have been with the company since before he bought it. "Our customers are everything to this company," he says, "and that's always top of mind with us. We have real loyalty to our customers, and we view every relationship as if it's going to be around for at least 30 years. That's the basis of all our decision making. We want to understand our customers' businesses, and we want them to understand ours. We like to keep things open and honest, and we're

convinced that it's mutually beneficial and the only way to do business."

An especially impressive feature of Plastic Mold Technology is the major investment the company has made in technology. "Our industry has changed dramatically, and keeps changing every day," Proos says. "One of the main reasons we've been able to stay at the top of our field is the significant dollars we've invested in computerized equipment, and the training necessary to keep our employees up to speed with it."

Each year, Plastic Mold invests a sizable percent of its total sales volume into the latest technology, and all the company's machines and equipment have been replaced within the past five years—signifi-

cant when considering that the sophisticated computers and software used by Plastic Mold can cost nearly $100,000 apiece, and machining centers, used to cut and contour steel, often cost more than $1 million each.

Proos' goal for the company's future is to continue its pattern of steady, conservative growth. "We'll continue investing in our company, our technology, and our employees," he says, "and we'll add to this company whatever we need to continue serving our customers. Our goal for the future is to be whatever the customer wants us to be, and do whatever the customer wants us to do. The way we look at it, if we take care of our customers the way we've always done, we can't help but be successful."

A COMPANY WITH ITS SIGHTS SET ON THE FUTURE, AMWAY Corporation is one of West Michigan's premier employers and the provider of a business opportunity enjoyed by millions of entrepreneurs worldwide. ■ With annual sales of $7 billion, affiliates in nearly 50 countries on six

continents, and a diverse product line ranging from home and personal care products to vitamins and food supplements, Amway and its two publicly traded sister companies, Amway Asia Pacific Ltd. and Amway Japan Limited, make up one of the world's largest direct selling companies. While it may be a household name in many places around the globe, the unique story of Amway's success may not be as well known.

Under the leadership of Amway Chairman Steve Van Andel and President Dick DeVos, who together form the Office of the Chief Executive, Amway is building upon the firm foundation laid by their fathers, Amway cofounders Jay Van Andel and Rich DeVos. Amway today supports more than 3 million independent business owners who have embraced the Amway business opportunity and market a broad array of Amway products, plus many other name-brand items, through its catalogs. Since 1990, Amway's sales have tripled and the number of international affiliates it operates has more than doubled.

Amway offers one of the broadest product lines in direct selling, making it a business opportunity that appeals to a wide range of people. In the United States, Amway

offers more than 450 Amway-brand products and thousands of famous-brand products through its PERSONAL SHOPPERS® Catalog. Manufactured at Amway's World Headquarters—which now stretches for more than a mile on its original site in Ada, Michigan—as well as at facilities in California, China, Korea, and India, Amway products are respected for their high quality.

Amway always has been known for its complete home care line, including SA8® laundry products; its ARTISTRY® Skin Care and Shaded Cosmetics line; and its nutrition and wellness products, including NUTRILITE® vitamins and food supplements. Amway's

home tech line, including high-quality water and air treatment systems, provides Amway distributors additional opportunities to expand their businesses, as do new co-branded products being introduced through unique arrangements with such companies as Rubbermaid and Waterford Crystal.

Amway continues to make tremendous strides under the leadership of Steve Van Andel and Dick DeVos, supported by the Amway Policy Board, which is comprised of Amway's cofounders and their eight children. Working in partnership with Amway distributors and employees, the corporation

Clockwise from top:
Amway Corporation is now led by Steve Van Andel, chairman (left), and Dick DeVos, president, who together comprise the Office of the Chief Executive.

Today, Amway World Headquarters stretches for more than a mile.

The Amway Policy Board, composed of the two cofounders and their eight children, was formed in 1992 and provides strategic direction for the corporation. Members include (from left, back) Cheri DeVos VanderWeide, Dave Van Andel, Doug DeVos, Nan Van Andel, Dan DeVos, Barb Van Andel-Gaby, (from left, front) Rich DeVos, Steve Van Andel, Dick DeVos, and Jay Van Andel.

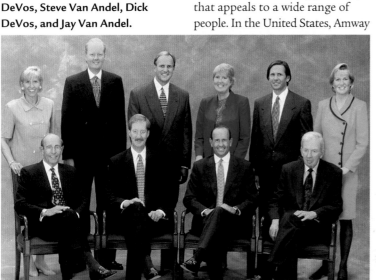

continues to thrive on the unique synergy derived from its person-to-person business. While the Amway of today may look strikingly different from the Amway founded in 1959, the spirit of Amway and the fundamentals and values on which it was founded have not changed.

IN THE BEGINNING

Rich DeVos and Jay Van Andel met when both were students at Grand Rapids Christian High School. While it was a business arrangement that brought the pair together—DeVos paid Van Andel a quarter each week for rides to and from school—it was their similar backgrounds, shared values and interests, and coinciding dreams for the future that made them fast friends. Early on, they decided they one day would start a company of their own.

Although World War II and separate tours of duty in the U.S. Army Air Corps interrupted the pursuit of their goals, the war also provided the seed for their first business. The unprecedented use of aircraft sparked a blaze of public interest in flying, so DeVos and Van Andel pooled their resources to purchase a plane and start a flying school—Wolverine Air Service.

The school was ready to open when it was discovered that the runways for a new airport would not be completed on schedule. In a show of creativity and determination that would come to characterize the pair throughout their lives, DeVos and Van Andel equipped their Piper Cub with pontoons and the Grand River became their landing strip. Their improvisation allowed them to open as planned—well ahead of their competitors—and laid the groundwork for the successful business the school would become.

FROM DRIVE-INS TO SAILING THE HIGH SEAS

After successfully launching their flying school, DeVos and Van Andel noted a lack of suitable restaurants nearby for students and visitors to their riverside venture. Inspired by a restaurant they had visited on a trip to California,

they created the Riverside Drive Inn—Grand Rapids' first drive-in restaurant.

Though both businesses thrived, DeVos and Van Andel decided to embark on a new adventure. They sold their businesses; bought a 38-foot, wooden-hulled schooner named *Elizabeth*; and, despite their inexperience on the high seas, set sail for South America. Though *Elizabeth* sank off the coast of Cuba, they continued on an adventurous trip through South America. They returned home to form the Ja-Ri Corporation and renew their search for the right business opportunity. They found it in a person-to-person sales opportunity marketing vitamins and food supplements manufactured in California by Nutrilite Products, Inc.

Over the next 10 years, Ja-Ri became a thriving, profitable business, and DeVos and Van Andel honed their business and presentation skills. They also continued

to develop their inborn talents for leadership, while cultivating the knowledge and principles on which they would found the Amway business.

AMWAY CORPORATION IS BORN

Realizing continued growth would require a larger range of unique products, DeVos and Van Andel began developing ideas for a new business venture. They founded Amway in 1959 in the basements of their homes, with a handful of distributors, a sales and marketing plan that drew on a person-to-person marketing strategy, and a single product—a biodegradable, all-purpose cleaner called L.O.C.

The new enterprise took on a life of its own, quickly outgrowing its tiny quarters and outpacing the most optimistic sales expectations of its founders. In 1960, the operation was moved to a small building on the corporation's current site in Ada. In 1962, Amway

The new company quickly outgrew the basements of the cofounders' homes and moved to a converted service station located at Amway's present site in Ada, Michigan.

After returning home from separate theaters of WWII, Rich DeVos and Jay Van Andel began their first business—Wolverine Air Service.

Clockwise from top left:
The 12,000-seat Van Andel Arena was made possible through a generous donation by Jay and Betty Van Andel, and through the tireless efforts of local business leaders, led by Dick DeVos, to generate public support and contributions.

Thanks to support from the Rich and Helen DeVos Foundation, Grand Rapids now boasts a leading medical center—the Helen DeVos Women's and Children's Center.

Amway cofounders Jay Van Andel (left) and Rich DeVos

became an international company when its first affiliate opened in Canada. By 1963, sales were 12 times the first-year sales.

Scrambling to keep up, the Amway complex grew rapidly, continually expanding to house much-needed manufacturing equipment and office space. In its first seven years, Amway completed 45 plant expansions just to keep pace with sales growth. In five years, the company's payroll expanded from a dozen workers to more than 500, supporting a burgeoning sales force that had multiplied to 65,000. During these early years, an average of 8,000 new distributors were signing up every month. Quickly, L.O.C. was joined by dozens of offerings within several distinct product lines.

The climate was ideal for the Amway opportunity. Increasing numbers of women looking for work outside the home swelled distributor ranks. Customers were

attracted by the convenience of shopping from their homes and the personal service provided by the thousands of Amway entrepreneurs. Consumers were becoming concerned about the effect of household products on the environment—and only Amway offered biodegradable detergents. Not even a catastrophic fire in the aerosol plant in 1969 could slow the skyrocketing growth.

GOING GLOBAL
Confident that the spirit of free enterprise and entrepreneurship would translate into any language, DeVos and Van Andel began expanding their international operations in earnest in the 1970s, adding affiliate markets in Australia, Europe, and Asia. Continued growth proved their confidence well founded, and the company continued its quest to bring the Amway business opportunity to people around the world. By the end of the 1980s, entrepreneurs supported by Amway were operating in 19 countries on five continents, marketing several hundred top-quality Amway products plus many more name-brand products through its catalog programs.

The strong growth in the 1980s was surpassed by the phenomenal expansion during the 1990s. Between 1990 and 1998, Amway's global sales tripled and the number of affiliates more than doubled. In the early part of the decade, leadership of the corporation was shifted from Rich and Jay to Dick and Steve, just as many independent

Amway businesses are now being passed on to the children and grandchildren of Amway's earliest distributors.

GIVING BACK TO THE COMMUNITY
As Amway evolved into one of the world's largest direct selling companies, it actively supported the communities in which it thrived. Throughout their lives, Rich DeVos, Jay Van Andel, and their wives have firmly believed that success is not measured by how much you get, but by how much you give, and the two couples have given generously to their community. From their earliest days, the struggling young men and their families faithfully donated a significant percentage of their earnings to help their churches, the community, and those in need.

Today, the Grand Rapids skyline and West Michigan community are enhanced by DeVos Hall, the Helen DeVos Women's and Children's Center in Butterworth Hospital, Van Andel Museum Center, and Van Andel Arena. These and many other undertakings were made possible not only due to financial contributions by Van Andel and DeVos, but also by their efforts and those of their families to galvanize community support. The Van Andel Institute of Education and Medical Research, a gift to the world from the Jay and Betty Van Andel Foundation, has brought cutting-edge medical research to the West Michigan area. Contributions from the Rich and Helen DeVos Foundation have helped make possible a downtown business campus of Grand Valley State University.

Nationally, Amway and Amway distributors have raised $23 million since 1983 to support Easter Seals and its mission to help people with disabilities achieve greater independence. Amway also is a national sponsor of Junior Achievement, and many of its employees and distributors volunteer their time and talents to support local Junior Achievement programs, which teach today's youth the basics of economics and free enterprise. Around the world, Amway affiliates support hundreds of projects and initiatives in their own communities that encourage a wide range of initiatives in human services, education, the arts, the environment, and athletics.

LOOKING AHEAD

As Amway looks to the next millennium and beyond, it continues to strive to bring the Amway opportunity and the spirit of free enterprise to people everywhere. With world-class products manufactured by world-class employees and distributed by world-class entrepreneurs, Amway is poised for a very bright future.

Steve Van Andel, Dick DeVos, and the entire Policy Board are dedicated to ensuring that Amway remains a global business leader by developing new products and new ways to support the businesses of its distributors.

The group remains committed to enhancing the unique relationship Amway maintains with the distributors it supports on every inhabited continent. From Asia and Australia to Africa and the Americas, Amway is dedicated to providing an opportunity that allows individuals to achieve their goals through a business of their own. And in West Michigan, where Amway's roots are firmly planted, the corporation and its founding families remain committed to the community and the people who are helping Amway forge ahead toward new goals and accomplishments in the 21st century.

Amway distributors offer their customers not only exceptional products, but also product education and outstanding customer service.

Amway's World Headquarters is the hub of an international business with operations in nearly 50 affiliate countries—each represented on the flag promenade, a popular tourist attraction.

ASTER FINISH CO. WAS FOUNDED BY JOHN MULDER IN 1959. Today, his family members continue to manage the company, supplying the ultimate in metal plating services throughout the Midwest. Automotive, appliance, plumbing, and hardware are just a few of the industries served.

Besides providing a superior corrosion resistant surface, Master Finish specializes in adding lustrous beauty to its customers' metal components. In this way, Master's plating process adds value through both extending product life and enhancing the product's beauty.

Through the plating process, copper, nickel, chrome, and nickel alloys are deposited onto zinc die cast, steel, and brass components. Customers' metal components are submersed in a series of baths to clean, neutralize, etch, activate, rinse, and plate the component parts. In each plating bath, an electrical current is applied to the parts, causing the metal suspended in each plating bath solution to deposit or "plate" onto the part's surface. Rigorous quality assurance procedures have earned Master Finish ISO 9002 certification.

In order to achieve Master's gleaming bright chrome finish, heavy metals are used, which, if improperly handled, can be hazard-

Automotive, appliance, plumbing, and hardware are just a few of the industries Master Finish serves. Besides providing a superior corrosion resistant surface, Master Finish specializes in adding lustrous beauty to its customers' metal components (top left).

The water that is separated from the metals is continuously monitored in-house, using a spectrophotometer to assure compliance with all discharge standards. The result is water so clean that the company's pet goldfish, Copper and Chrome, have grown and flourished in an environment of pure wastewater discharge (top right and bottom).

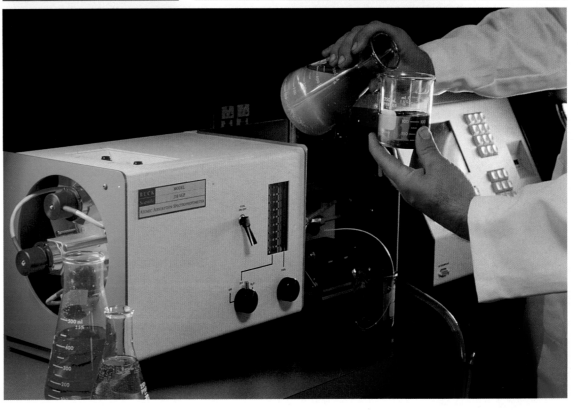

ous to the environment. Master Finish actively addresses these important environmental concerns. Certification to strict ISO 14001 environmental standards has been awarded to Master Finish. Ongoing, continuous testing assures day-to-day compliance with all discharge standards, and the heavy metal by-products from Master's process are never consigned to landfills.

The wastewater treatment begins with the collection of rinse waters, which are then pH adjusted. Heavy metals are then forced to precipitate out of the process wastewater. The heavy metals are then settled, removed, dewatered, and dried. The resulting material is a dry

powder, which is delivered to a smelter, which recycles Master's plating process by-product into new stainless steel. The water that is separated from the metals is continuously monitored in-house, using a spectrophotometer to assure compliance with all discharge standards. The result is water so clean that the company's pet goldfish, Copper and Chrome, have grown and flourished in an environment of pure wastewater discharge.

Master Finish Co. is proud of its role in adding value to its customers' high-quality products. Master's commitment to environmental responsibility assures a very bright future.

Through the plating process, copper, nickel, chrome, and nickel alloys are deposited onto zinc die cast, steel, and brass components. Customers' metal components are submersed in a series of baths to clean, neutralize, etch, activate, rinse, and plate the component parts.

EOPLE HIRE ATTORNEYS FOR A NUMBER OF DIFFERENT REASONS: To be their advocates and legal advisers, to counsel them, and to defend them when faced with a legal threat. Making a decision about whom to trust with these matters is an important and often difficult task. This is something Miller, Johnson, Snell &

Cummiskey, P.L.C. understands well. The firm is one of the largest law firms in West Michigan, yet its focus is not on size, but on serving clients at the highest level of integrity, honesty, and professionalism, and upholding values that reflect the best of the West Michigan community.

A COMMITMENT TO CLIENTS

Founded in 1959, Miller, Johnson has always emphasized building long-term relationships with its clients. "You can't have a successful law firm in a community like Grand Rapids based on the notion that you'll represent a client only once," says Bob Brower, managing member of the firm. "You have to develop ongoing relationships over long periods of time. That's the only way to become a trusted adviser and a confidant. That quality of relationship has always been our goal."

Along with its long-term client relationships, Miller, Johnson is known for its approachability and effective communication with clients. John Cummiskey, one of the

firm's founding members, says that has been the case since the firm started. "An attorney has to be able to communicate with clients in a way they understand," he says. "If clients can't understand us because we use a lot of legal jargon, then we can't be as effective at helping them."

Miller, Johnson has nearly 200 employees at its firm, 86 of whom are attorneys. This collection of attorneys is organized into three broad groupings: business, employment law, and litigation. Within those main groups, there are many different practice areas ranging from estate planning to intellectual property, real estate to health care, construction law to employee benefits, environmental issues to finance, government relations to immigration, and tax controversy and planning to manufacturing.

A COMMITMENT TO LEADERSHIP

Miller, Johnson has always been committed to a leadership role in the legal field, with three of the firm's attorneys having served as

state bar presidents, and numerous others as chairs of local bar associations and state and local bar practice sections. Throughout the firm's history, its members have been passionate about their firm's and their personal role in community leadership. Cummiskey, long known nationally as an advocate providing legal services to the poor, says that he has always encouraged other lawyers to provide time, resources, and money to help poor people who need legal services.

"People don't realize that at least 20 percent of the people in this country just don't have access to the legal system at all," says Cummiskey. "And the sad thing is, poor people have legal problems just like people of means, sometimes more so. They need access to the courts, and they need advice and counsel. It's up to us to help provide that." Through his efforts to provide support to Legal Aid, Cummiskey has become recognized as one of the best-known and most forceful voices in the nation on the issue of legal services for the poor, and

Miller, Johnson, Snell & Cummiskey, P.L.C., a full-service law firm, has grown since 1959 to more than 85 attorneys and maintains four locations including Grand Rapids, Kalamazoo, Southeast Grand Rapids, and Lansing. Leading the firm into the 21st century, Miller, Johnson's Management Committee includes (from left) Dave Gass, Mike Snapper, Carol Karr, and Bob Brower.

he is the namesake of the State Bar of Michigan's coveted award for pro bono contributions: the John W. Cummiskey Award.

A COMMITMENT TO THE COMMUNITY

The attorneys and staff who work at Miller, Johnson share personal commitments to the community. Some involvement is high profile, such as serving on the executive boards for various arts organizations and chairing community events. But many of the volunteer activities are low key, more hands-on, and more personal.

Miller, Johnson's attorneys and staff spend countless hours each year working on an individual basis with organizations like Heartside Ministries, Habitat for Humanity, Black Educational Excellence Program, Ronald McDonald House, and Indian Trails Camp. The firm supports its attorneys and staff, and strongly encourages their involvement in community activities.

A COMMITMENT TO THE FUTURE

Miller, Johnson is one of only two law firms in the state of Michigan that belong to Commercial Law Affiliates (CLA), a worldwide association of independent, midsize business and commercial law firms. Brower says this alliance gives the firm the ability to provide its clients

with a doorway to the world.

"This isn't an organization you can join simply by paying a fee," says Brower, "but rather, competition for admission is keen and we're regularly graded and evaluated. If we aren't up to par, we'll be asked to leave. Being a member of CLA has vastly increased our access to highly specialized lawyers in countries all over the world with whom we can almost instantly coordinate and refer legal matters. It's an invaluable service we can bring to our clients."

Looking ahead, Jon Muth, another Miller, Johnson member, says the firm's challenge will be to continue to grow and change,

while still holding on to its fundamental principles and values. "We've had the same basic philosophy for all these years," says Muth, "and we will remain committed to it: to render prompt and effective service, to creatively solve clients' problems, and to challenge ourselves with the need for constant improvement, but to maintain our humility and professionalism, never compromise our values, and always remain committed to give something back to the community. By adhering to our philosophy in deed and word, even though we may not be able to predict the future, we are confident that good things will happen."

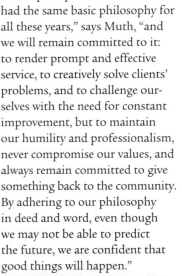

Clockwise from top left: The Employment Law Section of the firm, which counsels employers on complex and ever changing employment and labor issues, includes (from left) Peter Kok; Bill Fallon, chair; John Cummiskey; and Beth McIntyre.

Through its membership in Commercial Law Affiliates, an association of law firms worldwide, Miller, Johnson has the ability to coordinate and refer legal matters to attorneys in more than 70 countries. Litigation Section members include (from left) Boyd Henderson, chair; Jon March; Jim Brady; and Jon Muth.

Working with organizations of all types and sizes, Miller, Johnson strives to be approachable and communicate in nonlegal jargon. Business Section attorneys include (from left) Ken Hofman; Ron Roden; Jeff Ammon; and John McNeil, chair.

GRAND VALLEY STATE UNIVERSITY HAS A LONG LIST OF THINGS to be proud of: It is Michigan's fastest-growing public university; it has been repeatedly listed in *The Student Guide to America's 100 Best College Buys*, a book compiled by Institutional Research and Evaluation; its students are accepted into medical schools and other health fields at a rate that's twice the national average; its school of education supplies more of Michigan's administrators (principals and vice principals) than any other school in the state; and the list goes on and on.

For many people, Grand Valley's many attributes may not be common knowledge, simply because the school has come such a long way in such a short time. The school first opened its doors in 1963, with 224 students; under the direction of Arend Lubbers, who has been Grand Valley's president since 1969, the school's growth has been phenomenal, with an enrollment nearing 20,000 students.

CHOICES GALORE

In response to a changing world, Grand Valley State University offers a full range of undergraduate and graduate programs in such areas as liberal arts, communications, business administration, environmental research and resources, health sciences and medicine, education, engineering, social sciences, and government and public service. The school's impressive science complex totals nearly 300,000 square feet, with highly sophisticated instruments and extensive map and specimen collections. Grand Valley hosts international study programs in more than 10 countries; offers students an extensive library with more than 500,000 books, periodicals, reels of microfilm, compact discs, and on-line research; has a much higher computer-to-student ratio than the national average; and has expanded its student housing, designing apartment-like living centers instead of the typical dorm rooms.

Classes at Grand Valley are small, so students get acquainted easily and receive personal attention from their professors. About 90 percent of the school's classes have fewer than 40 students, 40 percent of them with fewer than 25 students. "There's a closeness here that you just won't find at the large universities," says Lubbers. "Professors and students really get to know each other." Unlike many large universities, classes at Grand Valley are taught by professors who specialize in teaching—not by graduate assistants.

MULTIPLE LOCATIONS

Grand Valley's main campus is located in Allendale, close to the

One of the most exciting developments at Grand Valley State University is the 15-acre campus expansion under way in the heart of downtown Grand Rapids (top right).

Grand Valley State University's Allendale campus is located between downtown Grand Rapids and Lake Michigan. "There's a closeness here you won't find at the large universities," says Arend Lubbers, Grand Valley president (left and bottom right).

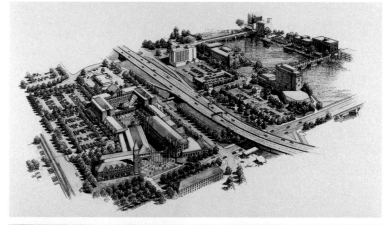

banks of the Grand River, amid 897 acres of rolling hills and wooded ravines. Students who live on campus are just 15 minutes from the city life of downtown Grand Rapids, and just 20 minutes away from the white-sand beaches of Lake Michigan.

In 1988, the Grand Rapids campus was established in response to demand for graduate programs, as well as for university services that were located downtown. Grand Valley's nine-story Eberhard Center has 43 classrooms, interactive classrooms, and labs; a library access office; and teleconference and conference facilities, as well as three computer labs. Graduate-level classes are offered in business administration, computer information systems, education, engineering, nursing, public administration, social work, and taxation. Several upper-level bachelor degree programs are also offered.

One of the most exciting developments at Grand Valley State University is the 15-acre campus expansion under way in the heart of downtown Grand Rapids. Known as the Grand Design 2000 Campaign, major fund-raising efforts helped Grand Valley achieve its goal of $15 million in private support for the downtown campus, which matched an estimated $35 million in public support from the state. The downtown campus is scheduled to open in 2000, and will be the new home of the Seidman School of Business—Grand Valley's highly acclaimed school of business and economics—as well as the university's International Trade Center and all of its graduate programs.

Keeping the Arts Alive

Known for its famous Cook Carillon, the only carillon in West Michigan, Grand Valley hosts regular performances by well-known local and renowned international carillonneurs. The university's annual Shakespeare Festival brings a week of celebration and high-quality stage productions to campus each September. The music department hosts several first-rate concerts, including a recital series by the top medalists in the Van Cliburn International Piano Competition. The free Arts at Noon series offers professional music, theater, and dance performances on campus throughout the year. The university's Performing Arts Center features an art gallery, the 490-seat Louis Armstrong Theater, and recently renovated music department

facilities, including a recital hall and a state-of-the-art music technology lab. The new Alexander Calder Art Center is home to the art and design department's array of programs, including ceramics, drawing, metalsmithing, painting, printmaking, and sculpture.

Grand Valley State University is looking forward to a prosperous future. Students who come to Grand Valley find exactly what they're looking for—a university that's small enough to give personal attention, yet big enough to offer students an excellent education and the choices they want, at a tuition they can afford. "We're proud of our growth," says Lubbers "and of the increasing opportunities we can offer students. As for the future, there's no doubt that there are exciting times ahead. But no matter how much we grow, we'll never lose the qualities that have made Grand Valley what it is today. That's what has always set us apart."

Grand Valley offers a full range of undergraduate and graduate programs in such areas as liberal arts, communications, business administration, environmental research and resources, health sciences and medicine, education, engineering, social sciences, and government and public service.

H OPE NETWORK BEGAN IN 1963 AS A WORK PROGRAM TO HELP A few psychiatric patients regain their self-confidence, dignity, and independence. Since then, the organization has grown to serve more than 6,000 people in Michigan who have disabilities or are disadvantaged by providing a wide variety

of vocational as well as residential programs, and medical rehabilitation, transportation, and housing services. Throughout the years, Hope Network's mission has remained the same: to enhance the dignity and independence of persons who have a disability and/or are disadvantaged. Hope Network's service to people is based on the Christian belief that all people are valuable and their intrinsic worth is determined by their Creator.

Hope Network serves people who have disabilities of all kinds, including mental illness; physical, developmental, and neurological disabilities; brain and spinal cord injuries or illnesses; and Alzheimer's disease and other forms of dementia. Hope Network also serves people who are terminally ill, people who have served time in prison, are homeless, have problems with substance abuse, or have experienced vocational injuries or other barriers to employment and community inclusion.

THE ORGANIZATION

Hope Network is composed of several entities: the Management

Services Organization, the affiliate members of the network, and other organizations throughout the state.

The Management Service Organization, governed by the board of trustees for the entire network, provides consulting and support services to organizations that belong to the network and to other organizations throughout Michigan. It assists organizations statewide in developing new services and streamlining their current operations to meet the ever changing needs and circumstances that arise in providing

services. Organizations work with the network through the Management Services Organization by way of partnerships, joint ventures, management contracts, and alliances.

Affiliate organizations are legal members of the network. They provide services to people in specific communities under the auspices of their local boards. Their unique contributions enrich the entire network, and benefit from the resources and expertise provided by the Management Services Organization and other network members.

Clockwise from top: Throughout the years, Hope Network's mission has remained the same: to enhance the dignity and independence of persons who have a disability and/or are disadvantaged.

Employment and Training Services provides adults and teens a wide array of employment services, including skill evaluation, vocational training, job placement, skill development, and from-welfare-to-work programs.

Medical Rehabilitation Services includes neuropsychology; occupational, recreational, and physical therapy; and independent living skill training.

Some organizations work on short-term projects, while others work with the intention of eventually becoming members of the network. Hope Network's rapid growth is attributed to high quality and efficient services that are a result of organizations working cooperatively to respond creatively to an ever changing and competitive environment.

THE SERVICES

Services are provided by approximately 2,200 caring and dedicated staff through person-centered assistance. Highly qualified professionals include psychiatrists, nurses, physical and recreational therapists, social workers, and direct care staff.

The services provided by the network can be organized into five general areas: residential services, medical rehabilitation, employment and training, transportation, and housing.

Residential Services provides a wide continuum of services from larger, highly staffed congregate homes to smaller, group homes to individual home ownership. Services are tailored to the individual's needs, which could include daily care, independent living skills training, psychological counseling, supervision, and opportunities to participate in work and other community activities. Many homes serve as transition homes that provide the residents with opportunities to grow into more independent living arrangements.

Medical Rehabilitation Services serves both children and adults, and provides residential and outpatient therapy for people who have sustained brain injuries, or have experienced other neurological or physical injuries or illnesses. Services include neuropsychology; occupational, recreational, and physical therapy; and independent living skill training.

Employment and Training Services provides adults and teens a wide array of employment services, including skill evaluation, vocational training, job placement, skill development, and from welfare-to-work programs. Work centers offer immediate employment

to people who need to regain stamina or develop work histories and experience. Supported employment provides supervised work experience in area businesses. Several hundred people gain meaningful, competitive employment every year.

Transportation Services provides specialized transportation services for people who are elderly, have disabilities, or are low-income passengers. The West Michigan fleet provides more than 460,000 rides a year.

Housing Services offers creative housing arrangements on a case-by-case basis for families or individuals who need accessible or affordable housing. Hope Network has developed low-income, specialized housing with the Department of Housing and Urban Development. Housing opportunities range from apartments in large complexes to single-family homes owned by the resident.

RESOURCES

Hope Network has grown into a $75 million network of not-for-profit corporations that serve a variety of people all over the state. Revenue from government entities, grants, and fees for services is earmarked for direct services. The network spends only 8 percent of its overall budget on administrative costs. The network is always

looking for creative ways to increase awareness and financial support from the community. In its 35-year history, Hope Network has seen major changes in its programs, the people it serves, and the public's acceptance of people who have disabilities. As for the future, the Hope Network philosophy that every person has value is one thing that will never change. "We will continue to respond to the community need and to give assistance to help people be healthy and strong citizens, and to foster their independence and productivity," states Herbert A. Start, president and CEO. "Hope Network was founded on this belief, and it is this belief that will carry us into the future."

Housing Services offers creative housing arrangements on a case-by-case basis for families or individuals who need accessible or affordable housing. Hope Network has developed low-income, specialized housing with the Department of Housing and Urban Development (top).

Work centers offer immediate employment to people who need to regain stamina or develop work histories and experience (bottom).

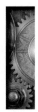

N 1926, HISTORY WAS MADE WHEN THE NATION'S FIRST REGULARLY-scheduled passenger flight took off from the main runway at Kent County Airport and flew from Grand Rapids to Detroit. ■ By 1960, passenger travel in the United States had grown to nearly 31 billion scheduled miles a year, and Kent County Airport was no longer able

to accommodate either the increased air traffic or the newer, larger, faster airplanes. The planning process began, and on November 23, 1963, the new Kent County Airport officially opened in Cascade Township. The total cost was approximately $7 million, and the airport featured two runways, a 10-story control tower, a huge hangar, offices for Northern Air Service, a 35-unit motel, a modern lighting system, and highly sophisticated electronic instrument landing and navigation equipment.

Today, airport amenities include scheduled passenger air service; air cargo, freight, and mail services; air charter service; U.S.

Customs Service; aircraft sales; flight instruction; aircraft maintenance; foreign trade zone; travel agency services; car rental; corporate aviation facilities; food and beverage concessions; a news and gift shop; and a golf course.

TOTALLY SELF-SUPPORTING

Today's Kent County International Airport is a county-operated facility that resembles a business in many ways, including its day-to-day operations. "The Kent County Department of Aeronautics operates the airport and is responsible to the Kent County government," says James Koslosky, aeronautics director for the Kent County Department of Aeronautics. "And although we are a county government department, the airport is entirely financially self-supporting. We generate the revenue necessary for the airport's operation and capital improvement through user fees and charges, and utilize no local, federal, or state tax dollars."

Kent County International Airport has a significant economic impact on West Michigan. The airport provides an employment base of more than 2,000 jobs and millions of dollars in payroll, with

a total economic benefit to the community in the neighborhood of $1 billion a year.

Approximately 160 commercial passenger flights fly in and out of Kent County International Airport every day, with close to 400 total takeoffs and landings. The airport can accommodate any size airplane, and is the second-busiest airport in Michigan and the 85th-busiest in the nation.

CONTINUOUS GROWTH

The airport's future challenge will be to keep up with the growth in West Michigan and to continue to meet the demand for world-class air transportation facilities. "We've undertaken an aggressive capital development program that will significantly improve our airport, and the service and facilities we provide to customers," Koslosky says. "In addition to adding a new north-south commercial service runway, this development program calls for a complete remodeling of the passenger terminal building, the construction of a new and expanded air cargo terminal, and the rebuilding of our current east-west primary runway. These projects make up the largest development initiative in the history of the airport, and will help us better meet the air transportation needs of West Michigan.

"But there's also something else that is important to us, and that's remaining a community airport. It's our goal to serve customers by providing them all the services they expect from a big city airport, while still offering the friendliness, convenience, and ease of use they'd find in a small-town airport. Even though demand will dictate that we keep growing, we hope to never lose that balance, because it's really one of the things that sets our airport apart from many others."

The control tower guides approximately 160 commercial passenger flights in and out of Kent County International Airport every day, with close to 400 total takeoffs and landings.

Today, airport amenities include scheduled passenger air service; air cargo, freight, and mail services; air charter service; U.S. Customs Service; aircraft sales; flight instruction; aircraft maintenance; foreign trade zone; travel agency services; car rental; corporate aviation facilities; food and beverage concessions; a news and gift shop; and a golf course.

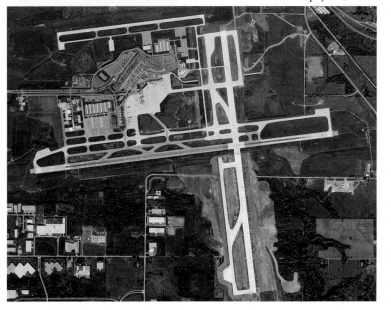

VICKERS DESIGNS, MANUFACTURES, SELLS, AND SUPPORTS electromechanical actuators and motors that are used to operate commercial and military aircraft doors, rudders, flaps, and controls for landing gears, throttles, and weaponry. The company has extensive engineering, manu-

facturing, testing, repair, and overhaul capabilities to produce these complex aerospace components.

TRACING THE COMPANY'S ROOTS

The company was founded in 1921 by Harry Vickers, a man known as an inventor, independent businessman, and international corporate executive. He developed many widely used hydraulic products, including a power steering system for cars and trucks, before forming the corporation that bears his name to this day.

In 1989, Vickers, Inc. purchased Grand Rapids-based Conductron, a subsidiary of McDonnell Douglas. Today, it is known as Vickers Electromechanical Division, and is part of Vickers, Inc.'s Aerospace Marine Defense Group. In 1996, Vickers purchased a competitive actuator manufacturer, Los Angeles-based Electrical Engineering Manufacturing Company (EEMCO), and moved the business to Grand Rapids in 1997.

COMMUNITY INVOLVEMENT

Vickers has a strong commitment to its employees and the community. Last year, nearly 10 percent of the company's workforce volunteered to work with Junior Achievement (JA) students from kindergarten through the 12th grade. Ron Modreski, Vickers vice president and general manager, is on the JA board of directors.

Vickers is an active member in the Manufacturing Council, a local network of manufacturers who meet regularly to share ideas and new innovations in technology. The council works with the Advanced Manufacturing Academy to provide high school students with certification programs and work site experiences.

Vickers is also actively involved in the Mulick Park Elementary

School Adopt-A-School program. Vickers provides volunteers for tutoring students in math, and reading, and for organizing computer workshops.

METEORIC GROWTH

Vickers is the largest manufacturer of electromechanical actuators on the Boeing C-17, the USAF's largest transport plane. The company serves nearly every major commercial and military aircraft manufacturer in the world. Since 1988, Vickers Electromechanical has doubled its sales, and the company is on track to double them again by the end of 1998.

Modreski feels that Vickers greatest strength is its employees. "We have a workforce that is committed to meeting customer requirements 100 percent of the time," he says. With the addition of EEMCO, the company expanded its facility by 26,000 square feet and created many additional jobs in Western Michigan.

Vickers is ISO 9001-certified, is a designated Boeing/McDonnell Douglas Certified Supplier, and holds a Federal Aviation Administration (FAA) Repair Station license to repair and service electrome-

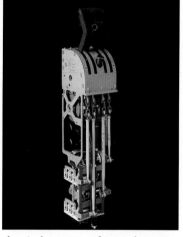

chanical actuators from other companies around the world. In 1997, Vickers parent company, Aeroquip-Vickers, Inc., was named by *Industry Week* magazine as one of the top 100 best-managed companies in the world.

LOOKING AHEAD

Vickers is aiming to be the supplier of choice for aerospace electromechanical systems. "Our goal is to develop applications from the front to the back of most major aircraft," says Modreski. "We'll continue to focus on providing our customers with the quality and service they expect, and we expect of ourselves."

Committed to quality, Vickers is aiming to be the supplier of choice for aerospace electromechanical systems technology.

Vickers designs, manufactures, sells, and supports electromechanical actuators and motors that are used to operate commercial and military aircraft doors, rudders, and flaps, as well as controls for landing gear, throttles, and weaponry.

WHEN IT COMES TO NAME AWARENESS, FEW COMPANIES in Michigan come close to Blue Cross/Blue Shield. Commonly referred to as the Blues, Blue Cross/Blue Shield of Michigan (BCBSM) is by far the best known, most widely recognized, and most universally

accepted health insurance company of them all. The company provides health insurance to virtually everyone—regardless of health status, age, or medical history. Although its name awareness is high, some people don't know that since 1991, BCBSM has had a West Michigan headquarters located in Grand Rapids.

DESIGNED TO WORK FOR EVERYONE

As the insurance company offering the widest range of health care products available today, Blue Cross/Blue Shield refers to itself not just as a health insurance carrier, but as a health benefit provider. Based on the type of coverage and services needed, customers can choose just the right plan to fit their own individual lifestyles and preferences.

Blue Managed Traditional is a plan that provides members with the largest network of physicians and the broadest possible access to provider care. The program includes complete freedom to choose physicians and hospitals, as well as flexible benefit designs and optional benefits for wellness and preventive care.

Community Blue PPO (preferred provider organization) is a plan that offers benefits delivered through a select number of providers who have been specially credentialed for their quality. It provides wellness and preventive care, and also offers members the option of choosing physicians outside the network if they pay higher out-of-pocket costs.

Blue Choice POS (point of service) is a benefit plan with built-in wellness and preventive care that is coordinated through a primary care physician within the Blue Choice network. Again, members may choose to see a nonnetwork physician for a co-payment fee.

Blue Care Network HMO is a health maintenance organization that offers members wellness and preventive care, with primary care physicians and specialists located throughout Michigan.

A unique addition to the Blue Cross/Blue Shield family is BlueWest, a program that combines managed traditional health care with wellness and preventive care. The program was designed as a direct result of input received in focus groups with West Michigan companies, and is reflective of the

Clockwise from top:
Blue Cross/Blue Shield (BCBSM) has had its West Michigan headquarters located in Grand Rapids since 1991.

Mercy Respite Center is one of the many community organizations that have benefited from BCBSM time and talent.

The Blues are a proud sponsor of the annual Tulip Festival.

features and services those companies asked for.

In addition to offering the widest possible range of health care options, BCBSM is one of the few insurance companies that take care of patients wherever they go: The widely recognized blue-and-white card is accepted throughout the world. "We have an extensive network, and it's our goal to do business with greater numbers of providers everywhere," says Charles Zech, Blue Cross/Blue Shield's vice president for West Michigan. Currently, 4.3 million people in the state of Michigan are covered by Blue Cross/Blue Shield products.

A STRONG COMMUNITY CONNECTION

Zech's office in the company's Grand Rapids headquarters is filled with photographs of employees participating in a variety of community events, and BCBSM strongly encourages everyone to become involved in one or more volunteer activities, giving awards to celebrate volunteerism.

BCBSM partners with two Grand Rapids schools, Dickinson Elementary and Academia de Español, and also supports Junior Achievement and a variety of other community organizations and events, including the American Cancer Society, Big Brothers/Big Sisters, Boy Scouts, Camp Fire Girls, Citizens for AIDS Awareness, Direction Center, Grand Rapids Symphony and Art Museum, Inner City Christian Federation, March of Dimes, Mel Trotter Ministries, YMCA, Project Rehab, Senior Services, Inc., Goodwill Industries, YWCA, and others.

THE FUTURE OF THE BLUES

Companies have come to recognize what an advantage it is having Blue Cross/Blue Shield serving West Michigan locally. "People realize that we're here, we're part of this community, and we have a definite presence in West Michigan," says Zech. "We're making it clear that we're here to serve our customers, to get to know them, and to help them get to know us."

West Michigan businesses and individuals are able to work with local BCBSM customer service rep-

Blues employees turn out in force to support the March of Dimes (top).

The Boys and Girls Club is another beneficiary of BCBSM efforts to support the local community (bottom).

resentatives and get claims settled locally, rather than having to deal with the Detroit office as in the past. And if rapid growth is any indication, it would appear that BCBSM's strategy of providing more localized service is working extremely well: In the past three years, membership in the company's various plans has increased by 27 percent, and the number of participating physicians has grown

from 55 percent in 1991 to more than 87 percent today.

BCBSM will continue to expand its presence in West Michigan. "We are committed to expanding our service, as well," says Zech, "We've been blessed with the trust and confidence of the people here, and as we grow, we'll continue to offer outstanding products and services. We're proud to be a part of West Michigan."

N THE EARLY 1960S, GRAND RAPIDS NATIVE WEB STILES SAW GREAT potential in this country for a new type of reconstituted wood product developed in Europe: an alternative to solid wood that was much less expensive and could be used to make high-quality furniture. Importing 32-square-foot sheets from Europe posed no problem. Once in the

Shaped furniture parts are manufactured on a Homag stationary processing center, one of a variety of machines supplied by Stiles Machinery, Inc. (top).

Serving as the link between overseas machine tool manufacturers and customers in the United States, Stiles provides a wealth of technical consultation and advice, and handles complicated issues associated with the language barrier, including currency, technology transfer, and transportation (bottom).

United States, however, few people in the field of woodworking knew how to deal with the material. So Stiles began contacting suppliers in Europe whose machines were equipped to handle the reconstituted wood panels. Ultimately, Stiles was importing both the reconstituted wood materials and the machinery needed to work with the wood—and Stiles Machinery, Inc. was born.

By the 1970s, Stiles started thinking about retirement and sold the company to a German conglomerate, Lohmann International. Soon, Lohmann sent Peter Kleinschmidt to the United States to run the new division. "Peter Kleinschmidt is the true pioneer of panel-based processing equipment in this country," says Steve Waltman, Stiles' vice president of sales and marketing. "He took what was a new and virtually unknown industry and grew it from a cynical beginning to a major U.S. industry."

In the late 1970s, U.S. acceptance of this wood product exploded, and the percentage of panel-based products more than doubled. The overall success of the industry has directly translated into enormous success for Stiles Machinery. In the mid-1980s, Kleinschmidt bought the company, and today, with sales exceeding $125 million, Stiles Ma-

chinery is considered the country's leading expert in high-tech woodworking solutions, distributing the finest woodworking and panel processing equipment available in the world.

UNIQUELY QUALIFIED

Perhaps what makes Stiles Machinery most unique is its breadth of expertise and experience. The top-quality equipment used for high-tech woodworking is primarily manufactured in Germany, Italy, and Japan. Stiles is the exclusive U.S. representative of the world-class suppliers located in those countries.

Serving as the link between overseas machine tool manufacturers and customers in the United States, Stiles provides a wealth of technical consultation and advice, and handles complicated issues associated with the language barrier, including currency, technology transfer, and transportation. Stiles also services the equipment it sells, and provides all necessary parts and technical training for customers.

"What we provide amounts to a whole lot more than just selling machines," says Waltman. "Customers need access to parts, service, or training on this highly specialized equipment. There has to be a link, and we provide it. That's invaluable to customers."

Stiles Machinery has four locations around the United States: its headquarters in Grand Rapids, two locations in North Carolina, and one in California. With more than 270 employees and service people located throughout the country, the company is twice as large as its nearest competitor. Stiles also maintains a network of sales partners, a second distribution group that helps the company increase its availability in select markets.

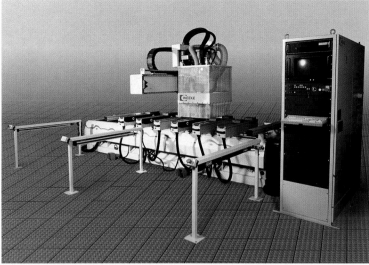

"We've made significant investments in facilities, people, and education," says Waltman. "We provide incredible support for our customers, but also for the industry at large." The company operates the Stiles Education Center (SEC), a comprehensive education facility with a staff of full-time instructors who constantly work with both customers and employees, as well as others employed in the woodworking industry. The SEC offers more than 30 accredited courses in all areas of the woodworking and panel processing business, from basic information through advanced programming and maintenance.

BRANCHING OUT

"We want to be able to service customers of any size," says Waltman, "so we've created four separate divisions of the company, each with its own specialty." The company's Altendorf America division handles several lines of high-quality, affordable equipment, such as panel saws and drilling and doweling equipment designed for the smaller shop. Another division, Holzma=U.S., is dedicated to providing panel saws and material handling equipment to cut primary panels into component parts. Holzma also offers management software to link machinery and manufacturing processes.

The third division, Stiles Machinery, is dedicated to serving larger businesses with high-production equipment, software, and systems. Stiles' fourth division, Customer Support Services, is dedicated to providing 24-hour parts support and the expertise of factory-trained field service representatives who provide customers with technical support and service.

While office furniture is important, Stiles also supplies businesses that produce kitchen cabinetry, store fixtures, point-of-purchase displays, and ready-to-assemble furniture, as well as serving the aerospace industry. "A unique aspect of our company is our relationship with the aerospace industry," says Waltman. "So much inside the plane is made of panels: the floors, the galleys, the dividing walls, the ceilings, and cargo holds. All these parts are produced on our equipment."

As for what's ahead, Waltman says the company will continue its commitment to education and to helping American manufacturers succeed by providing high-tech woodworking solutions that are safer, of better quality, and more accurate than ever before. "We've been raising the bar in this industry for more than 30 years," he says, "and we'll continue to do so. We have a vision for the woodworking industry. And when people buy into that vision, they're taking their businesses to the next level. We want to help them continue to do that."

Holzma=U.S., one of four Stiles Machinery divisions, is dedicated to providing customers with panel saws and material handling equipment to cut primary panels into component parts (upper left) for secondary machining. Weeke and Heian CNC machining centers, (top and bottom right) are part of Stiles' core product offering for high-output production. The machines size, drill, shape and contour parts in solid wood, engineered wood, plastics, solid surface materials, and nonferrous metals. The company's Altendorf America division handles several lines of high-quality equipment for smaller operations such as sliding table saws (bottom left), edgebanders, CNC machining centers, and drilling equipment.

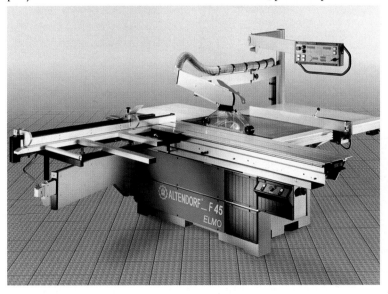

WHEN HE WAS JUST 25 YEARS OLD, HAROLD STEELE founded a Grand Rapids tool and die business he named HS Die & Engineering. For most of his young life, Steele had dreamed of becoming a race car driver, but when it came time to actually choose

his life's work, he opted instead for a different role in the auto field: building plastic molds and race car components. Today, the business he founded has grown into an $85 million company and has become one of the top plastic mold building companies in the United States.

TEAM HS DIE

Steele's love for the sport of racing is evident in nearly every corner of his company, and the slogan Team HS Die is emblazoned on hats, shirts, signs, and even floor mats. However, Steele says the nickname is really about his company's total commitment to teamwork, rather than racing. "Around here, the word 'teamwork' means we help each other do a better job by gaining from each other's knowledge and expertise," he says. "And for the record, we were talking about teamwork long before it became the industry buzzword.

We've always known our team is the key to our success. It's a big-picture focus, and it's gotten us where we are today."

Steele says his employees have been extremely loyal to the company, and some people have been with him since he founded HS Die & Engineering nearly 30 years ago.

"I've always stuck to the idea that I want to train and grow my own employees," he says. "I think of myself not as a mold maker, but as a molder of people. And when I hire employees, the main qualifications I look for are common sense and ambition. Consequently, we have a team of people who are the best in the business, and definitely our most valuable asset."

SUCCESS STORY

HS Die & Engineering's focus on teamwork has been a strong contributor to the company's continued success and growth. Today, there are a total of four plants and 350 employees, and Steele anticipates increased growth in the future. The company's primary customers are the Big Three domestic automobile manufacturers—General Motors, Ford, and Chrysler—as well as major foreign car makers such as Toyota, Mitsubishi, Honda, and Nissan. In addition, the company also serves nonautomotive customers, including appliance manufacturers, agricultural interests, and furniture makers.

HS Die & Engineering specializes in building plastic injection molds, as well as die-cast dies and aluminum and magnesium dies.

From its headquarters in Grand Rapids, HS Die & Engineering specializes in building plastic injection molds, die-cast dies, and aluminum and magnesium dies.

Today, the business Harold Steele founded has grown into an $85 million company and has become one of the top plastic mold building companies in the United States.

The company's main plant on Lake Michigan Drive has 135,000 square feet of production space and 225 employees, including engineers, skilled mold makers, and office staff. Plant 2, located in Walker, has 24,000 square feet devoted exclusively to mold making. Plant 3, which is next door to Plant 2, serves as a sampling operation where tools are sampled and molds are run. And the newest addition to HS Die & Engineering is located in Auburn Hills, Michigan, and is a 31,000-square-foot plant that primarily builds aluminum prototype molds for automotive customers.

FULL-SERVICE SPECIALISTS

One of the main qualities distinguishing HS Die & Engineering from its competition is the company's high-level engineering expertise and ability to act as a program manager on every project. "If a customer comes to us and asks us to do the instrument panel," Steele says, "we want to take care of every aspect of that instrument panel, from the initial design through building the prototype, and ultimately through final production. The same goes for door panels and the whole interior of the car. Because we have the ability to provide this level of comprehensive service, we can really streamline projects for our customers, and take the load off them."

When it comes to technology, HS Die & Engineering has always been on the cutting edge. In 1978, well before other companies were ready to jump into computerization, Steele began to make sizable investments in computerized technology, and today, the company's highly sophisticated computer-aided design/computer-aided manufacturing (CAD/CAM) system and other state-of-the-art equipment have grown to become an integral part of HS Die's tool building process.

A COMPANY WITHIN A COMPANY

Steele has incorporated his love of racing into his business. In 1990, he formed Team HS Racing, which has since become one of

the most successful ARCA (Auto Racing Club of America) stock car racing teams in the world. Since 1993, Steele's son Tim has been the head and chief driver for Team HS Racing, and he's won championships all over the country. Some of the team's trophies have come from well-known racing venues like Daytona Beach, Indianapolis, Atlanta, Charlotte, Las Vegas, and Michigan International Speedway (MIS).

Steele says there's a definite connection between his involve-

ment with racing and his tool and die business. "Car racing is a tough business," he says, "and those who do manage to make it to the top are the ones who aren't afraid to be competitive and who have a strong team behind them. This description fits HS Die & Engineering. We're convinced that by working hard, being competitive, maintaining a winning attitude, and keeping our team strong, we'll be even more successful in the future than we are today."

"Around here, the word 'teamwork' means we help each other do a better job by gaining from each other's knowledge and expertise," owner Harold Steele says.

ALCON FOAM IS KNOWN THROUGHOUT THE COUNTRY FOR THE versatility of its product—a product that's used for everything from flat roofing to recreational vehicles and garage doors to packaging. The product is expanded polystyrene (EPS), a plastic foam material that requires less energy to produce than paper

products, is 100 percent recyclable, and uses no ozone-depleting chlorofluorocarbons in its production process.

Expanded polystyrene was first used in West Germany and made its entry in the U.S. market around 1960. In 1965, two entrepreneurs, James Allen and Robert Foster, started Falcon Foam in a small building in downtown Grand Rapids and began to manufacture this new material. The company grew rapidly, and in 1966, moved into a 25,000-square-foot facility located in Byron Center.

In 1982, Foster left the $4 million business, and his interest was

At Falcon Foam, the manufacturing and cutting processes of expanded polystyrene (EPS) are highly accurate with close tolerances to the thousandths on length, width, and thickness. After the polystyrene expands and then ages for a period of time, it is loaded into state-of-the-art block molds, and steam is again applied. The end result: finished blocks of fused polystyrene foam that are ready for cutting to a wide variety of customer specifications.

bought out by brothers Dirk and Steve Buth. In 1995, Owens-Corning, a global building materials and glass composites company, purchased the business. The Buths continued to run the business until their retirement in 1997. The company today has annual sales of $40 million, employs 225 people, and is part of Owens-Corning's exterior systems business. The plant is operated by a management team of longtime Falcon Foam employees.

Expanded polystyrene can be used in a wide variety of applications from rigid insulation to custom packaging. The manufacturing and cutting processes are highly accurate with close tolerances to the thousandths on length, width, and thickness.

In its raw state, expandable polystyrene resembles table salt, and Falcon purchases it in 1,000-pound cartons. The material is first loaded into an expander machine, and steam is applied to activate the raw material and make it expand. Specialized equipment controls the amount of steam, which in turn determines the material's density. After the material expands and then ages for a period of time,

TED BOELEMA

TED BOELEMA

it is loaded into state-of-the-art block molds, and steam is again applied. The end result: finished blocks of fused polystyrene foam that are ready for cutting to a wide variety of customer specifications.

Expanded polystyrene is a product that's 100 percent recyclable, and Falcon Foam is proud of its environmental commitment. All of the scrap from production is recycled back into its own product and does not end up in landfills. The company doesn't stop with its own waste; it also takes back its customers' waste—at Falcon's expense—as well.

As for the future, Falcon Foam's goal is to become a national polystyrene company with the help of its parent company, Owens-Corning. Currently, the Grand Rapids plant services six states: Michigan, Indiana, Illinois, Wisconsin, Ohio, and Pennsylvania. In 1997, the company added another plant located in Los Angeles.

Under the well-known Owens-Corning brand name, Falcon Foam plans to keep moving into other markets and applications, looking into additional acquisitions, and building on its many years of success.

HS DIE & ENGINEERING INC.	1969
DVK CONSTRUCTION, INC.	1970
BELWITH INTERNATIONAL, LTD.	1972
YAMAHA CORPORATION OF AMERICA	1973
MICHIGAN WIRE PROCESSING COMPANY, INC.	1974
SUSPA INCORPORATED	1974
ADAC	1975
J.W. MESSNER INC.	1977
ROBERT GROOTERS DEVELOPMENT COMPANY	1977
GUS MACKER ENTERPRISES	1978
GEMINI PUBLICATIONS	1979
BENTELER AUTOMOTIVE CORPORATION	1980
FEYEN-ZYLSTRA	1980
CUSTER OFFICE ENVIRONMENTS	1981
DISTRIBUTION PLANNING INCORPORATED (DPI)	1981
AUTOCAM CORPORATION	1982
CPR/MICROAGE	1982
INTERFACEAR	1982
TOOLING SYSTEMS GROUP	1982
PROGRESSIVE DIE & AUTOMATION, INC.	1983
LEITZ TOOLING SYSTEMS, INC.	1984
WKLQ, WLAV, WBBL/MICHIGAN MEDIA, INC.	1984
SPECTRUM INDUSTRIES INC.	1984
RAMBLEWOOD EXECUTIVE SUITES	1985
THE RIGHT PLACE PROGRAM	1985
PAULSTRA CRC	1986
S.J. WISINSKI & COMPANY	1986
WINKELMANN ASSOCIATES-ARCHITECTS, P.C.	1992
ROHDE CONSTRUCTION COMPANY	1993
WORLDCOM	1996
NATIONAL CITY BANK	1998

DVK Construction, Inc.

THE AWARD IS CALLED THE PRESIDENTIAL EAGLE AWARD, OR "Nobilis Aquila." It is considered the highest possible tribute an American builder can earn, presented for vision, industry, loyalty, and overall standards of excellence. Only a few select companies are ever so honored, and DVK Construction, Inc.,

a leading general contractor in Grand Rapids for more than 25 years, is among them. The company displays the award proudly, and applies the high quality standards that it represents in every task it undertakes.

DVK Construction specializes in the commercial and industrial markets, serving major customers all over West Michigan. Over the years, DVK has earned a reputation for building excellence, as well as integrity, stability, and dependability. DVK Construction was purchased from the original owners in 1989 by Tim Timmer, Bob VanKalker, and Mark Anthony.

In 1990, Timmer died, and the company is currently owned by VanKalker and Anthony.

A Focus on Teamwork

According to VanKalker, president and co-owner of DVK, as much as 70 percent of his company's projects originate from repeat customers who know DVK and who have worked with the company before. He says there's no better measure of overall customer satisfaction. "When we do a job for a customer—any job, no matter how large or how small—we work on developing a long-term relationship," he says. "From the

very beginning, we think of it as a team effort."

Building customer relationships has been DVK's policy since the company was first formed back in 1970. At that time, one of the original partners, Warren Kuiper, had an opportunity to bid on a huge project: constructing the addition on an existing warehouse facility for Grand Rapids-based Elston Richards. According to VanKalker, winning that project was DVK's first big break, and the beginning of the company's long-term success. "Warren went in there and sold himself as a contractor the customer could depend on," VanKalker says. "Actually, I think he probably had more guts than ability at the time, but he believed in himself and what he could do. So he held his breath and just prayed the company could pull it off."

The project was, in fact, a huge success, completed on time and within the budget. Today, Elston Richards is still one of DVK's good customers, and DVK has constructed more than 1 million square feet of warehousing for the company.

DVK also enjoys a long-term relationship with Pridgeon & Clay, an automotive parts manufacturing company with which the company has worked for more than 25 years. DVK has completed renovations, additions, and various building maintenance needs for the company, handling jobs of every size from cutting a new door into an office to constructing a recent, 65,000-square-foot addition on Pridgeon & Clay's facility plant.

Building for the Future

VanKalker says that in the building industry today, there is much more emphasis on planning and on determining the most efficient

Bob VanKalker (seated) and Mark Anthony serve as the current owners of DVK Construction, Inc.

From its newly constructed corporate office, DVK continues its reputation for building excellence, as well as integrity, stability, and dependability.

Zondervan Corporate Headquarters is one of the many projects DVK Construction, Inc. has built.

use of space. "It's important for us to get to know the customer," he says, "but it's also important for us to develop an understanding of the customer's business. In the past, a contractor's job was just to make a building 'so high by so wide' and that was the end of it. That's just not enough anymore. We need to assume more of a consultant role, because intelligent space planning is key in how well a building works for a business."

Grand Rapids-based Allied Finishing turned to DVK for this type of consulting and planning help in the renovation of the one-story building its corporate headquarters had outgrown. Rather than incur the enormous expense of moving into another building, Allied hired DVK to do a major construction overhaul, which involved adding a second story to the existing building. DVK built the second story over a period of approximately four months. Because of DVK's careful planning and unique sequencing of each construction phase, Allied's business continued to operate as usual without significant disruption.

One of DVK's largest and highest-profile projects was building the new world headquarters for Zondervan Publishing House, a leading publisher of religious

The original founders of DVK Construction, Inc.—(from left) Warren Kuiper, Harvey Donker, Marvin Donker, and Owen VanKalker—received many awards for construction achievements.

books located in Grand Rapids. The total facility was 380,000 square feet, and it presented a unique challenge for DVK. "We actually started with a pre-engineered building," VanKalker says, "and then designed it to look like a conventional building, with a more traditional look. When we had completed the project, no one could tell the structure was actually made of metal." VanKalker says this technique achieves the cost-effectiveness and efficiency of using pre-engineered materials, but still achieves the rich look of traditional building methods.

IMPRESSIVE GROWTH
DVK Construction's sales volume has grown from $3 million in 1970

to average annual sales of approximately $20 million. In 1996, DVK earned the $25 million sales award given by American Buildings Company, including DVK as one of the top five contractors in the United States. The company's reputation for reliability and integrity continues to fuel growth.

According to VanKalker, DVK's goal is not necessarily to be the biggest, but rather the best. "We're contractors, but there's something a lot more valuable to us than the concrete and steel we work with. The most important thing is the trust we earn with our customers by partnering with them and developing long-term relationships. To us, there's nothing more important."

BELWITH INTERNATIONAL IS KNOWN AS THE WORLD'S PREMIER producer and distributor of quality cabinet and furniture hardware. As the largest marketer and distributor of this type of hardware in the world, Belwith International was founded in 1959 by Charles Belasco and Joseph Withers. After purchasing

a small hardware distribution company called Peabody Distributing, the two renamed it Belwith after the first few letters of their last names.

In 1972, Belasco and Withers sold Belwith to Grand Rapids-based Keeler Brass, the world's leading producer of furniture hardware and one of their major suppliers, and the company established its presence in West Michigan. Several years later, both Belwith International and Keeler Brass were ac-

quired by Babcock Hardware Group, and in 1990, Belwith International permanently relocated its corporate headquarters from Los Angeles to Grand Rapids.

GLOBAL MARKETING AND DISTRIBUTION

In addition to the products made at the Keeler facilities in Grand Rapids, Belwith sources the finest porcelains from Japan; fine die cast brass hardware from Taiwan, Hong Kong, and China; concealed

European hinges and drawer slides from Austria and Italy; wood turnings from Maine and New Hampshire; and solid brass drawer knobs and pulls from Jamestown, New York.

From Belwith's four distribution centers in Grand Rapids, Los Angeles, Tampa, and Toronto, the company provides its customers with an unparalleled selection of products, and it has a day-to-day philosophy about service: "It's our goal to make it as easy as possible for customers to buy from us," says Mark Pelley, Belwith's president. "We take their orders, and in almost every case, we can ship the order within 24 hours. That's a level of service our competition is hard pressed to match."

Belwith's order entry system is completely automated through electronic data interchange (EDI), and this system handles orders from 85 percent of the company's customers. "We handle more than 200,000 line items a month through our EDI system," Pelley says, "which is a major reason we're able to turn orders around so fast." At Belwith's fully automated—and completely paperless—warehouse, products are tracked with grocery-store-type bar codes and handheld scanner guns. Forklifts each have computers that are linked by radio to the main warehouse computer, allowing workers to easily know what shelves need stocking or what orders need to be filled.

Belwith's major customers include do-it-yourself home products stores, such as Home Depot and Lowe's, as well as retail giants like Wal-Mart, Kmart, and Meijer. And not only does the company source its hardware from all over the world, it also sells to customers all over the world. Stores in most every corner of North America carry Belwith's furniture hardware, as do home improvement stores

Belwith International is known as the world's premier producer and distributor of quality cabinet and furniture hardware.

Belwith employs its own staff of designers who remain constantly abreast of design innovations and who are associated with Color Marketing Group, an affiliation of 1,500 designers around the world who determine color trends for various industries.

located in Japan, China, France, and England.

FOLLOWING THE TRENDS

Hardware for furniture and cabinets is considered a fashion business, and Belwith International stays well ahead of design trends. The company employs its own staff of designers who remain constantly abreast of design innovations and who are associated with Color Marketing Group, an affiliation of 1,500 designers around the world who determine color trends for various industries. Pelley says his company uses these fashion and color predictions to make decisions about consumer preferences in decorative hardware.

"Current fashion and design trends have an enormous impact on the things we buy for our homes," says Pelley, "right down to decorative cabinet hardware. And consumers know that just by replacing hardware on their kitchen cabinets, their whole kitchen gets a face-lift for minimal cost. So, in order to be in touch with what the consumer wants, it's essential that we pay attention to trends, and then select hardware accordingly." To stay in touch with international design trends, Belwith regularly participates in trade shows such as Interzum and the international trade fair in Cologne.

TEAMWORK AND BELWITH'S LONG-TERM SUCCESS

In 1977, Belwith's sales were $5 million, and today, they exceed $75 million. Pelley says the credit for this success belongs to Belwith's employees. "In our company, we believe we're all in this together and we need each other to succeed," he says. "We're a true team, and there's a spirit of dedication here that's been around ever since the company first started. We communicate constantly, regularly share information with each other, and stay focused on our common goal, which is to help each other be successful in serving our customers."

Of the 170 Belwith employees, 110 work at the company's headquarters, and the average length of service is nearly 10 years. Pelley says Belwith's low turnover rate gives it an edge over the competition: "Our employees have an in-depth understanding of our products, how they're made, and how they're going to sell in the marketplace. This has definitely helped us maintain credibility with our customers, and build long-term relationships based on trust."

In the future, Pelley says Belwith International will continue to look at new markets and continue to increase its product line, adding new products based on fashion trends and customer demand. "Our focus has been, and will continue to be, on what customers want and need," he says, "and we'll continue to stay on top of the most current fashion trends and designs. Above all, we'll stay focused on our customers, continuing to build long-term relationships and striving to make it easier and easier for them to do business with us."

In addition to Belwith decorative products, the company also merchandises First Watch security products for every area of the consumer's home.

At Belwith's fully automated—and completely paperless—warehouse, products are tracked with grocery-store-type bar codes and handheld scanner guns. Forklifts each have computers that are linked by radio to the main warehouse computer, allowing workers to easily know what shelves need stocking or what orders need to be filled.

N GRAND RAPIDS, THERE IS A COMPANY WHERE PEOPLE MAKE BEAUTIFUL music together: Yamaha Corporation of America, a division of Yamaha Corporation Japan, the largest maker of musical instruments in the world. Located in Grand Rapids since 1973, the facility produces, distributes, and markets Yamaha woodwind, brass, and percussion instruments, as well as accessory items for the U.S. market.

In addition to producing more than 75 percent of the Yamaha wind instruments sold in the United States, the facility exports woodwind and brass instruments to the Canadian market as well.

THE GRAND RAPIDS DIFFERENCE

To complement its Los Angeles site, in 1972, Yamaha began looking for another location where it could find skilled manufacturing personnel with a strong work ethic and cultural appreciation. The company wanted the location to be in the Midwest, an area traditionally known as the heart of the U.S. band instrument industry. Grand Rapids was chosen and Yamaha began its operation with 25 employees.

While Yamaha's market share shows that the company understands the needs of America's musicians and music educators, that somehow doesn't tell the whole story. Each Yamaha and Deagan® instrument symbolizes the mutual respect that exists between those who make music and those who make musical instruments. The people of Yamaha know that musicians will play those instruments with an appreciation for detail and with a strong commitment to musical precision and grace. After all, this is the spirit with which the instruments are built.

At the 155,000-square-foot facility in West Michigan, Yamaha currently employs more than 260 people. Yamaha workers know that, through their craftsmanship, they are making a valuable contribution to the cultural life of their community and their country.

HIGH QUALITY AND VALUE

Yamaha prides itself on providing instruments of very high quality, while at the same time providing value. To achieve this quality, the company strongly believes in the practice of involving musicians in the manufacturing and assembly processes. After the instrument parts are made at the parent company, employees at the Grand Rapids facility assemble the final products. Tuning and adjustments are then done by skilled craftsmen who understand and can play the instruments, and who often play professionally.

The instruments manufactured by Yamaha are found in just about every musical corner of the country. The Juilliard School is one of Yamaha's customers, as is the Metropolitan Opera in New York City. And Yamaha instruments are also found in such prestigious orchestras as the New York Philharmonic, the Chicago Symphony, the Boston Symphony, and the Los Angeles Philharmonic, as well as the Grand Rapids Symphony. The University of Michigan and Michigan State University marching bands have purchased an extensive amount of Yamaha equipment. Eight of the Big Ten university marching bands also perform with Yamaha instruments.

At its 155,000-square-foot facility in West Michigan, Yamaha currently employs more than 260 people.

Yamaha workers know that, through their craftsmanship, they are making a valuable contribution to the cultural life of their community and their country.

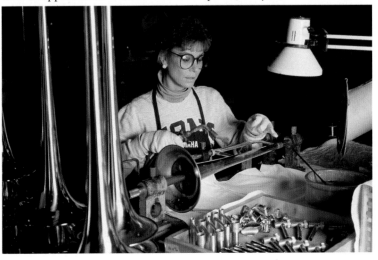

Yamaha does more than craft quality musical instruments. It works actively with musicians and music educators nationwide to advance band and orchestra music programs. Yamaha is donating a percentage of the sale of every band instrument to Project 2000, a consortium of respected music teachers and professors working to advance the music teaching profession by retaining and attracting qualified teachers, and by developing advanced teaching materials. Each summer, Yamaha also invites band directors and music educators from around the country to come to the Grand Rapids facility to learn about how the instruments are made and to offer their input through the Yamaha Listens program.

Yamaha also strives to educate the public on the beauty of making music. One innovative program Yamaha has created is called Music in Education™, which is geared primarily toward children in elementary and middle school. This interactive program uses a computer to teach everything from ear training to mu-

sic composition to playing songs on a keyboard. So far, the program has been used successfully by more than 4 million children who have developed a better understanding and appreciation for music because of it.

AN ENVIRONMENT WHERE PEOPLE CAN GROW

Any organization that cares about the long-term future must pre-

serve and invest in its resources—human, financial, and natural—and Yamaha is committed to the future. The company has established endowments to support musicians and musical programs at colleges and universities throughout the United States. Yamaha sponsors music clinics with professional artists, and contributes both money and time to a variety of local symphonies and arts organizations. And, finally, Yamaha does its part to preserve natural resources, from its state-of-the-art wastewater treatment facility to its comprehensive recycling program.

These initiatives, along with other programs, are what make Yamaha Corporation of America more than just a business. For those at Yamaha, it is important to tell the story behind Yamaha band and orchestral instruments—and the people who make them and the values they uphold.

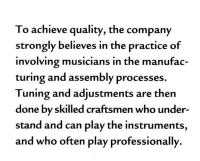

ABOUT 20 MINUTES EAST OF GRAND RAPIDS LIES THE TOWN OF Lowell, home to Michigan Wire Processing Company, Inc., a company that provides processed steel wire to the automotive, marine, and aerospace industries. Michigan Wire Processing, with 120 employees and two plants totaling

approximately 70,000 square feet, is considered an industry leader in providing customers with the highest-quality wire processing services.

THE BIRTH OF THE WIRE PROCESSING INDUSTRY

In the 1970s, when domestic steel and coal businesses were struggling to survive, many such companies began to divest themselves of certain operations in an attempt to control costs. An outgrowth of this was a specialty known as wire processing. In 1976, Michigan Wire Processing was begun in Lowell by Don Dietriech and Don Fizer. Both men had strong backgrounds in the steel industry and wanted to form a business of their own.

Dietriech and Fizer started out with one employee and provided steel wire processing services for just one customer. As demand increased, the business grew rapidly. Before long, the partners had built their first furnace and added annealing (heat treating) to the services offered. They also purchased a used truck to handle deliveries, and over the years, the business expanded.

In 1990, Dean W. Lonick joined the company as vice president/general manager. After the deaths of Dietriech and Fizer, Lonick became president and CEO. He describes his early years at the company as survival years. "When I first joined Michigan Wire," he says, "the whole wire processing industry was in a slump along with the rest of the economy, and business was tough. Then, after several years of stabilization, we had a strong growth period, and we're now growing at the rate of about 12 percent a year."

Michigan Wire's primary customers are located in Detroit, Michigan; Pittsburgh, Pennsylvania; Cleveland, Ohio; and Chicago and Rockford, Illinois, and include the major domestic steel mills. Other customers are end users and distributors of processed wire. The company currently provides three basic operations: clean and coat, a process that chemically removes an oxide layer on the wire's surface and applies coatings as a lubricant; drawing, a sizing operation that draws the wire through a die to change its size, shape, hardness, and tensile strength; and annealing, a heat-treating process that improves the workability of the steel in preparation for the customer's use.

All of the products manufactured from the wire are critical applications: high-grade fasteners, ball and needle bearings, suspension and drive train parts, fuel injectors, and engine internal components. There are thousands of different recipes for the preparation of wire to meet these individual customer specifications. "Our specialty is taking wire and doing virtually anything with it that our customers need—and those needs vary greatly," says Lonick. "Plus, we're always researching new processes and equipment designs, and we're determined to stay on top of the latest technology."

A FOCUS ON CUSTOMER SERVICE

Michigan Wire Processing's first priority has always been providing

Lowell, Michigan, located some 20 minutes east of Grand Rapids, is the home of Michigan Wire Processing Company, Inc.

Michigan Wire is very active in a variety of community-based youth programs.

Part of the services provided by Michigan Wire include a heat-treating process that improves the workability of the steel in preparation for the customer's use.

excellent service to its customers. "Our 'product' is actually the service we provide," Lonick says, "and we're known for our ability to handle whatever our customers need. That gives us a definite edge over the competition. And our service philosophy is shared by everyone in the company—it's just a way of life here, it's how we do things. We have an outstanding team of people who are all part of our commitment to customers."

Michigan Wire's two plants cover 23 acres outside Lowell, and the land surrounding them is covered with steel—approximately 20 million pounds. "Steel mills predict what their customers will need, and then roll the steel and store it in our yard," he says. "Then we take it from the raw state, perform the necessary work based on customer specifications, and ship the finished product just in time, using our own fleet of trucks."

D&D Trucking is an affiliate corporation that has 18 semitrailer trucks and a group of highly qualified drivers and maintenance staff. The fleet, which hauls exclusively for Michigan Wire, enables the company to react to customers' needs quickly and efficiently. "In the past, we were dependent on common carriers, and that meant we simply couldn't service our customers the way we wanted to. Our

truck fleet allows us to have absolute control of customer orders from pickup to delivery," says Lonick.

COMMUNITY TIES

"Giving back to the community is important to us," says Lonick, "and we do whatever we can—especially when it comes to helping kids. The principals of the company live here; our children go to school here. Our future is in our kids, and we have an obligation to help them prepare for it."

Some of Michigan Wire's beneficiaries include the local YMCA, several Little League teams, the Lowell Youth football team, the annual 4-H fair, yearbook sponsorships, candy sales, and just about any other cause that involves the community's children. The com-

pany even delivered lumber for Creekside Kingdom, a local playground in Lowell that was built wholly through the efforts of volunteers.

Between its two companies, Michigan Wire's annual sales are currently around $12 million, and Lonick says the company plans to continue searching for ways to expand its capabilities. "Because we want to keep providing our customers with the services they need," he says, "we'll keep looking at new products and exploring new acquisitions. But no matter what, one thing will never change: our focus on providing the very best service. That's always been at the heart of Michigan Wire Processing, and it will continue to be that way in the years to come."

Michigan Wire's speciality is to take wire and do with it whatever it takes to meet a customer's specifications.

NYONE WHO HAS DRIVEN A CAR, USED A WASHING MACHINE, been in a hospital, sat in an office chair, danced to a jukebox, made photocopies, lifted an automobile hatchback, or flown in an airplane has used products manufactured by Suspa Incorporated. Suspa's products touch the lives of

millions—even if the company name isn't familiar. Suspa, a name derived from the word "suspension," is a leading manufacturer of lift, support, damping, and adjustment devices for a wide range of industries.

BICYCLES, MOTORCYCLES, AND MOPEDS

Suspa's parent company, Suspa Compart AG, is headquartered in Germany, and was founded in 1950 to manufacture mechanical and hydraulic suspension elements for bicycles, mopeds, and motorcycles. The company later developed a suspension system for washing machines, as well as the first self-supporting gas cylinders used in office seating.

In 1974, Suspa decided to expand into the American market. The Grand Rapids facility opened, manufacturing pneumatic gas lift cylinders for automobile hatchbacks. Since then, the company has experienced phenomenal growth, and developed hundreds

of additional applications for its products.

ADDRESSING WORKPLACE CHALLENGES

Ergonomic studies have proved a direct correlation between worker comfort and worker productivity. More than ever, office furniture must adapt to the individual worker's height and weight, physical limitations or disabilities, and work styles, as well as specialized tasks required by the job. Suspa has made a concerted effort to continuously study and analyze ergonomic findings and integrate them into new product development.

One of the most crucial elements in the workplace is office seating that is comfortable and encourages good posture. Workers, particularly those who sit for long periods of time, need to be able to move around easily and make necessary adjustments to their chairs. Suspa's gas cylinders are a basic part of today's office

chairs, and enhance worker comfort by allowing adjustments in seat height, seat tilt, and back support. Today, there are millions of Suspa gas cylinders in chairs all over the world, and the company holds the dominant position in the U.S. office seating market.

Another workplace challenge that many businesses face is the need for varying heights in work surfaces, as well as workstations that are adaptable to the people who use them. Suspa has developed an innovative ergonomic lift system called MOVOTEC that can be used in a variety of work settings. Telephone operator stations, hospital surgical tables, industrial workbenches, conveyor platforms, drawing boards and drafting tables, and many other types of surfaces employ this unique system. MOVOTEC systems can also help companies comply with the Americans with Disabilities Act (ADA), by enhancing accessibility of customer service areas to people in wheelchairs, as well as those

Suspa President Erina Hanka makes it clear that the company's 200 employees deserve the credit for Suspa's excellent reputation. "Our people all take quality very personally. Everyone here cares so much about doing the best possible job."

having other mobility requirements. Suspa is the world's only manufacturer and distributor of MOVOTEC systems.

In addition to more obvious applications, Suspa's gas cylinders are found in less conspicuous places. Diaper-changing tables in public rest rooms are raised and lowered using the cylinders, and bumpy rides in two-wheeled bicycle trailers are cushioned using the same technology. They raise and lower storage covers on personal watercraft, allow service access to the interiors of jukeboxes, and hold open the covers of pickup truck toolboxes. Both hospital charting stations and the rollover protection systems in BobCat brand steer loaders utilize the cylinders. They also hold open flip-up doors, and assist with raising and lowering landing gear on kit airplanes.

Exciting Potential Ahead

Suspa President Erina Hanka says the company anticipates an exciting future with new products, new challenges and opportunities, and continued growth, particularly with small- to medium-sized companies. "We're very good at making from 20 to 20,000 pieces," she says, "and we feel there's an opportunity for us to grow along with growing companies." Suspa considers its customers to be partners,

and has been repeatedly recognized for consistent quality, on-time delivery, and superior service.

Hanka says the company is in an excellent position to compete globally. "We have frequent communication with our parent company in Germany," she says, "and also with our facilities in India, Taiwan, Singapore, and other areas. This gives us constant access to valuable information, and permits us to keep on top of the very latest in technology. It puts us in a better position to serve countries all over the world."

Hanka makes it clear that Suspa's 200 employees deserve the credit for the company's excellent reputation. "Our people all take quality

very personally," she says. "Everyone here cares so much about doing the best possible job. Our environment encourages and empowers people to make suggestions for making things work better. Everyone has an opportunity to change things."

Customers frequently visit Suspa's headquarters to share their expectations, and review areas of strength and opportunities for improvement with employees. "Our customers tell us they wish more suppliers were like Suspa," Hanka says, "because they know we're totally focused on them. Our mission is to make our customers more competitive and more successful. That means we can't help but be successful ourselves."

Suspa anticipates an exciting future with new products, new challenges and opportunities, and continued growth.

Frequent communication with its German parent company and other facilities in India, Taiwan, and Singapore gives Suspa constant access to valuable information, and permits the company to keep on top of the very latest in technology.

I N 1975, A SMALL COMPANY NAMED ADAC PLASTICS, INC. BEGAN IN GRAND Rapids. Consisting of three machines and six employees, the business specialized in producing plastic molded parts for the appliance and furniture manufacturers located in the Western Michigan area. Dan Trapp, who had purchased the company from its Detroit-based

ADAC delivers full-service capabilities, including the design, development, and manufacture of automotive products (left).

Research and development of future lighting projects are ongoing at ADAC (right).

owners, began to expand the business by specializing in substituting plastic for metal. The ADAC story had begun.

By the end of its first 10 years in business, ADAC had become a well-established custom injection molder; however, Trapp also noticed opportunities in the automotive supply business and saw potential for his company. He opted to sell a majority of his interest in the company to Richard Lacks and Ken Hungerford, with the agreement that Hungerford would assume the responsibilities of ADAC's president and general manager. The company's new president began shifting ADAC's focus toward developing full-service solutions for the automotive industry, and the company was well on its way to becoming a world-class supplier to the global automotive marketplace.

MORE THAN JUST A SUPPLIER
Today, ADAC employs several hundred people and functions as a preferred supplier to major

domestic automotive customers like Ford, Chrysler, and General Motors, as well as several international companies. In the last five years, the company has tripled its sales volume and is quickly approaching the $100 million mark.

Things have changed radically since ADAC focused solely on supplying customers with plastic molded parts. "We're now considered a part of our customers' extended enterprise, not just a supplier," Hungerford says. "In the past, customers designed and developed products, and we produced them. Now they consult us initially, asking for help to determine what they need. We've evolved into a company that fully serves our customers, making us a superior source of supply not only for today, but for the future as well."

ADAC is also well known for world-class quality: The International Organization for Standardization (ISO) has awarded the company with both ISO-9001 and QS-9000 certification for its high quality standards. In addition,

ADAC repeatedly has been recognized by major customers for continued product and service excellence.

EVERY PHASE OF DESIGN AND DEVELOPMENT
ADAC's products include complete module systems such as door handle assemblies, interior and exterior lamps, and functional assemblies, such as switch plates, trunk sill plates, and cowl grilles. Because of its sophisticated technology and expertise, one of the company's most valued services is its design and development capability. ADAC's Grand Rapids-based Design and Development Center, considered the firm's central engineering facility, employs some of the most talented people in the industry, including product designers and engineers, program managers, and tool and quality engineers. The facility has a total of 16,000 square feet, and uses the latest equipment for computer-aided design and computer-aided engineering (CAD/CAE), as well

Clockwise from top left:
Serving as ADAC's executive management team are (from left) Ken Hungerford, Don Bittner, Paul Koeneman, and Jim Teets.

ADAC supplies door handle assemblies to the global automotive marketplace with various finish options.

ADAC's advanced robotic paint system offers highly consistent film build control, greater transfer efficiency, and dirt-free products.

as the most advanced design software and testing capabilities for environmental, durability, material, color, and photometric testing.

Complete lighting systems are developed at ADAC's 8,000-square-foot Lighting Design Center in Livonia. The facility designs both exterior and interior lighting systems, as well as new and highly advanced lighting technologies, such as neon and fluorescent lighting systems. The center features an advanced, bird's-eye-view photometric light tunnel computer program, the first of its kind to be applied in automotive lighting.

State-of-the-art equipment abounds at ADAC's manufacturing facilities, which feature injection-molding presses; advanced robotic manufacturing processes; facilities for fully automated, product-specific painting; automated assembly equipment; statistical process control technology; and certified testing labs and equipment. Each manufacturing facility is highly specialized, and dedicated to its own individual product line.

The Saranac facility, where cowl grilles and functional assemblies are produced, features more than 95,000 square feet of manufacturing space, including the latest molding press technology and an advanced robotic paint system.

Lighting products are produced at ADAC's Grand Rapids manufacturing facility, where molding, finishing, and assembly operations are performed. All critical photometric testing takes place in this 75,000-square-foot plant, utilizing a computerized, 100-foot light tunnel.

The 230,000-square-foot operation in Muskegon specializes in manufacturing world-class door handle systems. This plant features the latest in molding, robotic, and material handling and drying technologies, in addition to a proprietary paint system.

In addition to its North American manufacturing operations, ADAC is supported by an additional facility located in the United Kingdom, an international network of qualified vendors and suppliers, and worldwide sales and service representation.

EMPOWERMENT AND TEAMWORK

The executive staff at ADAC has some definite ideas about the meaning of effective management. It believes that in order for the company to expect the most from its employees, it must provide a culture that fosters mutual trust and encourages teamwork. It believes in being visible, staying in close contact with employees, and working to keep communication lines open. And it believes in investing in employees with excellent pay, benefits, and incentives for education and training. ADAC is committed to training everyone in the company to solve problems and to make good decisions through continuous study of problem-solving techniques.

Hungerford is proud of ADAC's teamwork and the strong bond of partnership between management and employees that forms the key to the company's success. "We believe in continuous improvement, but it doesn't happen by itself," he says. "It has to start with us, by providing a culture for our employees that motivates them, and gives them incentives to keep improving our products and service levels for customers. Having this attitude is one of the main reasons for our success, and I believe it will make us even more successful in the future."

J.W. MESSNER INC.

DVERTISING AGENCIES DEPEND UPON CLIENTS: BANKS, MANU-
facturers, software companies, restaurants, retailers, and
thousands of other businesses, institutions, and associations. Clients pay agencies to create their corporate images,
to improve their name recognition, and to generate a desire

and sales for their products and services.

Nationally, the average length of the client/agency relationship is 5.2 years. By this measurement alone, J.W. Messner Inc. (JWM) is exceptional: The average length

of its client relationships is more than nine years, and several of its clients have worked with the agency for 17 to 20 years.

So, how has J.W. Messner Inc. maintained its stability for two decades in Grand Rapids? What is the JWM secret? The agency hasn't managed to avoid the occasional client loss; no agency can. But it also has constantly attracted new clients. Its billings, about $500,000 in 1978, hover around the $100 million mark today.

"We never take anything for granted," Board Chairman Jim Messner says. "We remember when we weren't big, and we still don't feel big. I don't remember we're this big until I take people on a tour of our agency. Our challenge,

I think, is holding on to who we are. The closer you come to success, the further away you can get from what makes you successful. Continuity—keeping the intensity of our business philosophy alive, and transmitting it as we've grown to more than 120 associates spread out across the country—that's the biggest challenge."

STEADY GROWTH
At first glance, continuity would not seem to be a problem for the company. Messner, with 12 years' experience in advertising under his belt, started J.W. Messner Inc. in 1977 with assistant Dee Winter and broadcast producer John Weitzel. Winter is still Messner's assistant and Grand Rapids office manager, and Weitzel now heads the company's Seattle office. From day one, J.W. Messner Inc.'s headquarters has been in the historic Waters Building in downtown Grand Rapids.

However, today the agency's 120-plus associates also work in Seattle, Oakland, Los Angeles, Minneapolis, Cincinnati, Charlotte, Pittsburgh, and Buffalo. Many first proved their talents in the huge national agencies that congregate in Los Angeles, Chicago, and New York City. Others have demonstrated excellence in regional agencies, or have firsthand experience in clients' industries and various other disciplines. The result? A depth and breadth of advertising experience unlike that of a typical ad agency.

"We succeed for two reasons," says Messner. "One, we're a group of people doing things we like to do. That naturally attracts clients. Two, everyone here is willing to do the right thing, the best thing, for our clients, no matter what size the client is. We invest the

"We believe that an agency's greatest assets go out the door at the end of each day. That's why we invest heavily in smart, talented, experienced people who not only do their jobs well, but also love what they're doing. And that naturally attracts great clients," says J.W. Messner Inc. Board Chairman/CEO Jim Messner.

From an inch away to shots from the sky, J.W. Messner Inc.'s creative production teams go to any length, anywhere, to capture the perfect imagery on film or video for their clients' television commercials and audiovisual needs.

time and the personal involvement and the money it takes to serve our clients' best interests.

"And people figure that out about us fairly quickly. We bring in a visitor here, and they don't walk out remembering any one ad or fancy high-tech piece of our equipment as much as they talk about the esprit de corps. They remember the environment, the atmosphere."

Doing Things Right

Longtime Messner partner Tom Quinn, who retired in 1997, had a sign on his office wall that read: "Right is right, even if nobody does it. Wrong is wrong, even if everybody does it." "That says everything," Messner affirms. "Doing what's right, for our clients, for our associates, for our industry."

Obviously, the agency is doing many things right. In 1996, J.W. Messner Inc. became one of only 13 agencies in the country approved to work on Chevrolet Dealer Marketing Group (DMG) accounts, such as longtime client Mid-America Chevy Dealers, based in St. Louis. Today, the agency creates TV, radio, newspaper, outdoor, and direct mail advertising; creates and maintains Web sites; and buys media for 76 DMGs, comprising 1,832 Chevrolet dealers. These DMGs make up 11 out of a total of 26 Chevrolet Area Marketing Groups in the country.

Consumer product advertising is another of J.W. Messner Inc.'s strengths. It has launched successful consumer products such as Kitty Litter, Tidy Cat, and Scoop Away cat litters, and helped the Grand Rapids-based Video Tyme chain grow so successful that it was purchased by Blockbuster. The agency's advertising for Georgia-Pacific consumer products increased the market share of their Angel Soft brand bath tissue from the fourth- to the second-leading brand in the category.

Messner admits that being in Grand Rapids has its drawbacks. "Not being able to fly direct to Grand Rapids from anywhere, that's our biggest handicap," he

says. "People ask us why we haven't moved our headquarters to Chicago or Detroit. But the answer is simple. Quality of life. We attract talented people from big cities who are fed up with fighting the traffic and the parking and the noise. We all enjoy living here in West Michigan. When I'm flying back here and the flight attendant says, 'Welcome to Grand Rapids,' that's a beautiful sound."

In the offices of J.W. Messner Inc. are state-of-the-art digital video editing equipment, color copiers, and a complete digital audio recording studio. Also, there are a lot of people who are enjoying what they do. The hours can be long, and the work hectic, but cheerfulness pervades the agency.

The company is generous with its benefits, which of course helps morale; but more than that, each associate is polite, enthusiastic, and confident. Messner is proud of the fact that "people don't put up with bad attitudes around here."

"Attitude is everything," says the sign on Messner's desk. If there's a secret to his company's success, perhaps that explains it best.

Creative JWM teams follow defined marketing, brand, and creative strategies to deliver their clients' messages in compelling, on-target communications via multimedia channels including television, radio, newspapers, magazines, direct mail, point-of-sale displays, brochures, and annual reports, to name a few.

Investing in the latest technology allows JWM's creative teams to bring creative concepts to reality with unparalleled quality, efficiency, and expediency.

One of the company's fastest-growing divisions is J.W. Messner Interactive, which launches and maintains client sites on the World Wide Web, such as a Web site home page for a salmon marketing alliance.

THE STORY OF ROBERT GROOTERS DEVELOPMENT COMPANY IS one that the company's namesake is proud to tell. It is the story of how a young entrepreneur and his wife invested endless amounts of ambition, energy, and drive to beat the odds and build a successful and prosperous business

Robert Grooters is proud to be a part of the Grand Rapids community, and is excited about playing a role in the city's future growth. "We have the greatest community in the country," he says. "People here care about quality, and they work with pride. They really want to help this city succeed. It is the energy, enthusiasm, and generosity of the people here who have helped Grand Rapids get where it is."

Perhaps the greatest testament to Robert Grooters Development Company's determination is Bridgewater Place, a world-class office showcase located on the banks of the Grand River in downtown Grand Rapids (top right).

The lobby of Bridgewater Place, which was designed by Sharon Grooters, won a major architectural award, and the building, which has the largest installation of Norwegian blue pearl granite in the world, has been praised as one of the finest office buildings in the Midwest (bottom right).

through hard work and perseverance. In essence, it is the story of the American dream happening in Grand Rapids.

HUMBLE BEGINNINGS

Robert Grooters' career began in the grocery industry, where his night job involved loading and unloading trucks in the warehouses of Spartan Stores. During the day, Grooters was very active in several different business ventures. The first business was a sandblasting company. This was followed by a copper recycling company, a foundry, and later a transformer company. Through his experiences with these enterprises, he gained solid business knowledge.

Grooters is quick to give credit to Sharon, his wife of 35 years. They were married at a young age and have been working side by side as a team all along the way. He states, "She was my business partner from the beginning, and we are still a strong team today."

Presently, Robert Grooters Development Company is the premier developer and owner of industrial real estate in West Michigan. The company was founded in 1977 by Robert and Sharon Grooters, and in slightly more than 20 years, it has grown to one of the largest independently owned development companies in the United States.

Grooters says that a real estate developer is actually a visionary: someone who isn't afraid to pursue a dream and take risks. He states, "When we started out in this business, I used to knock on doors with a picture in my hand of what I thought a building would look like, and people would look at me and say, 'Yeah, right. You're going to build this?' But I never let other people's lack of belief stop me from what I knew could be accomplished."

A TENANT IS A DIAMOND

Grooters says that knowledge gained from his retail grocery background has been useful to him as a real estate developer.

"In the grocery business, you learn about high volume, low margins, and customer service, and we apply those same principles to our business," he says. "By building a high volume of larger buildings, we can amortize the cost over more square feet, and offer the lowest possible cost to our tenants

in order to help them obtain the maximum value from their space."

There were several lessons learned from the grocery business about customer service. "When it comes to our customers, service is everything," Grooters says. "We work closely with our tenants to understand their businesses, and basically become their partner— their right arm. In fact, our motto is A Tenant Is a Diamond, which is a pretty good indication of how valuable our customers are to us.

This applies to every one of them, whether they lease 100 square feet or 150,000 square feet."

Approximately 75 percent of the company's growth has been from repeat business, which is illustrated by a tenant retention rate of approximately 90 percent. Grooters feels that these statistics are the direct result of the company's attitude toward customers.

BEFORE AND BEYOND BRIDGEWATER PLACE

From 1977 to 1994 Robert Grooters Development constructed approximately 3 million square feet of industrial space, nearly all of which was sold to a real estate investment trust (REIT) in 1994.

During the 1980s, the company had its first experience with office space constructing Horizon Drive Office Park. This development consisted of six 30,000-square-foot buildings for a total of nearly 200,000 square feet of office space. This development was sold in 1996.

Perhaps the greatest testament to Grooters' determination is Bridgewater Place, a world-class office showcase located on the banks of the Grand River in downtown Grand Rapids. The first phase of this two-phase project consists of 405,000 square feet in a 17-story tower. The attached 1,400-car parking deck serves to accommodate the 1,200 people who work in the facility. The lobby, which was designed by Sharon Grooters, won a major architectural award, and the building, which has the largest installation of Norwegian

blue pearl granite in the world, has been praised as one of the finest office buildings in the Midwest.

Grooters says that bringing the building to fruition was no easy task. "When I initially talked about what I had in mind," he says, "people said I was crazy. At the time there were only seven of us in the company, and no one thought we could ever pull off such a major project." Today, Robert Grooters Development employs 20 people, seven of whom are exclusively devoted to Bridgewater Place in the areas of management, maintenance, sales, finance, marketing, and construction.

After the completion of Bridgewater Place, and subsequent to the sale of 3 million square feet of industrial property, one would perhaps think that Grooters would have scaled back and relaxed, but his metabolism simply wouldn't allow that. During the four-year period of 1994 through 1997, the company has constructed seven new industrial parks through-out West Michigan for a total of nearly 6 million square feet of new industrial and high-tech office space. In addition, another 4 million square feet of development is projected during the next 18 to 24 months, part of which will be in two new industrial parks. By the end of that period, the company will have constructed more than 100 buildings in its 20-year history.

Grooters says that he is proud to be a part of the Grand Rapids community, and is excited about playing a role in the city's future

growth. "We have the greatest community in the country," he says. "People here care about quality, and they work with pride. They really want to help this city succeed. It is the energy, enthusiasm, and generosity of the people here who have helped Grand Rapids get where it is."

As to the future, Robert Grooters Development Company will continue to develop its vision. "Today, we are at a level beyond what anyone thought we could accomplish," Grooters says. "In a way, our business is kind of like a game of Monopoly: You have to have big dreams and be willing to take risks. You also have to be constantly looking for people who aren't afraid to play the game along with you. That's how dreams are built."

Presently, Robert Grooters Development Company is the premier developer and owner of industrial real estate in West Michigan. Norton Shores Industrial Park (left) and South Holland Industrial Park (right) add to the company's total area of nearly 6 million square feet of new industrial and high-tech office space.

Northridge Industrial Park is another Robert Grooters project.

N 1974, SCOTT MCNEAL, A HIGH SCHOOL JUNIOR, AND HIS YOUNGER brother Mitch were masters of their driveway basketball court in Lowell, Michigan. Their passion for the game led them to start a three-on-three basketball tournament, which, over the next two decades, grew from a hobby into the largest, most well-known

three-on-three tournament in the country.

HOOP DREAMS

Scott McNeal, dubbed "Gus Macker" by high school friends, and Mitch McNeal never anticipated their Gus Macker 3-on-3 Tournament would become a nationwide event. They were simply looking for something to occupy their time during spring break in 1974. "Our parents' house was the neighborhood hangout for us and our friends," says Scott. "We'd play basketball in the driveway all the time, but got tired of playing each other for nothing. So we got 18 of us together, had six captains choose teams of three, and each threw a dollar into the pot. We played a double elimination tour-

nament in our driveway, and the winning team got the money."

The following year, 30 kids signed up to play, and year after year, the Gus Macker 3-on-3 Tournament grew. In 1978, the Macker Basketball Association was registered as a nonprofit organization, and in 1979, some makeshift baskets were put in the street to accommodate 90 teams. TV-8 came from Grand Rapids to cover a story on the tournament, which by then included T-shirts for the players and a Miss Macker pageant.

THE BIG LEAGUES

Thanks to word of mouth and local media, 1980 saw 500 players participate in the Gus Macker 3-on-3 Tournament, and winners started receiving trophies. Then the national media got wind of the event. "*Sports Illustrated* wrote a great story in 1985," says Scott, "and it had such a huge impact on the tournament, it brought people to Lowell from all over the country. People started asking if we could put a tournament on in their towns." The tournament was also featured on ABC's *Wide World of Sports*, on ESPN, and in *USA Today*.

Lowell is only so big, however, so in 1987, the main tournament moved to Belding, which was aptly nicknamed Mackerville U.S.A.

That year also marked the first year the tournament was played in other towns—five in 1987. The corporate offices were later moved to Grand Rapids, and by 1996, there were more than 75 tournaments throughout the country with a total of about 200,000 players.

The Gus Macker 3-on-3 Tournament has also been successful in raising money for charities throughout the country. "At each tournament site, there's a local organizing committee that runs the event with our help," says Scott. "That committee donates proceeds from the event to a local charity." Since 1992, charitable donations from these tournaments have exceeded $3 million, and proceeds from the Grand Rapids tournament have gone toward the Grand Rapids Public School System's Pay-To-Play program, enabling kids to participate in sports without having to pay out of their own pockets.

As Gus Macker Enterprises moves into the future, Scott and Mitch McNeal are making sure it remains what it was in 1974—fun. "This is a community event," says Scott. "It started in a small town, and we'll continue with a small-town mentality. I still live in Belding, and my wife schedules the teams. It's a family event, and we're going to keep it that way."

In 1974, Scott McNeal, a high school junior, and his younger brother Mitch started a three-on-three basketball tournament, which, over the next two decades, grew from a hobby into the largest, most well-known three-on-three tournament in the country. As Gus Macker Enterprises moves into the future, Scott and Mitch McNeal are making sure it remains what it was in the beginning—fun.

BENTELER AUTOMOTIVE IS A SUBSIDIARY OF BENTELER AG, a 120-year-old, family-owned company headquartered in Paderborn, Germany. The parent company is well known throughout Europe as one of the leading manufacturers of chassis systems and other automotive products. In 1980,

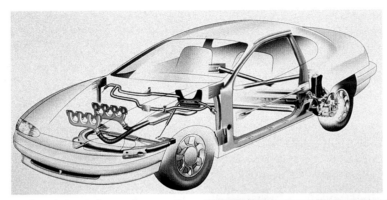

Benteler AG established its U.S. corporate headquarters in Grand Rapids, and today, Benteler AG's U.S. operations include more than 700,000 square feet of manufacturing facilities located in Grand Rapids and Kalamazoo, as well as sites in Goshen and Fort Wayne, Indiana.

THREE DIFFERENT SYSTEMS
In 1997, Benteler Automotive Corporation produced its 100-millionth door beam—an astounding achievement that no other company in the world has managed to attain. Today, the company is one of the leading door beam producers in the world, manufacturing nearly 100,000 of these steel beams per day to protect vehicle passengers from side impact collisions.

Besides protecting occupants in a collision, Benteler is also in the business of protecting the environment and improving fuel economy. The company serves major automotive customers by designing and producing entire systems for the chassis and stainless-steel, front-exhaust areas. Systems are tailor-designed, based on individual customer need, and Benteler has its own in-house prototype capabilities, as well as tool-and-die, stamping, and testing abilities in all three product areas.

In the impact management area, Benteler produces more than 125 different types of door beams, as well as cross-car beams, quarter panel reinforcements, door reinforcements, and instrument panel supports. In the production of its impact management systems, the company uses highly sophisticated laser cutting technology and robotic welding, for which it holds patents for both the spiral cut and taper cut designs. In order to ensure optimum safety and to meet stringent government regulations, Benteler has invested heavily in test equipment,

performing regular crash tests of its systems for structural integrity, strength, and durability.

Benteler's chassis systems feature innovative technologies in product design and manufacturing, such as the company's unique process for developing precise and efficient structural components. The use of a hydroforming process originally developed in Europe enables metal parts to be formed through intense water pressure, resulting in tubular parts that are dimensionally accurate and consistently superior to stamped parts.

Benteler is also known as a world leader in producing fabricated exhaust products that meet or exceed government-mandated emissions standards, as well as customer durability requirements. The company holds patents on a unique air-gap technology, which is designed to significantly reduce outer temperatures of exhaust components, decrease air pollutants, and reduce engine noise. Benteler has also formed a partnership with the U.S. Department of Energy's National Renewable Energy Laboratory (NREL) to produce a new catalytic converter, which promises to cut engine emissions by at least 50 percent, thus substantially reducing air pollution.

Quality is another area in which Benteler is a world leader. The company is QS 9000 certified by the International Organization for Standardization, and the walls

of Benteler's corporate headquarters are lined with quality awards received from major customers like Ford, General Motors, Chrysler, and Honda.

CONSISTENT GROWTH
Benteler has experienced about 20 percent growth per year, with U.S. sales currently in excess of $350 million annually. The company also has technical license agreements with Aisin Takaoka, a major manufacturer of exhaust manifolds in Japan, and Young Shin Co. Ltd., a major producer of door beams in Korea; Benteler is the first automotive supplier to penetrate the Korean market.

As a world leader in product development, safety, and superior advanced technology, Benteler Automotive is poised for even greater success in the future.

In addition to producing door beams, Benteler Automotive serves major automotive customers by designing and producing entire systems for the chassis and stainless-steel, front-exhaust areas (top).

Benteler is known as a world leader in producing fabricated exhaust products that meet or exceed government-mandated emissions standards, as well as customer durability requirements (bottom).

TURNING A STODGY CHAMBER OF COMMERCE PUBLICATION INTO A major city magazine is no simple task. But taking the same type of publication and turning it into an award-winning investigative and creative magazine is indeed a rare accomplishment. In 1980, Gemini Publications succeeded in this

task when it launched *Grand Rapids Magazine*, which was originally owned by the Grand Rapids Area Chamber of Commerce and known simply as *Grand Rapids*. John Zwarensteyn, Gemini's CEO and publisher, tells of how the magazine earned the nickname Publication of Second Opinion: "When I first launched *Grand Rapids Magazine*," he says, "the city had only one print news entity: the *Grand Rapids Press*. I knew we needed another publication in this city, one that would probe community issues and be more investigative, and that offered readers a second opinion on local issues. With *Grand Rapids Magazine*, we immediately began publishing articles that were challenging and thought provoking, as well as entertaining, and it wasn't long before people began to sit up and take notice. The magazine definitely had a major impact, right from the beginning."

THREE AWARD-WINNING PUBLICATIONS
Today, *Grand Rapids Magazine* is known as a lively, authoritative, high-quality publication that's

designed to inform, amuse, and entertain its readers, and to help them get the most out of living in Grand Rapids. Each issue includes lively columns and articles, colorful photography and graphics, and service features that guide the reader to the interesting sights and sounds around town.

Covering such topics as political and social issues, crime, the environment, the arts, and education, as well as essays on people, organizations, and communities, the magazine is always interesting and entertaining. It also features the popular *Dining Guide*, which presents objective reviews of the area's restaurants, as well as a *Calendar of Events* that keeps readers up to date on the latest concerts, theater attractions, art exhibits, and other attractions in and around Grand Rapids. The magazine's annual dining awards are coveted by all of the area's restaurants.

Gemini's second publication was launched in 1983. It was targeted exclusively at the area's business community. Initially published as a monthly newsletter, the *Grand Rapids Business Journal* immediately became popular with West Michigan business readers. A survey conducted nine months after the publication's initial appearance confirmed the *Business Journal*'s growing popular-

ity: "That survey confirmed our belief that there was a definite need for the *Business Journal*," says Zwarensteyn. "Based on our findings, we decided to alter the format to a monthly newspaper tabloid. Our original intent was to take the *Business Journal* from a monthly to a semimonthly, and eventually to a weekly. But we did a second survey a year later, and the results were so positive that we decided to scrap the semimonthly interval and go immediately to a weekly. It was risky, but it has proven to be a wise decision." The survey also determined that readers wanted more news articles, which don't really fit in a magazine format, so the *Journal* became a weekly tabloid.

In 1989, Gemini added a third publication to its stable: *Grand Rapids Parent Magazine*. Geared to today's active parents, this monthly magazine focuses on the interests and needs of parents, as well as those of professionals who work with parents and children. Columns spotlight people and agencies that strive to enhance family life in the Grand Rapids area, and articles introduce community professionals who set the agenda on education, child care, business and investment planning, the environment, and other issues. There are also stories for and about children,

Gemini's award-winning design and production staff produces more than 5,000 pages of editorial, advertising, and marketing ideas every year. Gemini's publications have won more than 50 national design, photography, and art awards since 1980.

as well as a monthly calendar of events that lists and describes family-oriented activities in Grand Rapids.

All three Gemini publications have repeatedly demonstrated a high degree of top-notch journalistic efforts, and all three have won numerous prestigious national editorial and design awards. *Grand Rapids Magazine* has won three separate national awards for general excellence, as well as awards for design excellence and editorial excellence in investigative journalism. The *Grand Rapids Business Journal* has won a total of seven national awards, including two general excellence awards as the number one local business journal in the United States. Since 1990, *Grand Rapids Parent Magazine* has won a total of 44 national awards for editorial content, news writing, design and graphics, feature writing, individual columns, and overall general excellence. No other local parenting magazine in the country has won as many national awards.

STEADY GROWTH

When Zwarensteyn first started Gemini Publications and launched *Grand Rapids Magazine*, circulation consisted of approximately 2,000 subscribers. That number has now grown to 14,000 paid. "Our monthly readership may exceed 100,000," says Zwarensteyn, "which makes us one of the larger city magazines in the country, based on paid circulation per capita for the size of

the market. Our goal is to exceed 20,000 paid subscribers by the year 2000, and we have every reason to believe we'll get there."

Growth has been equally successful for Gemini's other two publications. The *Grand Rapids Business Journal* started out with 2,000 charter subscribers in 1983, and today it has 7,000 subscribers and more than 30,000 readers. *Grand Rapids Parent Magazine*, which started out with a circulation of 6,000 in 1989, has now climbed to more than 24,000.

Zwarensteyn says each of the Gemini publications has enjoyed continued success and growth, and he expects more of the same

in the future. "From the beginning, we've believed in giving Grand Rapids superior publications that have a high degree of journalistic integrity," he says. "The many national awards we've won against major market publications show that we've accomplished that goal. Our readers—as well as our advertisers—know they can count on us to deliver what we say we'll deliver.

"This is an exciting time for us because Grand Rapids is rapidly becoming a major international business and financial center. And as the area grows, we grow. This is certainly the right place for us. And this is where we intend to stay, grow, and prosper."

Clockwise from top: Daily and weekly editorial department meetings keep staffers updated on current developments. The editorial staff has won more than 50 national writing and general excellence awards.

Gemini Chief Executive Officer and Publisher John Zwarensteyn reviews financial progress with members of the business and administrative staff.

Promoting and distributing Gemini's entire stable of publications and getting new subscribers keep the marketing and circulation staff busy.

ARLIN FEYEN AND BOB ZYLSTRA MET IN 1974 WHILE WORKING with other volunteers to help renovate an inner-city house that was donated to their church. When the house was finished and sold, other projects started to appear. The endeavor grew rapidly and eventually earned its own

name: Project Conserve. The efforts of this team of volunteers spawned a multimillion-dollar housing rehab organization that would become known as the Inner City Christian Federation.

Feyen and Zylstra continued their volunteer work for several more years, and in 1979, they explored the idea of starting their own business. By 1980, they had a business plan for a new electrical contracting firm that would make the industry a better place by setting new standards of excellence and integrity. Today, Feyen and Zylstra have built a company

J. REUS PHOTOGRAPHY

that's grown far beyond an electrical contracting firm. With 230 employees and five separate, specialized divisions, Feyen-Zylstra provides customers with an unmatched range of electrical, electronic, and communication services.

AN INTEGRATED APPROACH

According to Zylstra, customers today need different kinds of electrical and electronic wiring. "With all the new technologies available," he says, "the electrical and electronic requirements have changed dramatically. The owner of a building typically needs an electrical contractor, a cabling contractor, a telephone service agent, computer system specialists, and a technician to install the security system. Not only is scheduling these services a hassle for the customer, but the end result may be a rat's nest of wiring. Our company assumes responsibility for every aspect of the project from start to finish, integrating a whole array of systems while making sure things are streamlined and well coordinated, taking the burden off the customer."

Feyen-Zylstra's five divisions were originally treated as separate entities. Uniting them as one company under the Feyen-Zylstra umbrella means a tremendous breadth of expertise is available to the customer. The company's Applied Power Systems (APS) division handles the basic wiring—coordinating commercial, industrial, and design/build electrical services from concept through installation. Voice Data Systems (VDS), the telecommunications arm of Feyen-Zylstra, designs and installs fiber-optic and network electronics systems, handles telephone and computer cabling, and provides telephone systems including expertise for moves, additions, and changes in service.

System Engineering (SE) specializes in control panel design/build and installation, working with manufacturers who use highly sophisticated automation. Tri-Tech Security (TS) designs and installs electronic security systems. And Residential Electrical Services (RES) responds to the needs of residential customers, providing expertise on electrical layout and service upgrades, lighting design,

Clockwise from top:
Plaza Towers, the tallest building in the Grand Rapids skyline, underwent a complete renovation involving co-ordinated efforts of three divisions from Feyen-Zylstra.

One of Feyen-Zylstra's early successes is the 50 Monroe Building, a contemporary landmark in downtown Grand Rapids.

Warehouse lighting and power were installed by Applied Power Systems, the electrical construction division of Feyen-Zylstra. The company provides contracting services for many clients with facilities located in Grand Rapids, including United Parcel Service, Gordon Food Service, and the Amway Corporation.

▶ VANDERLENDE PHOTOGRAPHY, INC.

automated energy management, and television/audio/video controls.

ALL IN A DAY'S WORK

Feyen-Zylstra's experience and unique combination of talents has earned the company some high-profile projects, like the 33-story Plaza Towers in downtown Grand Rapids. Three different divisions shared the tasks during the building's renovation, including implementing all electrical construction, replacing and upgrading the security systems, and handling telephone and communication concerns. Along with this project came some especially tough challenges, such as removing the entire 33rd floor and roof containing AirTouch Cellular's antennas and switching equipment, and WOOD-TV's antennas and equipment—all without shutting the companies down. In addition, Feyen-Zylstra handled the installation and maintenance of aircraft warning lights on top of the tallest crane on the Grand Rapids skyline.

The company faced another challenge when it tackled the United Parcel Service Regional Distribution Facility. Feyen-Zylstra's APS division installed an automated system capable of sorting 27,000 packages per hour, with a voice-activated zip code entry system. One of this project's biggest hurdles was the required length of conduit/wire runs without splices, as well as the physical congestion of multiple conveyor systems installed at various heights. One of the greatest benefits that resulted

from the project's completion was the prestigious ABC Construction Award for Electrical construction worth more than $1 million.

The Gordon Food Service Distribution Facility, a fast-track project, involved installing light fixtures and conduits at heights of 96 feet during frigid winter weather. The facility features more than five miles of conveyor systems with large variations in temperature, so proper insulation and sealing were essential. "With this project, if the electrical system wasn't done correctly, you'd end up with 10-foot-long, two-ton icicles protruding from different penetrations in the walls," Zylstra says. This project also won an ABC Construction Award for Feyen-Zylstra, and was cited as "a real showpiece of how an electrical system should be installed."

THE COMPANY LOOKS AHEAD

Feyen-Zylstra is the trendsetter in the electronics/electrical contracting business. "People perceive us

as being ahead of the trends, the ones to duplicate," says Feyen. "Typically, we're two years ahead of our competition." The company has enjoyed steady growth at the rate of about 25 percent annually, and concentrates most marketing efforts on building repeat business with existing customers. "With every project we do, we consider it an investment in the future, because every satisfied customer will tell someone else. We focus on building our clients—not our number of projects."

The company's long-term goal is to be perceived as the number one electrical and electronics contractor in West Michigan. "That doesn't necessarily mean we'll be the biggest or the cheapest," Zylstra says. "It means that because of what we have to offer, and the integrity we're known for, we can offer clients the best value, the highest quality, the most professional service, and basically a higher level of specialized expertise than anyone else in the business."

Clockwise from top left:
A Voice Data Systems technician installs a circuit board in a panel of a telephone voice mail system.

An electrician monitors the power on a substation. Twenty-four-hour emergency service is one of many ways Feyen-Zylstra meets its customers' needs.

Applied Power Systems provided power and controls for these pump motors.

DAVE CUSTER IS FOND OF SAYING THAT HIS DEALERSHIP HAS a commonsense approach that focuses on the customer: learning to understand what customers need and want, providing extraordinary service, and following through on promises made. "Really, it's so simple it's almost profound,"

explains Custer, "because without the customer, we wouldn't be here. We stay focused on that—and from a philosophical standpoint, that makes us unique."

In business since 1981, Custer Office Environments is West Michigan's largest office furniture dealership, and this works to the

Led by (from left) Bob Cramer, vice president and general manager; Dave Custer, president; and Greg Wolf, vice president of finance and administration, Custer Office Environments has been awarded the prestigious Steelcase Exemplary Dealer Award twice by excelling throughout stringent customer audits, site visits, and Steelcase evaluations.

company's advantage. "Being the biggest has never been our goal," says Custer, "because our goal is to be the best. But, I must admit our large size has helped us provide customers with services and capabilities that small firms just aren't able to offer."

MORE THAN JUST FURNITURE

One of Custer Office Environments' greatest strengths is its ability to create not just offices, but total office environments. Custer's talented and highly qualified staff, which includes 26 degreed interior designers, works closely with customers from the earliest possible stage to plan and design offices, making the best possible use of space. Based on the customer's budget and individual tastes and preferences, the designers can specify and procure everything needed for the office environment including furniture, floor covering, wall covering, painting, window

treatments, ceiling and lighting, signage, even artwork and accessories, and will then follow the project through to the very end, supervising delivery and installation. And Custer is able to work with any size customer, from the two-person office to the 1,000-person office in West Michigan or anywhere in the country.

Another service Custer provides is asset management services, which involves picking up and storing furniture for customers who are short of storage space, and then providing delivery and setup when the furniture is needed again. The dealership also provides move management services, interior updating and modification, and complete planning and reconfiguration of existing office space when a business needs to change or expand.

A major part of the dealership's ability to provide total office environment solutions is having an

Custer Office Environments' talented and highly qualified staff, which includes 26 degreed interior designers, works closely with customers from the earliest possible stage to plan and design offices, making the best possible use of space.

in-depth understanding of how a workplace can and should be used from a physical standpoint. "We specialize in understanding businesses and how people work within them," says Custer. "A big part of our job is studying people's individual work styles to learn how they work now, and which tools could help them be more effective within the workplace." Using today's computer technology and a program developed by Steelcase called Workplace Performance, Custer's designers are able to study and audit pertinent information about a business and plan a better and more effective office environment.

FROM TRAINEE TO BUSINESS OWNER

Custer started at Steelcase Inc. as a management career trainee, eventually working his way up to the level of regional manager for the Detroit region. When a large Detroit Steelcase dealer with a branch in Grand Rapids declared bankruptcy in 1981, Custer—with the help of Steelcase—purchased the assets of the Grand Rapids dealership and formed Custer Office Environments. First-year sales were just under $3 million, and included jobs that really helped launch the dealership. Says Custer, "In 1981, the Amway Grand Plaza

hired us to manage the procurement of things they needed for the new and renovated hotel, and we bought everything they needed—furniture, beds, even clock radios. It was a far cry from office furniture, but it was a big project that really jump-started us."

After 17 years of steady growth, Custer's sales are in excess of $36 million. The dealership has 140 employees, and in addition to the main showroom in Grand Rapids, Custer also has locations in Battle Creek, Kalamazoo, Benton Harbor, and Grand Haven.

Custer's main furniture line is Steelcase; in addition, Custer also carries 100 other lines such as Baker, Sligh, and NuCraft—furniture that fills the more unique and unusual niches that customers want and need. The dealership's warehouse outlet is open to the public, and caters more to smaller, budget-conscious business owners.

Custer's stunning, two-story Grand Rapids showroom, located in the 70-year-old former Bixby Office Supply building in the heart of downtown, is an example of the creativity and talent the dealership provides to customers. With more than 21,000 square feet, the showroom has been planned and laid out to illustrate the virtually endless possibilities in creating today's office environments, and it also

acts as a working showroom for Custer's employees.

RECOGNIZED EXCELLENCE

In 1993, Custer Office Environments applied for the prestigious Exemplary Dealer Award, a Steelcase award that represents the highest possible honor a dealership can earn and is awarded to only three dealers out of 500. In order to qualify for the award—which can be won only once every three years—a dealership must excel throughout stringent customer audits, site visits, and Steelcase evaluations that rate qualities such as customer satisfaction, marketing innovations, financial strength, and overall dealer performance. Custer won the prestigious award in 1993 and again in 1996.

When asked about his vision for the future, Custer returns to his commonsense approach to customer service: "Quite simply, our customer is king. So of course our goals for the future revolve around customers—to be able to serve them even better by providing more flexibility with office planning, design, and furnishings, and to provide even more integrated office environment solutions, from one single source. We believe that's the key to really providing our customers with the best long-term value for their money."

WHEN MOST PEOPLE SHOP FOR GROCERIES, OFFICE supplies, cosmetics, or pet foods, they are unaware how the merchandise made its way from the manufacturer to a warehouse and finally to the store. However, everybody is sensitive to price increases

and no one is happy when their favorite products are not in the store. Helping to keep prices down and the products in stock are sophisticated material handling systems used by manufacturers, distributors, and retailers.

Engineering and constructing these systems is the specialty of Distribution Planning Incorporated (DPI). DPI is one of the country's

leading providers of material handling systems used in warehouses and distribution facilities. Its well-earned reputation is proved by the 200-plus systems it has designed and installed nationwide.

HISTORY

DPI was founded in 1981 by four engineers who, for almost 20 years, had worked together designing

material handling systems. During DPI's early years, James E. Bonthuis, David L. Neu, Robert V. Riddle, and Donald A. Schneider represented a major conveyor manufacturing firm, engineering and selling the manufacturer's material handling systems to grocery distribution companies.

By the late 1980s, the company's growth led it to reassess its business strategy. DPI had developed the capability to provide material handling systems that integrated complementary technologies. In 1987, DPI altered its original strategy and became a systems integrator, with the ability to plan, design, engineer, sell, and install material handling systems using equipment from numerous material handling manufacturers.

As a systems integrator, DPI often works in a design-and-build relationship with its customers. In this capacity, DPI is responsible for defining the customers' mate-

DPI is one of the country's leading providers of material handling systems used in warehouses and distribution facilities. Its well-earned reputation is proved by the 200-plus systems it has designed and installed nationwide.

◀ DAVE HANKS, MARQUETTE PRESENTATIONS

◀ DAVE HANKS, MARQUETTE PRESENTATIONS

The company's engineering staff includes mechanical engineers, electrical engineers, and civil engineers. A highly trained design staff, using sophisticated graphics and engineering software, supports the company's systems engineering.

DAVE HANKS, MARQUETTE PRESENTATIONS

THE BUSCHMAN COMPANY

rial handling requirements, as well as designing and providing the material handling system.

MECHANIZING WAREHOUSES

The company defines its business as mechanizing warehouses. DPI's systems are used to receive, store, select, and ship products quickly and efficiently. These systems typically consist of pallet racks, rack-supported structures, various types of powered conveyor equipment, computer controls, and electronic peripherals.

The company's customers are located across the country, from California to New Jersey and from Florida to Wisconsin. The company's projects range in size. DPI has designed and installed a material handling system for a large California-based supermarket chain. For this customer, DPI engineered and installed nearly eight miles of conveyor, 7 million pounds of pallet rack, and several high-speed sortation systems in a 1 million-square-foot facility. However, DPI also provides smaller, simpler systems when the customer's requirements are less demanding.

DPI is also equipped to work with companies when they need to increase the capacity of their existing systems. These projects are often the most challenging, since the customer usually needs to continue operating even as its

systems are being disassembled and upgraded. It is in these projects that DPI's years of experience designing and engineering systems solely for distribution facilities proves invaluable. A keen understanding of a warehouse's day-to-day operations is critical when the requirement is to upgrade a system without interrupting the customer's operations.

A TEAM WITH THE RIGHT COMBINATION

DPI is headquartered in Grand Rapids and has a sales office in Chicago. The company has 34 employees, of whom 24 are in systems sales/engineering, three are in field installation, and seven are in administration. The company's engineering staff includes mechanical engineers, electrical engineers, and civil engineers. A highly trained design staff, using sophisticated graphics and engineering software, supports the company's systems engineering.

The company has purposely sought out people with the right combination of skills, attitude, and integrity that mirror the company's priorities. Also key to DPI's success is the staff's experience in the material handling industry, which averages more than 12 years.

The company works hard to provide an environment in which each employee is treated as an in-

tegral member of the team. DPI encourages its staff to be creative, using its abilities and experience to develop effective solutions to customers' needs.

NO END IN SIGHT

Although DPI's revenues are in excess of $20 million annually, the company's founders remember the challenges of DPI's early years. Focusing on the customer instead of on DPI's success or growth continues to be the company's guiding principle.

This attitude was recognized in 1997 when DPI was honored as one of the fastest-growing companies in the 1997 *Michigan Private 100*, a study which ranks Michigan companies according to their five-year growth rates.

With a future that has never held more promise, DPI is committed to meeting its customers needs with the excellence that has become its hallmark.

Clockwise from top left:
The company defines its business as mechanizing warehouses.

DPI's systems are used to receive, store, select, and ship products quickly and efficiently. These systems typically consist of pallet racks, rack-supported structures, various types of powered conveyor equipment, computer controls, and electronic peripherals.

In 1987, DPI became a systems integrator, with the ability to plan, design, engineer, sell, and install material handling systems using equipment from numerous material handling manufacturers.

O THE CASUAL OBSERVER, THE SHORT HISTORY OF AUTOCAM Corporation may look like a classic overnight success story. Started in 1982 as a division of Autodie Corporation and taken public in 1991, the company has experienced constant and often meteoric growth. Building on a sales base of $8 million in 1991, the company expects to top $150 million by 2000. But what looks like business serendipity is really the result of hard work; shrewd, strategic planning; and an extraordinary, company-wide commitment to quality.

A HISTORY OF RAPID, STRATEGIC GROWTH

Autodie created Autocam in 1982 to produce close-tolerance, specialty metal alloy components. In 1988, recognizing its tremendous potential, John Kennedy, Autodie's CFO, purchased the new division. Under Kennedy's leadership, the company quickly gained a foothold in the highly competitive automotive market, starting with a contract to produce fuel-injector components for the AC Rochester Products division of General Motors. By the time of its initial public stock offering in 1991, Autocam was well on its way to becoming a world-class leader in precision-machined components. In the years since, the company has experienced an annualized sales growth rate of 18 to 20 percent.

Autocam's extraordinary success is largely the result of an unwavering commitment to the revolutionary ideas of renowned quality expert W. Edwards Deming. From the beginning, the young company was driven by a firm belief in the value of continuous improvement. As the company grew, Deming's ideas translated into increased productivity, improved processes, higher employee morale, and, ultimately, lower production costs. In turn, these factors combined to make the company increasingly competitive. Soon, the young company was in a position to expand and diversify outside its automotive base. Armed with a clear sense of the company's capabilities and competencies, Autocam's management team began to target strategic opportunities for growth.

THE FUTURE DEMANDS DIVERSIFICATION

Autocam entered the computer electronics market through an important contract with Hutchinson Technology, a world leader in rigid disk drive components. The success of this partnership encouraged the management team to pursue additional opportunities outside the automotive market. In 1992, the company purchased the assets of a California-based contract manufacturer of precision-machined components for the electronics and medical device industries. This new operation enabled Autocam to diversify further into high-growth, nonautomotive markets. Currently, the Hayward, California, facility supplies precision components to the ophthalmic and cardiovascular surgical device industries.

Today, even though it has pursued other opportunities successfully, Autocam still considers automotive its primary market. The company enjoys a very competitive, long-term position in this large and diverse global market, particularly in the areas of fuel and braking systems. Autocam has strong relationships with three of the industry's top manufacturers, and has won the prestigious GM and Hitachi Supplier of the Year awards for three consecutive years. In 1996, the company achieved QS 9000 well ahead of its competition.

Predictably, Kennedy and his management team attribute their success in automotive and other markets to the company's continuous-improvement mind-set. Over the past 10 years, Autocam has never strayed from its early focus on quality. In order to maintain this focus, the company continually analyzes its ability to meet—even anticipate—customer demands. Usually, in today's high-pressure global markets, this means providing a competitively priced product. To stay competitive, Autocam has occasionally found it more expedient to acquire, rather than develop, additional capabilities.

Autocam Corporation corporate headquarters is located in Kentwood.

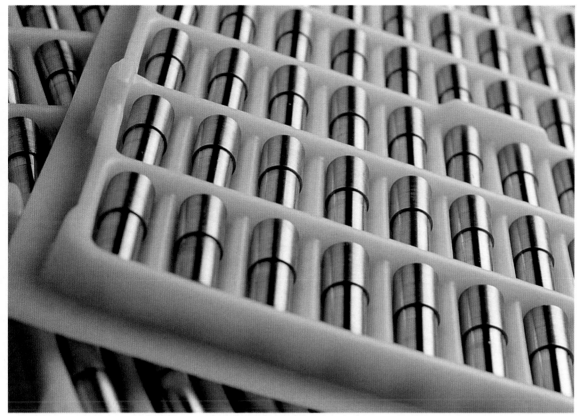

Autocam manufactures precision-machined components for the automotive, computer, and medical industries.

Such strategic acquisitions and partnerships enable the company to offer a wide range of value-added services without compromising profitability.

In 1997, Autocam acquired the Hamilton Group, a highly successful precision-machining operation based in Gaffney, South Carolina, and Dowagiac, Michigan. Hamilton was an appealing partner because it had highly complementary braking systems customers and core competencies. This acquisition strengthened Autocam's position with the global automotive industry and enabled it to move into the fast-growing southeastern U.S. region.

The Hamilton acquisition was quickly followed by the decision to build a new, 50,000-square-foot manufacturing facility in Marshall, Michigan. Finally, in 1998, Autocam moved outside U.S. borders with a Brazilian partnership that further diversifies the company's product mix. These initiatives are just the start of an all-out campaign to become a more full-service supplier to companies throughout the world.

An Empowering Work Environment

Thanks to participatory management, sophisticated training programs, and a generous benefits program, Autocam is one of West Michigan's most respected employers. For two consecutive years, *Forbes* magazine named Autocam one of America's 100 Best Small Companies—a tribute to the company's employee-centered corporate culture.

The company's work environment is based on the philosophy that employees are more productive and more valuable when they are empowered to make decisions. At Autocam, employees are given objectives and data, then are left to create solutions that improve the work process. Kennedy and his management team respect their employees, and it shows. Company facilities are so clean, well-lit, and streamlined that they defy traditional machine shop stereotypes.

With a mere 10 years of corporate history under its belt, Autocam has grown into one of the world's premier precision-machining companies. And the company's future appears even more promising. Confident of reaching its ambitious growth goals, Autocam is firmly in control of its future.

Autocam uses the latest CNC grinding and multispindle turning equipment to achieve superior surface finishes and ultraprecise dimensional tolerances. The finished components are used in a wide range of high-tech applications.

ccording to Fred Reichheld, author of *The Loyalty Effect: The Hidden Force behind Growth, Profits, and Lasting Value*, firms that concentrate on keeping good customers and productive employees are the ones that will be most successful over the long run. In Grand Rapids,

CPR/MicroAge offers excellent proof of the accuracy of this assessment.

When Jerry Engle began Computer Products and Resources, Inc. (CPR) in 1982 as a computer service organization, he developed four simple operating principles that would guide his company: respect the individual, provide the best level of service possible for customers, constantly strive for new ways to better serve customers, and provide an open and honest working environment for employees so they are motivated to do their best.

By remaining steadfast in his dedication to these principles, Engle has been able to keep good customers, keep productive employees, and move CPR from a two-person business operating from a card table and lawn chairs to a company ranked among the top 100 fastest-growing small businesses in Michigan six times from 1989 through 1997. Today, CPR/MicroAge has grown at an average rate of 29 percent each year since 1992. And the four principles upon which Engle founded his business are still the guiding forces behind the company's success.

THE CUSTOMER KNOWS BEST
Engle's vision for CPR in 1982 was simple: provide business customers

with the best on-site computer repair service their money can buy. The company became so good at doing this that CPR's customers began asking Engle not only to just service, but also to supply computer systems. After a year's worth of researching his options, Engle decided to become a MicroAge franchise. MicroAge Computer Centers, Inc.—a leading computer distributor headquartered in Tempe, Arizona—offered the perfect way for CPR to maintain its impeccable service standards while providing its customers with what they were asking for in a new computer supplier. In 1988, CPR became CPR/MicroAge.

Today, the company services and sells a multitude of computer brands—including Compaq, Digi-

tal, Hewlett-Packard, IBM, NEC, and Toshiba—as well as software, printers, and other hardware and peripherals. CPR also employs more than 130 personnel—or "teammates"—and maintains a 4-to-1 ratio of service people to salespeople.

As part of his company's dedication to customer service, Engle believes in extensive training for all his teammates. "Corporate America needs to have a greater emphasis on training its workforce," he says. "Up-front planning is so essential. By up-front planning, we reduce the amount of things that can go wrong. We train toward the customer's needs first; second, we train toward industry needs and requirements; and third, we train toward our employee needs."

With nearly 100 Customer Support Engineers dedicated to supporting large and general business networks throughout West Michigan, CPR/MicroAge is staffed with the professionals needed for network consultations, installations, and high-end connectivity. The company maintains a staff of Microsoft Certified Professionals, Novell Certified Network Engineers and Administrators, and more than 70 A+ Certified Technicians. CPR/MicroAge is a Novell Platinum Authorized Reseller, a Citrix Gold

Clockwise from top:
CPR/MicroAge Founder and President Jerry Engle attributes the success of his company to working with loyal partnering customers, teammates, and vendors. The company has earned a reputation within the community built on trust and respect.

CPR/MicroAge's Customer Support Engineers are authorized to repair a variety of desktop business computers, printers, and laptop computers.

The Quality Integration and Configuration Center at CPR/MicroAge processes and tests more than 10,000 computer systems per year before delivery and installation.

All photos by Huyck Photographic Imaging, Inc.

Laptop repair is the most intricate and complicated type of computer repair.

Partner, a Compaq Systems Service Provider, and a Microsoft Solution Provider.

STAYING AHEAD OF THE GAME

Few industries have had as great an impact on the business community as the computer industry—and few have changed as rapidly. For this reason, CPR/MicroAge maintains an in-depth focus on this very complex industry. "Technology changes like lightning," Engle says. "We understand how our customers have invested in this technology, and we're positioned to lead them into the future so they get the best possible use of their investment."

Helping CPR/MicroAge's customers calculate and understand total cost of ownership (TCO) for their computers is a key factor in achieving the firm's goals. The TCO may vary from five to 25 times the original purchase price, and as much as 47 percent of this total figure is often spent on end user support. "We try to convey to our customers/partners all the things they must consider: training needs, realistic implementation dates, and the importance of a master plan," says Engle. "This is a major implementation and

roll-out. We truly help our customers leverage their investment."

AND GROWTH CONTINUES . . .

In the early 1990s, many computer experts were predicting doom for computer dealers like CPR/ MicroAge because of the advent of the mail-order market and computer superstores, as well as corporate downsizing. Rather than panicking, however, Engle bucked the advice and trends that said to scale back. He instead decided to invest in his company's infrastructure by adding new equipment, new facilities, and new people. He predicted that if customers were downsizing, there was a greater likelihood they would outsource to CPR/MicroAge those things they formerly had employees do. Engle stuck to his course and continued

to provide the exceptional service on which his company had built its reputation.

Today, CPR/MicroAge's mission statement reads: "We are committed to establishing and maintaining lasting partnerships with our customers, teammates, and vendors by understanding their needs and expectations; performing consistently to the highest standards of quality and ethics in a friendly and professional manner; and demonstrating leadership in the changing world of technology." At CPR/MicroAge, this mission is a way of life. By remaining focused on it and by following the four principles Engle established back in 1982, the company is poised to continue its remarkable growth and success well into the next millennium.

Call Center Agents at CPR/MicroAge respond to more than 80,000 customer calls per year. The Call Center processes service calls, help-desk support calls, and general sales inquiries.

 NE OF THE BIGGEST CHALLENGES FACING TODAY'S OFFICES IS dealing with the seemingly endless mass of wires and cables. In fact, the average office has literally miles of wiring to accommodate computers, printers, multiple phone lines, fax machines, photocopiers, and, of course,

lighting. And while planning an office layout in a relatively new building is a tough challenge, trying to integrate today's technology into an old building can be nothing short of a nightmare. However, Interface Architectural Resources—better known as InterfaceAR—has the ideal solution: an innovative product known as access flooring, which allows wires and cables to be neatly organized beneath the floor, keeping them out of sight and out of people's way.

InterfaceAR is part of Atlanta-based Interface, Inc., a global leader in the worldwide commercial interiors market. Interface, Inc. specializes in floor coverings, fabrics, specialty chemicals, and interior fabrics and upholstery products, including Guilford of Maine, Stevens Linen, Toltec, and Intek.

DEVELOPING A VISION FOR TOMORROW'S WORKPLACE

InterfaceAR is recognized throughout the world as a leader in developing solutions that help today's offices prepare for the ever increasing demands of a high-tech future. The company, which now has 135 employees and nearly $35 million in annual sales, made its first Grand Rapids appearance in 1996, when it purchased Grand Rapids-based C-TEC, a leading manufacturer of raised floor systems since 1982.

InterfaceAR has a variety of solutions for businesses that help them cope with changing technology needs. The company's raised floor systems can turn the floor of an office into a grid of perfectly routed wire and communication cables, linking an entire office to

printers, modems, and servers without any exposed wiring. In addition, the floors allow heat and conditioned air to be efficiently distributed, providing the quality and flexibility needed to maintain a productive business environment.

InterfaceAR flooring can be found in many Fortune 500 companies in the United States, including Lockheed Martin, Boeing, Hughes Aircraft, IBM, GTE, and Owens Corning. Two of the company's most challenging installations have been 26 stories of the World Trade Center in New York City, and the Kennedy Space Center in Florida. InterfaceAR also has a worldwide distribution of its products, with its largest foreign markets in the Far East and the Middle East.

According to Rich Kroko, InterfaceAR's president, the com-

InterfaceAR's raised floor systems can turn the floor of an office into a grid of perfectly routed wire and communication cables, linking an entire office to printers, modems, and servers without any exposed wiring. In addition, the floors allow heat and conditioned air to be efficiently distributed, providing the quality and flexibility needed to maintain a productive business environment.

pany's products offer customers the ability to be flexible within a constantly evolving, high-tech environment. "One of the biggest challenges businesses have to deal with is their churn rate," he says, "which refers to how fast people move around inside offices. Today, with all the wiring and cabling requirements, reconfiguring an office can be very disruptive and costly. With our access floors and electrical systems, power and data are totally flexible, and can literally be picked up and moved with a minimum of disruption."

Kroko says this applies not only to new buildings, but to older structures as well. "A great deal of our work is on existing buildings," he says. "We're able to take an outdated building—even a building that's 200 years old—and without doing major renovations, bring it up to modern specifications with our products." Kroko also states that "the company has the ability to easily update its products, and its Intergy Modular Power Distribution System, a simplified wiring system with 'plug and play' technology, virtually eliminates the need for conventional fixed hardwire and conduit."

A TRULY GREEN COMPANY

According to Kroko, "Interface is very concerned about environmental responsibility. We have a corporate objective of continuously doing more with less, and achieving sustainability, which means we're working toward things like generating zero waste, using renewable materials and energy sources, eliminating toxic emissions, improving logistical systems to cut down on transport needs, and serving as a good example for other companies to follow. That attitude permeates this company, and it constantly influences how we feel, how we think, and how we act." InterfaceAR's newest product line—Tri-Tec—is made from 100 percent recycled aluminum and is also recyclable itself. The company is driving all products in this direction.

Interface, Inc. has representatives in several environmental and business groups, including the U.S. Green Building Council, World Business Council for Sustainable Development, and Business for Social Responsibility. In addition, the company's chairman, Ray Anderson, is cochair of the President's Council for Sustainable Development.

No one knows for sure what the future holds for businesses, but one thing is clear: Change will be omnipresent, and technology will continue to evolve at the speed of light, giving businesses new challenges in keeping up with the pace. InterfaceAR will continue to develop products that meet the needs of all types of businesses, offering them flexibility and innovative solutions to meet these constantly changing conditions.

Access flooring allows wires and cables to be neatly organized beneath the floor, keeping them out of sight and out of people's way.

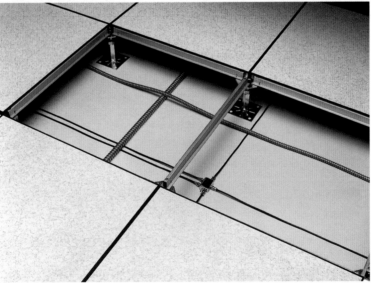

InterfaceAR is recognized throughout the world as a leader in developing solutions that help today's offices prepare for the ever increasing demands of a high-tech future.

N 1982, BROTHERS-IN-LAW DREW BOERSMA AND KURT VANVELS DECIDED to go into the business of manufacturing dies. They were in their early 20s and collectively had about eight years of experience in die making—but they also had very limited capital. Armed with confidence, a strong faith in God, and a willingness to take risks, the pair borrowed some

money and bought a two-stall garage in Comstock Park. Advanced Tooling Systems, Inc. (ATS), the business they started there, has since added two expansion companies—Engineered Tooling Systems, Inc. (ETS) and Mold Tooling Systems, Inc. (MTS). Together, they form Tooling Systems Group (TSG). Each company has its own niche in the manufacturing of tooling for the automotive and furniture industries. Together, the three divisions generate annual sales in excess of $15 million.

HUMBLE BEGINNINGS

Boersma believed so strongly in the potential of starting a tool and die shop that he talked VanVels into leaving college to become his business partner. After securing a location, the two started looking for basic toolroom equipment. Finding most of what they needed in a newspaper classified ad, they hauled their inventory in an old pickup truck and later spent their Saturdays painting it.

Boersma and VanVels still needed a tryout press before they could open. Because presses are costly, the two expected opening to be delayed. However, a chance drive led them to exactly what they needed. "We were out driving one day and passed a local die shop where we noticed an old clunker press sitting outside," explains Boersma. "We bought the thing for practically nothing and had an excavator haul it over to our

shop. Suddenly, we realized we had the equipment, so there wasn't anything standing in our way. We were in business."

Boersma intended to keep his night job while making sales calls for the new business during the day. Almost immediately, customer contracts started coming in, and after only three months, he quit the night job and joined VanVels full-time. By the end of the first year, business had grown so rapidly—thanks to word-of-mouth advertising from satisfied customers—that the two had hired 15 employees. "We had to hire people fast in order to keep up with the work coming in," Boersma says. "When you do a good job for people and you treat them fairly, it doesn't take long for word to get around. Most of our business has always been repeat business."

TOOLING SYSTEMS GROUP

The success of ATS in the 1980s led the way for ETS and MTS in the 1990s. ATS builds medium to large sheet metal stamping dies; ETS builds small to medium sheet metal stamping dies; and MTS specializes in zinc die castings, plastic injection molds, and hydroforming, an innovative process that uses high-pressure water to inflate steel tubes. While each company operates as an independent corporation, they share resources whenever possible in order to maximize efficiency. A key ingredient for the success of the new divisions has been on-site managing partners at each company—Dan Van Enk at MTS and Jim Grotenrath at ETS.

TSG customers are primarily first-tier automotive suppliers, or companies that supply fenders, floorboards, dashboards, door components, and shifter knobs to the automobile industry. The group also supplies dies directly to the

Mold Tooling Systems, a division of Tooling Systems Group, moved into its new facility in 1997, and has more than 16,000 square feet of manufacturing space to produce injection molds, die cast dies, and hydroform dies.

Engineered Tooling Systems is currently the newest member of the Tooling Systems Group, and builds sheet metal progressive and line dies.

furniture industry for making parts such as table legs, seat components, and desktop brackets, as well as various dies and molds for appliance manufacturers.

THE TEAM

Boersma and VanVels are related by marriage, and a strong sense of family permeates the entire company. "When someone asks us about our greatest asset, I automatically tell them about our people," Boersma says. "Our employees are an outstanding bunch—the backbone of our business. We spend a lot of time nurturing our relationships with them. At most larger tool and die shops, the management team is isolated, and has very little to do with employees. It couldn't be more different here."

TSG encourages teamwork both on and off the job. Boersma and VanVels say that being involved with employees on a personal level helps enhance relationships and keeps the group cohesive. Many employees team up to play softball, basketball, and hockey, as well as to participate in the company golf league.

AN EYE ON TECHNOLOGY

The TSG companies are committed to remaining abreast of the latest technology and investing in the resources necessary to stay

at the top of their industry. All designs are done by computer, and the company has key employees in the CAD/CAM (computer-aided design/computer-aided manufacturing) areas who continuously research and make recommendations about technology. "In our field," says Boersma, "technology is key, and we're prepared to make whatever investments we need to stay current. We send our employees to national trade shows and encourage them to join user groups. They really know what's going on out there, and when they come to us with ideas and recommendations, we listen."

Word of TSG's technical expertise and capabilities has spread, and business is coming in through

new channels. The group has had major automakers suggest to their first-tier suppliers that they turn to TSG for their dies and injection molds.

Boersma and VanVels say they're sometimes astounded at the growth they've achieved, which averages about 15 to 20 percent per year. The company has come a long way since 1982, when the goal was to have 20 or 30 employees and enough money to pay the bills and put food on the table. TSG's goal for the future is steady, managed growth; continued dedication to employees; and 100 percent customer satisfaction. "We've been blessed," says Boersma, "and with God's help, we'll continue to be successful in the future."

Clockwise from top left: At Advanced Tooling Systems, cranes up to 25 tons are utilized to move dies to computer-controlled mills or to load a truck for shipping.

CNC (computer numerically controlled) mills are an integral part of the tool and die industry, and Advanced Tooling Systems, Inc. has six.

The Advanced Tooling Systems tractor/trailer travels through many of the eastern states. The truck is utilized by all of the members of the Tooling Systems Group for enhanced delivery to the customer.

DAVE RASMUSSEN HAS NO DOUBTS ABOUT THE CURRENT STATE of U.S. manufacturing. The Progressive Die & Automation (PD&A) president is adamant about the importance of manufacturing in the U.S. economy, and in just 15 years, he has catapulted his tool and die business to the very top

of the industry. When Rasmussen bought the company in 1983, there were 18 employees and less than $1 million in annual sales volume. Today, there are two separate companies, a total of 240 people, and more than $32 million in sales.

TWO COMPANIES, TWO SPECIALTIES

PD&A's specialty is designing and building sheet metal stamping dies, which are used to stamp or shape metal into car parts such as brackets, shields, seats, or trunk components. As much as 80 percent of the company's business is supplying these dies to first-tier automotive suppliers, which manufacture parts for major automobile makers. The company also serves several major appliance manufacturers, and its prototype division is involved in some rather unique projects.

PD&A's sister company, Quality Die & Mold Corporation (QD&M), was purchased in 1996 with the intent of creating a full-service supplier to the larger tier-one companies. QD&M designs and builds plastic injection molds used to make plastic, rubber, and other nonmetal parts. As with PD&A, QD&M's primary customers are first-tier automotive suppliers, but the company also supplies molds to office furniture manufacturers, consumer products manufacturers, and toy companies.

THRIVING ON CHALLENGES

The aggressive nature of PD&A sets it apart from the competition, and Rasmussen pursues large, complex projects. This enterprising attitude was a definite factor in landing a $7.5 million project with Johnson Controls, the larg-

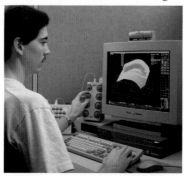

est maker of automobile seats in the world and the exclusive supplier of seats for the resurrected Volkswagen Beetle, which will be produced in Mexico in 1998. Based on several criteria, Johnson wanted to find a single supplier to develop and manufacture the dies, as well as to manage the entire tooling program.

"Because of all the safety and strength issues, automobile seats are made up of many parts," says Rasmussen. "A variety of stamping dies are needed to manufacture them. Johnson turned the whole project over to us for several reasons. Our engineering, manufacturing, and project management capabilities were to a level that gave us the ability to handle the complete project. We took much

From its headquarters in Grand Rapids, Progressive Die & Automation, Inc. has catapulted to the top of its industry through its commitment to CAD/CAM technology, a clean working environment with wire E.D.M., and large CNC capabilities on a bridge mill.

of the burden off their shoulders, which saved time and kept costs down."

PD&A also played a key role in the initial production run of the Saturn automobile. In the late 1980s, when manufacturing began, PD&A was awarded tooling contracts for approximately 50 separate parts.

AN ATYPICAL ENVIRONMENT
PD&A doesn't look like a typical tool and die shop. The offices are beautifully decorated, and the plant itself is extremely clean, with glossy, painted floors; plenty of lighting; and an organized work flow. Rasmussen's intention is to create a work environment of which his employees can be proud. This applies not only to aesthetics, but also to PD&A's philosophy, which is one of shared responsibility, employee empowerment, and trust. Consequently, turnover is extremely low, and in the history of the company, no employee has ever been laid off.

The company has made significant investments in new technology and has always been willing to accept risks and tackle new challenges. In 1986, drafting boards were removed from the building when PD&A made a total commitment to developing all its dies using computer-aided design (CAD) and computer-aided manufacturing (CAM) technology. This sort of forward thinking keeps PD&A in touch with the latest technological advancements, and has made the company a highly respected leader in the tool and die industry.

LOOKING AHEAD
Since Progressive Die & Automation was formed, it has experienced steady and continuous growth, and Rasmussen says he expects this to continue. The company is targeting markets outside the United States, particularly in areas projected to see large increases in automotive business, such as Mexico, India, South America, and China. Through his active involvement with the National Tool and Machining Association (NTMA), Rasmussen is constantly in touch with both national and

international trends in the tool and die business. Slated to become the NTMA chairman of the board in 1999, Rasmussen will represent the association and the trade.

Rasmussen sees a bright future for PD&A and QD&M, and the role they play in the U.S. economy. "Manufacturing is the backbone of America," he says. "It's what built this country, and what made it great. Manufacturing is a vital part of our economy, and we have everything to gain by making sure it stays here and remains healthy."

PD&A succeeds largely through teamwork with employee involvement in the decision making process.

PD&A has made significant investments in new technology and has always been willing to accept risks and tackle new challenges.

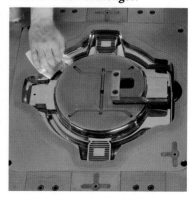

THE CRAFTSMEN WHO MAKE SPECIALIZED PRODUCTS FROM wood—such as dining room furniture, a gleaming boardroom conference table, ready-to-assemble office and residential furniture, and kitchen cabinets—depend on sophisticated precision tooling to do their jobs. They need the highest-quality

tooling available to render the best results in their woodworking, and for this, most turn to Leitz Tooling Systems, Inc.

Leitz manufactures a wide variety of precision industrial carbide-tipped and diamond tools, from saw blades to router bits to insert tooling for all types of industrial processing machinery. All Leitz tools are manufactured in accordance with stringent German safety standards, using sophisticated machines for manufacturing efficiency and to ensure the highest possible quality. Leitz continuously analyzes ways to improve such things as user friendliness, safety, tooling accuracy, and cost-effectiveness.

Leitz USA is a division of the Leitz Group, which is headquartered in Oberkochen, Germany, and is the world's largest manufacturer of tooling for the woodworking industry. Since the parent company's founding more than 120 years ago, it has continued to specialize in the development and manufacture of precision tooling, for all segments of the woodworking industry.

BRANCHING OUT

The decision to open a branch of Leitz Tooling Systems in Grand Rapids—the company's first entry into the U.S. market—came in April 1984. Since Grand Rapids has always been known as "the

furniture city," it seemed natural for the company to establish itself locally. Today, the Grand Rapids Leitz facility provides tooling systems for manufacturers in all segments of the woodworking industry, including residential and office furniture, boats, hardwood and laminate flooring, custom kitchen and bath cabinets, and almost anything else that is made from wood.

Since the company first moved here, Leitz has opened 10 other locations around the United States and one in Canada. These branch locations, called service centers, operate as regional sales offices and service facilities for resharpening tooling.

SERVICE BEYOND THE SALE

Terry Jacks, Leitz Tooling Systems president, says the company excels by providing customers with specialized support both during and after the sale. "Most tooling companies who primarily distribute tooling do not understand proper sharpening techniques and won't make the necessary investments in sophisticated machinery to do the job correctly," Jacks says. "We back our tooling 100 percent, with precision resharpening processes that guarantee the

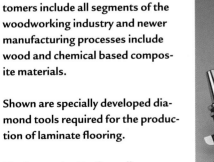

Clockwise from top:
Leitz Tooling Systems, Inc., located on Grand Rapids' southeast side, manufactures high quality "tooling solutions" for customers throughout North America. Current customers include all segments of the woodworking industry and newer manufacturing processes include wood and chemical based composite materials.

Shown are specially developed diamond tools required for the production of laminate flooring.

The innovative Profix tooling system utilizes interchangeable carbide tipped knives that can be used on moulders, routers, shapers or tenoners.

tools will perform exactly the same way they did when they were new."

Jacks says it is the company's goal to work with customers as early as possible in the selection of a new machining process. "The industry considers us consultants, not just salespeople," he says. "Customers make huge investments in expensive machinery, but without the correct tooling concept, that machinery will not function efficiently. We can make the entire system work that much better by providing the best tooling solution possible, right from the beginning."

For an example of this service, Jacks points to a major laminate flooring manufacturer located in Washington State. The manufacturer approached Leitz early in the process design, asking for advice regarding problems that arise due to the complex nature of its product. The protective overlay materials used in laminate flooring are highly abrasive, which dulls the tooling very quickly. Leitz evaluated the company's proposed manufacturing process and encouraged it to reconfigure the machine to allow for a much more efficient tooling solution.

"People who don't involve us early enough can make terrible mistakes with tooling configurations," Jacks says. "When the product can't be cut precisely, the customer ends up with a very low quality, expensive product." Leitz's early involvement saved the laminate flooring company several hundred thou-

sand dollars in the long run and dramatically improved product output. Jacks says the company has been thrilled with the results that Leitz helped it achieve.

Closing the Gap

Leitz USA imports tooling from five manufacturing plants in Germany and Austria. Each Leitz facility produces specialized products for individual market segments. This specialization focuses energy and resources for the most cost-effective tooling solutions for tomorrow's manufacturing.

Lower-volume, quick-delivery products like profiled inserts, custom carbide-tipped tools, and polycrystalline diamond tools are produced in Grand Rapids. The same manufacturing machinery and standards are used in the United States as in Europe. Various CNC and EDM machines are utilized in the manufacturing process to provide the necessary

product quality as well as versatility. The flexibility of this production plant allows custom tools, from simple to sophisticated, to be manufactured to meet customers' demanding delivery schedules.

Sales in the United States have grown dramatically since Leitz first located in Grand Rapids, and the number of employees has doubled over the past four years. The company has plans to continue opening additional service centers in other locations around the country. Yet Jacks says no matter how large the company gets, the focus will still be on quality, both in tooling and in relationships formed with customers. "Our slogan is 'the worldwide leader in tooling solutions,' because there's a big difference between just selling tools and providing solutions. We want to be perceived as a tooling partner, not just a tooling vendor. We consider that the very best measure of our success," says Jacks.

Clockwise from top left: All Leitz service centers utilize computer controlled sharpening machines to recondition sawblades to original specifications.

A comparator, capable of measuring to one-thousandth of a millimeter, is used to check the profile integrity of a carbide tipped tool manufactured in Grand Rapids.

State-of-the-art electronic discharge machines are utilized to manufacture and service polycrystalline diamond tooling.

NE QUALITY THAT A RADIO STATION NEEDS MORE THAN any other is the ability to adapt to constant change. And few have had to cope with as much change as Grand Rapids' Rock Network, WKLQ/WLAV/WBBL. What these three stations have in common—besides the same parent company, Michigan Media, Inc.—are the radical changes they've experienced since 1993. Yet, in spite of these changes—or maybe even because of them—the stations are stronger than ever, with ratings that continue to climb.

WKLQ ARRIVES IN TOWN

On March 1, 1984, Bloomington Broadcasting Corporation, Michigan Media's predecessor, established a new radio station in Grand Rapids with the call letters WKLQ. Its original format was pop music, also known as Top 40, which primarily attracted the 18- to 34- year-old market. In 1990, after six years of continued ratings success, station management decided to compete directly with station WLAV by switching to an album-oriented rock (AOR) format.

According to Bart Brandmiller, president and general manager, this was a bold move. "WLAV had essentially owned the AOR market since the 1970s," he says, "and we literally took it away from them. It's just one example of how fast things can change in radio." The AOR format became successful for WKLQ, making it one of the most popular stations in Grand Rapids.

In 1994, Michigan Media, as the company was now known, bought out the competition, acquiring WLAV and filling a niche that had been sorely lacking in the Grand Rapids market by focusing the station on classic rock. Simultaneously, WLAV-AM changed its call letters to WBBL and became Grand Rapids' first 24-hour, all-sports station. The Michigan Media Rock Network had been formed.

THE ROCK NETWORK FOCUS

Brandmiller says it's the stations' priority to cater to the public. "The more we understand what listeners want, the better we can serve them," he says. "We're very focused on that. I think this is one of our greatest strengths, and it's also one of the biggest reasons we've been so successful."

Just as important as pleasing listeners is building strong bonds with advertisers. "We let our advertisers know up front that it's our purpose to do a whole lot more than just sell commercials," says Brandmiller. "We want to work with customers to help them grow their businesses."

Brandmiller admits that pleasing both the listening audience and advertisers can be a challenge. "And although this is often a delicate balance, it's necessary in order to be successful," he says.

AGGRESSIVE AND DARING

When WKLQ lost its popular morning show to a competitor, it was perhaps the station's biggest test of coping with the change inherent in the world of radio. Brandmiller admits that at first it was tough. "In this business, we build strong bonds with our listeners," he says, "and listeners become very loyal. When something they've become accustomed

The Rock Network sponsors a wide variety of community events.

WLAV's Blues on the Mall starts every June and is a regular Grand Rapids happening on Wednesday nights through August, often attracting as many as 6,000 to 7,000 fans.

to changes, they react, and not always positively. When that happens, we have to be ready to react to their concerns—fast."

Within a few months, WKLQ's new morning show was the popular and controversial *Howard Stern Show* from New York. Brandmiller talks about Grand Rapids' reaction: "We actually talked to many people before bringing the show to town, and we continue to monitor the public's reaction today. What we've discovered is that even though Grand Rapids is known for being conservative, it's not as ultraconservative as people think. Howard's show is controversial, but people really do like it, and the ratings have been excellent."

Summer in the City

Thanks to WLAV, on a summer night in the center of downtown Grand Rapids, a person can hear Chicago-style blues music. The station's Blues on the Mall starts every June and is a regular Grand Rapids happening on Wednesday nights through August, often attracting as many as 6,000 to 7,000 fans. And on another night during the summer in Grand Rapids, courtesy of WKLQ, people can hang out downtown and listen to the sounds of a live alternative rock band. Summerstock is a weekly series of free downtown concerts, featuring up-and-coming national bands who are usually promoting a new recording.

What's Next?

The stations constantly look for new ways to monitor what listeners want, and one way to do this is with preferred listener cards. WLAV's VIP Card and WKLQ's Player Card allow listeners to qualify for premiums and free merchandise, get special seating for concerts, and benefit from other perks. For the stations, these cards mean better tracking of listener information. "In the old days," Brandmiller says, "listeners would fill out forms that sat in big plastic bags, and the information never got used. This new, high-tech system allows us to create a database of our listeners, so we can monitor who they are, and know their preferences. It's a tremendous way to keep in touch with our listening audience."

Staying in touch with listeners is the stations' key to future success. "What it boils down to is, our product is free—all listeners have to do is push a button to turn us off," Brandmiller says. "So we're very aware that their concerns and interests are what we have to cater to. We've been doing that all along. And we intend to keep getting better in the future."

On summer nights in Grand Rapids, courtesy of WKLQ, people can hang out downtown and listen to the sounds of a live alternative rock band. Summerstock, a weekly series of free downtown concerts, features up-and-coming national bands who are usually promoting a new recording.

FOR PEOPLE WHO LIVE IN MICHIGAN, DRIVING IN THE WINTER CAN be a major challenge. The roads are often snow covered and slippery, and over the course of the season, massive amounts of salt are dumped onto roads to keep them clear. But for vehicles, the salt can be deadly—voraciously eating away at

a car's finish, and causing rust and corrosion within a matter of days. Fortunately, there's an answer to this problem in the form of electro-deposition coating, or E-Coat. And this is the specialty of a Grand Rapids company called Spectrum Industries Inc. For more than 15 years, Spectrum has led the industry in this innovative process that protectively coats the metal parts of automobiles, and helps them withstand harsh climates by providing a superb barrier against rust and corrosion.

A COMPANY THAT'S GROWN FAST

With a background in the tool and die industry, Jay Bassett began his entrepreneurial ventures by starting his own tool and die shop in a garage with equipment he'd purchased and rebuilt himself. While attend-

ing Ferris State University, Bassett discovered he had a natural talent for engineering, and as his tool and die business continued to grow, he began to do his own design work as well. In 1979, Bassett founded another business, a small manufacturing company, to make steel shelving for Revco, which later bought the company from him. In 1983, Bassett sold his tool and die business, and turned to a new venture.

When Bassett first started Spectrum in 1984, he had 40,000 square feet of space, 30 employees, and first-year sales of approximately $300,000. Today, his company has three plants devoted exclusively to E-Coat: two in Grand Rapids and one in Belding, Michigan. The Grand Rapids plant alone has 130,000 square feet, and has gone through

five separate renovations to create additional space. The three plants together have more than 400,000 square feet, and companywide, Spectrum has 430 employees and total annual sales of $32 million.

The E-Coat process is truly state-of-the-art technology. Developed originally as a primer, E-Coat can function as either a primer or a finish coat, and conforms to complex parts so well that it provides a superior finish anywhere it's applied. A water-based coating, E-Coat is not sprayed on, but is applied by dipping the parts into a paint bath, which is electrically charged so the paint solids are attracted to and adhere to the metal surface. The dipping process results in a uniform paint thickness with minimal waste, and also allows the coating to cover hard-to-reach areas, which

Both the new corporate headquarters for Spectrum Industries Inc. and the home of the flagship plant for the Electrodeposition Division are located in this facility on Plymouth Avenue Northeast.

means superior resistance to corrosion and humidity.

A Niche in Cubic Finishing

In 1992, Spectrum Industries branched into another process called Cubic finishing, the decorative painting process used primarily to create a wood-grain effect in automobile interiors, but also used for many other patterns on a wide range of materials. The process had originally been developed by Cubic, the Japanese company that invented it. Today, the company has two Grand Rapids plants and 100,000 square feet devoted exclusively to Cubic finishing.

Using the Cubic process in automobile interiors enables designers to use less expensive and more versatile materials to a greater advantage. Injection-molded plastic with a burled wood finish adds richness and depth to an automobile's interior, but at a fraction of the cost of real wood.

A Team That Makes the Difference

Spectrum Industries uses a unique team concept in its work environment that Bassett says has been extremely effective for the company. "About five years ago, we started the team concept," he says, "and we've been able to improve our customer service immensely because of it. By using teams, everyone takes a personal responsibility for their own work and a personal responsibility for satisfying the customer—sort of like smaller companies within the company. I'm definitely convinced this has been great for our business all around."

Each Spectrum customer is assigned a specific team composed of three to five people who run their own operation, make decisions autonomously, and work exclusively with that customer. The teams meet with customers on a regular basis both at Spectrum and at customer plants, and become familiar with the customers' particular parts, needs, and quality requirements, ensuring a higher level of service through their in-depth knowledge.

Bassett also says the company has a Points for Defects program, which is an incentive for team mem-

Directing the company is the executive committee composed of I. Jay Bassett, president and founder (seated), and his sons Kevin Bassett, vice president of the Spectrum Cubic operations (left), and Keith Bassett, vice president of the Electrodeposition operations (right).

Additional members of the executive committee are (from left) Jim Douma, controller; Pat Cannon, marketing manager; and Tim Braniff, facilities director.

bers to keep quality levels high. Employees scrutinize parts that come in from customers—usually tier-one automotive suppliers—and identify defects before the parts make their way to the line for coating. Then, about every 60 days, prizes are awarded to employees based on the number of points they've accumulated.

Bassett says there's plenty of potential for Spectrum Industries in the future, particularly with the Cubic process. "We're a team-oriented company that's focused on the customer," Bassett continues, "and with both our E-Coat and Cubic operations, we've proved that we're committed to investing in the people and technologies necessary to remain a leader in our industry. In the future, we anticipate more growth and expanded capabilities to serve our customers even better than we do now."

T IS A PEACEFUL PLACE, QUIET AND SERENE, WITH A CREEK THAT winds throughout the property. The surrounding 200 acres of wooded land are filled with tulips and daffodils in the spring and a medley of colorful wildflowers in the summer. There is a small, private lake that is ideal for fishing and trails that are perfect for

biking, cross-country skiing, or simply walking through the woods. Wildlife is abundant and includes rabbit, raccoon, ducks, geese, and a variety of birds—including snowbirds. This is a place where people feel very much at home and sometimes don't want to leave. It is Ramblewood Executive Suites, located just minutes from the heart of downtown Grand Rapids.

BUSINESS TRAVELER'S HAVEN

For people who travel often, being away from home for long stretches of time can be both tiring and stressful. And as any business traveler knows, staying in hotels and living out of a suitcase gets old very quickly. Ramblewood Executive Suites offers guests an attractive and comfortable alternative to hotel living: spacious, fully furnished one- and two-bedroom apartments located amid beautiful natural surroundings.

Guests at Ramblewood Executive Suites enjoy such amenities as full kitchens, weekly maid service, convenient laundry facilities, complimentary continental breakfast, and use of a 55,000-square-foot

health club that features both indoor and outdoor tennis courts and a full fitness center with indoor pool. There's also a junior Olympic-sized outdoor pool and the poolside Splash Cafe, where guests can relax with a sandwich and an ice-cold drink.

HOW IT BEGAN

Ramblewood was originally built in 1970 by a group of developers whose goal was to design and build attractive, high-quality apartments and town homes that complemented the area's natural surroundings. The Ramblewood community continued to prosper through consistent growth and expansion. As the need increased for both short- and long-term business accommodations, Ramblewood developers began planning another kind of expansion that would offer a more desirable and comfortable alter-

Clockwise from top: Ramblewood Executive Suites is not a temporary home, but an award-winning lifestyle full of activities for those passing through.

Nancy Lane (left) and Rita Garton are professionals in catering to Ramblewood's distinguished Executive Suites guests.

Ramblewood has 82 executive suites set in a peaceful and serene wooded area available with private entrances and fireplaces.

native to hotel living for nearby corporations and business travelers. Ramblewood Executive Suites was formed in 1985 with a total of 55 suites, and today this number has grown to 82. Occupancy has consistently been high, with an average guest occupancy rate of more than 93 percent.

CUSTOMER DIVERSITY

According to Nancy Lane, Ramblewood's leasing and marketing director, a typical customer is generally someone who visits as a guest of a Grand Rapids company, or business travelers staying in Grand Rapids for extended periods of time. "We've hosted business guests from all over the world," Lane says. "People come to us from places like Great Britain, Japan, Germany, and India. We've had diplomats from Nigeria and engineers from Saudi Arabia and China. And as for the United States, we've had chocolate salesmen from Nestlé, buyers from a carrot company, and salespeople from Sara Lee and Coca-Cola. And we've had some pretty famous guests, too— but I can't say who they were."

Lane says the guest roster isn't always limited to business travelers. "We sometimes have people staying with us who need temporary lodging, such as those whose homes are being repaired after a fire," she says. "And then there's also our group of regular summer residents who return year after year. We call them snowbirds, because they're seniors who have made their per-

manent homes in warmer places, like Florida, and who return to Michigan for the summer. They come back to visit with their children and grandchildren, and also to escape the Florida heat."

SERVICE EMPHASIS

With all the amenities Ramblewood Executive Suites has to offer, the staff still consider excellent service by far their highest priority. "We want our guests to feel perfectly at home, and to keep coming back," Lane says, "so we always go the extra mile for them." Whatever guests need—from transportation advice to directions to a list of the city's best restaurants—the Ramblewood staff are available to help find the answer. "We may not immediately have all the answers to our guests' questions," Lane says, "but we won't stop looking until we find what they need. We pride ourselves on that level of service."

As for the future, there's plenty on the horizon for Ramblewood Executive Suites. Plans include increasing the number of suites to 100 or more; attracting more guests who stay on a daily basis, in addition to those who stay for the longer term; and expanding services such as housekeeping and technology accommodations. But Lane emphasizes that Ramblewood's most important goal for the future is to continuously provide even higher levels of service. "Quite simply, our whole reason for being here is to serve our guests, and it's essential that we constantly remain focused on them. If we do that, then our priorities are in order. And everything else will fall into place."

With the kind of growth Ramblewood has experienced so far, and the phenomenal success it has achieved over the years, the future looks incredibly bright.

Clockwise from top left:
The executive cottage has a Jacuzzi, washer/dryer, and private yard area.

Indoor and outdoor swimming are only a portion of the many amenities available at Ramblewood's 55,000-square-foot tennis and health club.

The executive suites are tastefully furnished to provide all the comfort and convenience of home.

T ONLY TAKES A FEW MINUTES WITH BIRGIT KLOHS TO BECOME CON-vinced of what a healthy, thriving city Grand Rapids is. As president of The Right Place Program, Klohs heads up an organization having the sole function of keeping businesses as well as attracting them to the community. "Grand Rapids is a business-oriented city with a

strong work ethic, excellent people, and support from the community that is second to none," she says. "This is a first-class city, for a variety of reasons. I strongly believe there are many opportunities to be successful here."

CREATED BY BUSINESS, FOR BUSINESS

The Right Place Program was created in 1985 by a group of business and community leaders who were committed to improving the economic prosperity of this community. At that time, the unemployment rate in Michigan was hovering around 17 percent with Grand Rapids' unemployment at 10 percent, and it became apparent that in order for the area to once again thrive, a focused economic development strategy was needed.

The group put together a strategic plan, the result of which was the formation of The Right Place Program. And since the organization was formed, it has had a profound impact on the economic vitality of this community: Over the past 10 years, Grand Rapids' unemployment rate has dropped to slightly more than 3 percent—the

One of Grand Rapids' many, successful, family-owned businesses, Nicholas Plastics continues to grow and make investments in the area.

Continuous growth over the past decade has placed Lacks Enterprises among the 12 largest manufacturers in Kent County, with more than $210 million in annual sales and an employee base of nearly 1,750 (left).

The Rapistan Systems Technology Center serves as a development and test facility for new material-handling system products and software (right).

lowest it's been in 24 years. The number of jobs has risen by 38.4 percent, with 17.5 percent of those in the manufacturing sector.

The mission of The Right Place Program is to "develop opportunities for economic growth in areas of quality employment, productivity, and technology in Greater Grand Rapids through leading business expansion, retention, and attraction efforts." Working primarily with local manufacturers, the organization's 16 employees regularly call on 40 to 50 companies per month.

Klohs says The Right Place focuses on these manufacturing

companies because they're the community's economic base. "Grand Rapids is an extremely strong manufacturing community," she says. "People may not realize it, but nearly 29 percent of our jobs here are in manufacturing, which is twice the national average. We're committed to keeping these businesses here in this community, and helping them continue to thrive."

The Right Place Program helps its customers by providing them with continuous support—assessing their needs and working with them on future plans, as well as offering assistance if the compa-

nies are planning an expansion and need a new building, want to remodel an existing facility, need to hire additional employees, are facing tax abatement or zoning issues, or just about any other needs the companies might have.

"We consider ourselves a 'first call for help' for our customers," says Klohs. "It's our goal to regularly keep in touch with them and offer them enough support so they'll have an incentive to stay here. Because we were created by business for business, our approach is very customer focused."

AGGRESSIVE MARKETING

In addition to ongoing customer support, another important function of The Right Place Program is regular marketing of Grand Rapids, not only to domestic companies who are considering expanding here, but also to international companies. "We are very systematic about getting in front of these customers," says Klohs. "We don't do mass anything—we carefully target the customers we want to entice to come here according to the kind of industry and/or products they make, and how well the company would fit within our community." The Right Place Program staff regularly conducts seminars in countries outside the United States, as well as attending focused trade shows, an approach that has been very successful.

The competition faced by Klohs and her staff is enormous, as touring teams from other states regularly come to Grand Rapids seeking to entice local businesses to relocate elsewhere. That's why The Right Place Program concentrates its efforts on building and nurturing relationships with Grand Rapids' businesses.

"We regularly call on our customers and say to them, 'Look, if you're planning an expansion, and you have customers elsewhere, we want you to at least turn to us for the facts so you can comparison shop, and see what we can do for you,'" says Klohs. "We have strong relationships with more than 1,000 manufacturers in Kent County, and it's our priority to keep those relationships healthy and strong, and to keep those businesses right here in our own community. We want them to trust us and let us know when they need help.

I think it's this person-to-person approach that really makes the difference."

THE FUTURE

Klohs says The Right Place Program will continue working to keep Grand Rapids economically strong as a world-class manufacturing center. "This community is very fortunate to have such a strong business base with such a high number of manufacturing companies," she says. "In good times, we might tend to take these businesses for granted, but we should never forget that they always have a choice to locate somewhere else. We're now economically very healthy and prosperous. It will continue to be the mission of The Right Place Program to keep it that way, well into the future."

Clockwise from top left: American Seating Company, a local manufacturer of auditorium and transportation seating along with office and laboratory furniture, supplied a large portion of the public seating used in the new Van Andel Arena in Grand Rapids.

Amway's wide array of products includes a complete line of skin care and cosmetics; nutrition and wellness products; a complete home care line; and home tech products, including a high-quality water treatment system and a complete line of stainless steel cookware. These products are manufactured at Amway's World Headquarters, which now stretches for more than a mile on its original site in Ada.

Behr Industries Corporation, a German supplier of interior wood parts for luxury automobiles, chose Grand Rapids for its first U.S. location.

WITH ALL THE COMMERCIAL REAL ESTATE COMPANIES around, it is not easy to be the best. It takes such qualities as years of experience, extensive education, solid commitment to superior customer service, high qualifications, a professional staff, and the willingness to work hard for clients no matter how large or how small the project. To Stan Wisinski, these qualities are second nature, and this type of thinking has earned S.J. Wisinski & Company the distinction of being the largest commercial, industrial, and investment real estate firm in West Michigan, with exclusive property listings of more than $200 million annually.

Wisinski, the company's founder and president, says he can hardly remember a time when he wasn't in real estate. At the age of 20, while a liberal arts and business student at Aquinas College, he felt he needed to focus on a career. "I started talking to people, and the subject of real estate kept coming up. I found it interesting, and started investigating. I liked it and just kept going."

Wisinski earned his real estate license in 1960 and joined the Westdale Company. After working in residential real estate for four years, he moved to commercial real estate, founding Westdale Commercial Investment Company. He formed S.J. Wisinski & Company in January 1986. From the very beginning, this new business venture flourished. Less than a year later, it ranked as one of Grand Rapids' largest commercial, industrial, and investment real estate firms.

Wisinski says he has no secret for success other than hard work, commitment, and dedication. "When I decided on real estate as a career," he says, "I made a commitment to learn the business from A to Z, and to continue learning as much as possible. That's still my philosophy after all these years."

Clockwise from top:
In order to deal with the complex nature of commercial real estate, S.J. Wisinski & Company forms long-standing relationships with clients, gaining a thorough understanding of their businesses.

The company has earned the distinction of being the largest commercial, industrial, and investment real estate firm in West Michigan, with exclusive property listings of more than $200 million annually.

Stan Wisinski says, "I believe our facility is an important part of our image."

DIVERSE SERVICES FOR LONG-TERM CLIENTS

S.J. Wisinski & Company is a full-service brokerage company specializing in the sales, leasing, and site selection of commercial, industrial, and office properties throughout West Michigan. The company markets vacant land, existing structures, conversions, new construction, and build-to-suit properties. Since the company has focused on brokerage, and not development, it has established a strong relationship with many local, regional, and national developers in the provision of real estate services. S.J. Wisinski & Company also offers complete property management services.

In order to deal with the complex nature of commercial real estate, the company forms long-standing relationships with clients, gaining a thorough understanding of their businesses. To accomplish this, Wisinski's 30 licensed brokers are highly qualified, trained specialists. More than two-thirds of the firm's brokers have been in the commercial and industrial real estate business longer than 10 years—some for as many as 35 years. They thoroughly understand the market, from the most relevant statistics to the premier properties to environmental concerns and requirements. The brokers have an in-depth knowledge of the community and know what it takes to bring buyers, sellers, owners, tenants, lenders, and investors together.

Wisinski himself is an example of the best in the business. He received the Society of Industrial and Office Realtors (SIOR) designation, and was the first in the state to receive the dual industrial/office designation from that organization. He also holds the Certified Commercial Investment Member (CCIM) designation, and was the first person in West Michigan to receive this designation. He has won a Distinguished Sales Award from the Sales and Marketing Executive Club of Grand Rapids, has been voted Realtor of

the Year by the Grand Rapids Real Estate Board, has won the Society of Distinguished Real Estate Professionals Award from the Grand Rapids Real Estate Board, and was formerly named Michigan Commercial Realtor of the Year. His name has appeared in *Who's Who in America, Who's Who in Finance and Industry in America,* and *Who's Who in the World.*

THE RIGHT IMAGE

Wisinski believes that a polished, professional image is important in commercial real estate because it sends a positive message to clients. This concept was kept in mind in the design of the company's headquarters, located on East Paris Road just north of 28th Street. The 11,200-square-foot building features an abundance of win-

dows and skylights. Wisinski says, "Clients who visit the company often comment on the building and its uniqueness." It manages to tastefully attract the right kind of attention. He says, "I believe our facility is an important part of our image."

With the tremendous growth that is occurring in and around Grand Rapids, Wisinski sees many opportunities ahead and expects continued growth for his company. "We're excited about our business and the future," he says. "As Grand Rapids and the lakeshore communities grow closer together, this area will continue to grow and prosper. We're excited to be a part of it all, and plan to continue providing the absolute best in commercial and industrial brokerage services."

Clockwise from top:
Weekly sales meetings offer the opportunity to share market information.

Hard work, commitment, and the dedication of sales associates and their support staff helped make the company a success.

S.J. Wisinski & Company believes that a polished, professional image is important in commercial real estate because it sends a positive message to clients.

TECHNOLOGICAL LEADERSHIP, WORLD-CLASS QUALITY, AND A totally integrated involvement with customers. These are lofty objectives for any company, but they're a way of life at Paulstra CRC. In fact, they're at the heart of the company's business philosophy, and a primary reason that Paulstra has become one of the world's leading suppliers of antivibration products for automotive giants such as Ford, General Motors, and Mercedes-Benz.

AN INTERESTING HISTORY

Paulstra CRC's parent company is Paris, France-based Hutchinson, a world leader in rubber manufacturing with more than 18,000 employees and $2 billion in annual sales. The company's story actually begins with Hiram Hutchinson, an American businessman who traveled to France in 1850 and started a large rubber product factory near Paris. Originally named the Compagnie du Caoutchouc Souple (Flexible Rubber Company), the company's name was later changed to A. Hutchinson et Compagnie, and then shortened years later to Hutchinson.

Hutchinson's original business was manufacturing boots, shoes, and clogs, and by 1857, production had reached 14,000 pairs per day. New rubber items continued to be added to the product line—such as hoses, tubes, and mats—and during the same time, Hutchinson expanded its European presence by opening a plant in Germany. The company also began developing products for customers in the United States. Through the years that followed, Hutchinson continued to grow and expand, with additional products being added and other factories being opened in Europe. In 1910, the company developed the first balloon fabric for airships, and for many years, Hutchinson was alone in mastering the manufacture of this fabric. In the late 1940s, Hutchinson began importing machinery from the United States and, throughout the ensuing decade, further expanded its manufacturing to include highly resistant rubber hoses.

ACQUISITION OF PAULSTRA

In 1974, in an effort to strengthen its position in technical industrial markets, Hutchinson acquired Paulstra, a French company that specialized in rubber-bonded engine mounts for the aircraft industry. As the company's business began shifting more toward the automotive industry, Paulstra began developing antivibration technologies for use on automobile engines that closely resembled those used on aircraft engines.

In the mid-1980s, at Ford Motor Company's request, Paulstra began to develop hydraulic mount technology for select Ford vehicles manufactured in North America.

The company's three tech centers— two in France and one in Grand Rapids—are staffed by highly qualified and talented metallurgical, rubber, and electrical engineers who are devoted to researching and developing technology to keep Paulstra CRC on the leading edge of its industry.

It was during this time that the company saw an opportunity to further strengthen its relationships with North American customers, and in 1986, Paulstra set up its first U.S. operations by acquiring the assets of Grand Rapids-based Corduroy Rubber Company, which it renamed Paulstra CRC.

According to Yves Huet, Paulstra CRC's president and CEO, purchasing the Grand Rapids company was an important and strategic move for Paulstra. "When we decided to establish operations here in the United States," he says, "our decision to purchase the assets of Corduroy Rubber Company was based on the fact that it was already making antivibration products, as well as a variety of other rubber products, and was very experienced in this industry. But another important factor in our decision was the employees, who were—and are—a group of very motivated and highly skilled people who are a tremendous asset to our company. This is a team of very dedicated people, who are the key to Paulstra CRC's continued success."

Since it was acquired by the parent company in 1986, Paulstra CRC has more than doubled its annual sales, which now exceed $100 million. It has manufacturing plants in Grand Rapids, Cadillac, and now Ithaca, as well as a sales office in Livonia, and the company employs more than 500 people. According to Huet, one major

strength is the company's commitment to remain abreast of the very latest technology.

"Our success over the past 10 years is directly related to our continued investment in sophisticated machinery and technology," says Huet. "We also have developed an innovative product called active mount that is state of the art, and combines the technology of hydromount and electronics. We've also developed technology that lets us simulate automobile engine vibrations through the use of highly sophisticated computers, which allows us to determine where and what kind of antivibration mounts we have to design. Our customers look to us as the technology experts, and they usually consult with us very early in the development process."

Paulstra's advanced manufacturing equipment includes new-generation computerized injection presses, modular assembly robots, transfer dies, and integrated workstations. The company's three tech centers—two in France and one in Grand Rapids—are staffed by highly qualified and talented metallurgical, rubber, and electrical engineers who are devoted to researching and developing technology to keep Paulstra on the leading edge of its industry.

When it comes to what's ahead for Paulstra, Huet says he envisions continued growth and success. "What's most exciting is that

our company is going more and more toward globalization," he says. "That presents us with enormous opportunity because as automobile manufacturers continue to expand their presence globally, they will choose suppliers who can meet their demands and who understand that cars are different, engines are different, and cars are driven differently in other countries than they are here. It's always been the philosophy of this company to be wherever our customers need us to be. That's how we got here, and that's how we will continue to serve our customers in the future. We're excited about our future here in West Michigan."

Paulstra has become one of the world's leading suppliers of antivibration products for automotive giants such as Ford, General Motors, and Mercedes-Benz.

ROHDE CONSTRUCTION COMPANY

T SEEMS THAT SOME COMPANIES ARE JUST DESTINED TO SUCCEED. THAT is certainly the case with Rohde Construction Company, which has grown more than 50 percent per year since it was founded in 1993. The company's specialty is developing multiple-based housing, which includes apartments and town homes, hotels and motels,

communities for the elderly, retail chain outlets, and university student housing. Focusing on this type of housing, Rohde Construction recognized a total volume of under $6 million at the end of its first year of business. By its fifth anniversary, Rohde's volume had risen to $48 million, and the company had become one of the largest multihousing contractors in the state.

A Wealth of Experience

Rohde Construction's founder and President Mark Rohde has spent nearly 30 years in this segment of the construction business, and his company has more experience in the construction of multifamily and elderly housing than any in West Michigan. Rohde's ability to assist an architect with value engineering and

A university-owned housing project, Laker Village Townhomes, incorporated 29 town house buildings and two community buildings, housing 876 students on the Grand Valley State University main campus. University housing is one of the specialties of Rohde Construction Company.

The Crossings Townhomes—a 114-unit rental town home project in Portage—is an example of the diverse types of multiple-based housing Rohde constructs. The company is the largest such housing contractor located in West Michigan.

accurate early estimates of construction cost has made the company an integral member of development teams. Rohde says that this approach has been invaluable in building loyalty and long-term relationships with the company's growing list of repeat clients.

One of Rohde's highest-profile projects was the development of the Grand Valley State University student housing program. The Living Centers, which accommodates well over 500 students, was a part of the concept that created a more contemporary and comfortable approach to student housing than traditional dormitories. Rohde also created a 29-building town house community called Laker Village, which houses an additional 850 students.

Another of Rohde's major projects was the Marsh Ridge Elderly Community, a 150-unit complex that features both apartments and town homes for the elderly. The complex is situated in a parklike setting, and includes two ponds with fountains, a comfortable community facility, and a charming gazebo.

As Grand Rapids continues to grow and thrive, Rohde Construction will grow and thrive with it.

With a commitment to the community and a true mastery of its specialty, Rohde Construction will continue providing West Michigan with the very finest in multiple-based housing well into the next millennium.

Lloyd's Bayou, a 111-unit retirement community, is representative of a number of elderly housing projects Rohde Construction has built throughout the state. Rohde is a leader in the construction of housing for the elderly.

As part of its multiple-based housing expertise, Rohde Construction builds motels throughout the state of Michigan, such as the Sleep Inn Motel in Kentwood.

WORLDCOM HAS COME A LONG WAY SINCE ITS HUMBLE beginnings in 1983. In a coffee shop in Hattiesburg, Mississippi, four men outlined the details for a long-distance company. There—after a waitress suggested the name LDDS for Long Distance Discount Service—

Over the years, WorldCom has aligned itself with some of the world's leading communications companies, creating a single vendor that can provide everything a business needs—from local to long-distance telephone service, as well as Internet access.

WorldCom's predecessor was born. In April 1985, Bernard Ebbers was named president of the Mississippi-based enterprise, and WorldCom started on its path to becoming a communications giant. Acquiring more than 40 communications firms and operating in more than 50 countries, the company has grown to include 200 offices around the world, 17,000 employees, and some 500,000 business customers. In 1997, WorldCom's combined annual revenues equaled $7.3 billion.

MERGERS

WorldCom has always done what is best for business, and it is this philosophy that created the industry's first major, full-service provider. Over the years, WorldCom has aligned itself with some of the world's leading communications companies, creating a single vendor that can provide everything a business needs—from local to long-distance telephone service, as well as Internet access. In 1994, WorldCom merged with IDB, which gave the company a strong international presence, and in 1995, a merger with WilTel Network Services made WorldCom a leader in data services while adding 11,000 miles of fiber-optic cable to the network. Joining with MFS/UUNET in 1996 allowed WorldCom to break into the local arena and acquire the world's largest Internet Service Provider. And, in 1998, a merger with CompuServe and ANS Communications significantly enhanced the company's ability to offer complete Internet services. The acquisition that same year of St. Louis-based Brooks Fiber Properties, which maintained offices in Grand Rapids, expanded WorldCom's local fiber-optic networks and switching facilities.

NETWORKS

WorldCom has the most advanced family of networks in the industry, including 20,000 route miles of owned U.S. fiber, access to 30,000 route fiber miles, 4,000 miles of digital microwave facilities, long-term capacity in virtually every undersea fiber cable, and worldwide satellite coverage. And, the company is constantly upgrading to maintain its position as a leader in the industry.

Today's business and financial leaders are identifying WorldCom as tomorrow's communications leader. In 1997, *Fortune* rated WorldCom as number two overall in highest return to investors, and the *Wall Street Journal* ranked the company as the top telecom stock on its Shareholder's Scoreboard. Listed at number 309 on the Fortune 500, WorldCom was also added to Standard & Poor's 500 Index in 1996.

INDUSTRY FIRSTS

WorldCom has pioneered the development of many technologies that have now become standard in the industry. The company was the first public frame-relay service, fractional T-1 service, and commercial Internet service provider, and the first provider to use a switched-based backbone. It was also the first company to offer Metro Frame Relay, an ATM, and services for both Web-based and ATM network management.

And now, WorldCom has brought about a new reality: a single company capable of providing full-service, facilities-based communications. True to its motto, WorldCom is "One Company. A World of Solutions.SM"

BRIAN WINKELMANN ALWAYS KNEW HE WANTED TO BE AN architect. By the time he was eleven, he had designed a house for his parents with an indoor garden "to keep summer inside all year." Winkelmann has accomplished his dream of becoming an architect—today, Winkelmann Associates-

Architects, P.C. is an award-winning firm that's well on its way to becoming one of the top architectural firms in the state.

EXPERIENCE AND TALENT

Winkelmann entered the architectural field in 1980, and has gained respect in the industrial, multi-family residential, and commercial properties fields. While working for another local architectural/engineering firm, Winkelmann was the lead architect for the impressive Bridgewater Place. He then became design architect of the Great Lakes Chemical Corporation world headquarters in West Lafayette, Indiana, a stunning 100,000-square-foot structure with three floors cantilevered over a lake.

After founding Winkelmann Associates-Architects, P.C., Winkelmann steered his firm to specialize in building renovation and historic preservation. When Dwelling Place purchased the run-down Herkimer Hotel on South Division, it was Winkelmann Associates that painstakingly restored the 103-year-old building to its original state, uncovering wood-work and preserving the grandeur of the main floor. Today, the Herkimer is listed in the National Register for Historic Structures.

Along with traditional architectural design and historic renovation, Winkelmann Associates specializes in space planning and design-build for a variety of businesses. "We see ourselves as a 'translator of space,'" says Winkelmann. "We like to get to know our customers, and to understand their businesses. We make it a priority to understand what they're not telling us, which is often the real key to finding solutions for them."

RECOGNITION IN THE FIELD

The impressive collection of awards Winkelmann Associates has re-ceived are a good indication of what the firm has accomplished. In addition to Brian Winkelmann's being listed in Who's Who of Executives and Professionals, the firm's work on the Herkimer Hotel appeared as the center spread in *Preservation Shore to Shore*, the State Historic Preservation Office annual report, and was rated one of the 10 best renovation projects in the state. Both the Herkimer Hotel and the Great Lakes Chemical headquarters building each won the Distinguished Building Award from AIA. Great Lakes also won

the Eagle, the National Award of Excellence from Associated Builders and Contractors.

Winkelmann plans to continue his firm's growth, but will balance that growth so he can keep doing what he's best at. "I don't want to end up the manager of a massive architectural firm," says Winkelmann. "I want to be an architect. When people hire Winkelmann Associates, they get me, and I plan to keep it that way. I'll never grow the firm so big that I become an ivory tower architect. I'll always put my customers first."

Among the many projects in which Winkelmann Associates has been involved are (clockwise from top) the Herkimer Hotel, the Michigan Bulb Company's corporate head-quarters addition, and Robert Grooters Development Company's Norton Shores Industrial Park.

ATIONAL CITY IS A BANK THAT BLENDS EXPERTISE FOR CORPORATE banking and retail banking. The bank has had an enviable performance record in the delivery of its banking services since it was founded in 1838 in Cleveland, Ohio. National City purchased First of America Bank in 1998 and will make a significant banking contribution to the West Michigan market. The bank's key philosophy is servicing customers and fulfilling their financial needs.

CONSISTENT PERFORMER

National City is a $78 billion bank holding company, and the company serves markets in Ohio, western Pennsylvania, Kentucky, Michigan, Illinois, and Indiana. In addition to the bank's delivery of core banking products, National City has been an innovator in developing a subsidiary company called National Processing, Inc., which provides processing services for merchant credit cards, airline tickets, check guarantees, and receivables and payables for many large corporate customers throughout the United States. The company also has a full-functioning leasing company, investment company, and commercial finance subsidiary. National City has been instrumental in providing mutual fund services, and it manages its own proprietary mutual funds called the Armada Mutual Fund Family. National City operates 40 full-service branch facilities, as well as operating automated teller machines, and has partnered with

National City Bank's main branch is located on Monroe Avenue in downtown Grand Rapids.

With branches conveniently located throughout the Grand Rapids area, National City Bank offers a full range of services to its customers.

Grand Rapids grocer Meijer, Inc. to open branch banks inside Meijer stores throughout West Michigan.

THE YEARS AHEAD

Ken Hoexum, National City regional president, believes Grand Rapids will become the model city of the future, because it exemplifies how well the private and public sector can work together. "The Midwest, with all its manufacturing capacity, is now respected as an area that drives our country's economic strength," Hoexum says. "People in the Midwest have integrity, high values, and an excellent work ethic, and the people in Grand Rapids are the best possible example of that. It's a wonderful community, and we're proud to be a part of it."

As for National City's future role in Grand Rapids, Hoexum is excited about the years ahead: "At National City, we will grow as the community grows, continuing to add products and services to meet our customers' needs. We'll continue to explore new technology and look for ways to do business faster and more efficiently. But we will never lose the one quality that makes us first: our caring, personalized attitude toward customers. It's what really differentiates us from other banks. And it will always be something that sets us apart."

Roger Bickel, a Bingham Farms, Michigan-based freelance photographer, specializes in travel and nature stock photography. His travel photos cover most of the 50 states, and his nature photos feature the flora and fauna of Michigan. Bickel's work has appeared in Towery Publishing's *Cincinnati: Crowning Glory*, *Greater Detroit: Renewing the Dream*, and *Discover Columbus*; such periodicals as *National Geographic Traveler*, *Better Homes and Gardens*, *Woman's World*, and Delta Air Lines' *Sky*; and books published by Houghton Mifflin, Barnes & Noble, Insight Guides, and Children's Press.

Dianne Carroll Burdick received a bachelor of fine arts degree from Western Michigan University and an associate of fine arts degree from Grand Rapids Community College. Specializing in portraiture, photojournalism, and fine art photography, she is employed by the *Grand Rapids Press* and does freelance work for such clients as Smiths Industries Aerospace, the Public Museum of Grand Rapids, Seyferth & Associates, Inc., the Grand Rapids Area Chamber of Commerce, Frederik Meijer Gardens, the Grand Rapids Ballet, the Frey Foundation, Grand Valley State University, and the *Detroit Free Press*. Burdick's work also has been featured in numerous exhibitions and competitions. Originally from Ann Arbor, she moved to the area in 1960 and is currently renovating a 120-year-old house in the Heritage Hill District.

Dennis Cox is an award-winning travel and location photographer in Ann Arbor whose images have appeared in numerous publications, including *Smithsonian*, *Time*, and *Newsweek*. A member of the Michigan chapter of the American Society of Media Photographers, he was the recipient of the 1997 Travel Photographer of the Year award, given by the Society of American Travel Writers. As director of China Photo Workshop Tours/Photo Explorer Tours, Cox has been leading tours to China since 1981 and to other photogenic world destinations since 1996.

Grace Davies, a New York-based photographer, received an associate degree from the Fashion Institute of Technology of the State University of New York and a bachelor's degree from Hunter College of the City University of New York. Her photography files consist of more than 20,000 images of scenics, geology subjects, nature, pets, and gardens. Recently, Davies photographed the scenics of Beaver Island in West Michigan; the birds and plants of Cape May, New Jersey; the rain forests and the Indian River in Dominica; and the turtles and geology of the Cayman Islands. Her images have been included in many publications, such as *Historic Traveler*, *Habitat Magazine*, *Time*, *New Choices*, the *New York Times*, and the *Newark Star Ledger*, and in books published by Harcourt Brace, HarperCollins, Macmillan/McGraw-Hill, Oxford University Press, Prentice Hall, and West Educational Publishing.

David J. DeJonge, a lifelong resident of Hudsonville, Michigan, enjoys taking pictures of people. His clients include Meijer, Inc. and Blue Cross/Blue Shield, and his images have been published in *Grand Rapids Magazine*, *Michigan Living*, and the *Grand Rapids Press*.

Lisa Haverdink is originally from Grand Rapids, but spent several years in Oklahoma where she received a bachelor of science degree in nursing from the University of Central Oklahoma. An adjunct instructor in pediatrics at a local nursing school, she is developing her recently discovered interest in photography at Grand Rapids Community College. Haverdink specializes in nature transparencies and outdoor photography, and she is learning to shoot, develop, and print with black-and-white film. One of her images was chosen and displayed at the 1997 visual arts competition at the annual Grand Rapids Festival of the Arts. Haverdink also is interested in organic gardening and preventive health care.

William J. Hebert is a former high school biology teacher who became interested in photography while traveling during his summer vacations. A native of Michigan, he specializes in location assignments and stock photography, and his work often sells as fine art. Hebert spends approximately four months of the year completing assignments out of the country, and

in his spare time, he plays classical and jazz guitar and composes music.

Bill Hill, a lifelong resident of Grand Rapids, worked as a commercial artist for more than 40 years. Since his retirement, he has produced nature slides for use in magazines, books, and calendars. The recipient of numerous local, state, and national awards, Hill acquired his photography skills through programs, workshops, field trips, monthly camera club competitions, photography books, and magazines. His images have appeared in a variety of places, including advertisements for Kodak Ektachrome film; an instruction booklet for Kodak; the dust jacket of *Petersen's Big Book of Photography*; Grand Valley State University's annual report; a brochure cover for Great Lakes Hydraulics, Inc.; the *Grand Rapids Press*; the Grand Rapids sesquicentennial poster; Christmas cards for Integra Printing Inc.; the cover of the first issue of *Quality of Life* magazine; and *Lake 'N Trail Magazine*, *Birder's World*, and *Michigan Magazine*. His work has also been exhibited at the Grand Rapids Public Library, the Blandford Nature Center, the Frederik Meijer Gardens, and the Casa de Teatro in Santo Domingo.

Jim C. Hill, a marketing representative for LuDann Education Services, is also a self-taught photographer specializing in capturing local sports on film. He shoots the West Michigan Whitecaps, the Grand Rapids Griffins, the Grand Rapids Hoops, and the First of America Classic on the PGA Senior Tour, and he is the photographer for the Van Andel Arena and DeVos Hall. Though he has taken pictures for numerous companies and universities, as well as local, regional, and national publications, Hill is best known for his photograph of Michigan's game-winning field goal against Notre Dame in 1994.

Hillstrom Stock Photography, established in 1967, is a full-service stock photography agency based in Chicago. Its files include images of architecture, agricultural backgrounds, classic autos, gardens, and high-risk adventure/sports.

Richard Hirneisen loves taking pictures of people in their environments, whether they are in a factory in China, on a farm in Iowa, in an office in Tokyo, or at a lab in Brussels. A graduate of Wayne State University, Hirneisen claims he is never bored behind the lens of a camera, and his client list includes such prominent names as Ford Motor Company, Kmart, the University of Michigan, and Nissan North America. His images have also been included in Towery Publishing's *Greater Detroit: Renewing the Dream.*

Steve Huyser-Honig, an editorial photographer and member of the American Society of Media Photographers, specializes in travel and location photography. His newspaper credits include the *Anchorage Daily News, Miami Herald, New York Post,* and *San Francisco Examiner.* Magazine credits include *Car & Travel, Harrowsmith Country Life, Home & Away,* and the *International Journal* of the W.K. Kellogg Foundation. His images have also appeared on the Web sites of Great Outdoor Recreation Pages and the Nature Conservancy. Among his clients are resorts, museums, convention and visitors bureaus, colleges, and nonprofit agencies. He and his wife, Joan, a writer, often work on joint assignments, in which they frequently include their two sons.

Brad Iverson, originally from Seattle, earned a bachelor's degree and a master's degree from Wayne State University. His fine art photography, portraits, and essays on social realism have been featured in such publications as *Camera, Afterimage,* and the *New York Times,* as well as in permanent collections at the Bibliothèque Nationale in Paris and the Archives of American Art, a bureau of the Smithsonian Institution. Iverson lives in Huntington Woods.

Brian Kelly has lived in Grand Rapids since his infancy. A self-employed photographer, he earned an associate degree in arts, with a concentration in photography, from Grand Rapids Community College. His specialties include architecture and abstract cityscapes, home and corporate office environments, and interior design. Among his clients are Amway Hotel Corporation, Plaza Tower Associates, Burgler Advertising, United Bank of Michigan, and the Grand Rapids Foundation.

Fred L. Kleiboer, a former Peace Corps volunteer in Ponape, Micronesia, is a native of Grand Rapids who studied photography at Grand Valley State University. Self-employed at Kleiboer Photography, he specializes in human interest, editorial, public relations, children's portrait, black-and-white landscape, and urban scenic photography. His work has been published in *On the Town* magazine and *West Michigan Magazine,* and his clients include Butterworth Hospital and McLaren Hospital. A married father of three, he has bicycled from Grand Rapids to Nova Scotia.

Balthazar Korab moved to the Detroit area in 1955 after attending L'École des Beaux-Arts and L'École de Louvre in Paris. Specializing in architectural photography, he was awarded the American Institute of Architects medal for photography, and his work has been exhibited in Rome and Turin, Italy. In 1994, President Bill Clinton presented a portfolio of 12 of Korab's photographs to President Árpád Göncz of Hungary— Korab's native land—as a presidential gift. His images have also appeared in Towery Publishing's *Greater Detroit: Renewing the Dream* and *Toronto Tapestry.*

Michael Morin, the proprietor of his own studio, specializes in product brochures and architectural photography. Moving to the Grand Rapids area in 1984, Morin received the Kodak Photographic Excellence Award in 1990 and 1991 through a Professional Photographers of Michigan competition. His work was also featured on the cover of the August 1994 issue of *Professional Photographer* magazine.

Diane Bosley Taylor, originally from Holland, Michigan, moved to Grand Rapids in 1975. She studied illustration and photography for two years at Kendall College of Art and Design, received a bachelor of arts degree and a secondary teacher's certificate from Michigan State University, and took classes at Western Michigan University and the Leys School in Cambridge, England. Specializing in travel, landscape, and floral images, she is the proprietor of DBT Photography. She has sold photos of Rome to *Kids Discover* and *Relax* magazines, and has images published in various textbooks,

including *Death to Life* and *Human Geography.* In addition to selling a wallsized display photo for a convention of private schools, Taylor has sold images at local arts and gift shops, as well as dynamic graphics for clip art. Recently diagnosed with multiple sclerosis, she values the beauty around her now more than ever.

Don Van Essen, a self-employed photographer from Minnesota, specializes in commercial, studio and product, underwater, and nature photography. An attendee of Maine Photographic and Professional Photographers of America workshops, he has had images published in *Lake 'N Trail Magazine, Michigan Magazine, Michigan Out-of-Doors, Great Lakes Fisherman,* and *Professional Photographer.* The recipient of numerous Addy awards, Van Essen has also received the International Association of Business Communicator's Award of Excellence. His memorable experiences include taking pictures of sharks and the Berlin Wall.

Dan Watts has been a commercial photographer and audiovisual producer for 20 years, working for the office furniture, health care, and advertising industries. He has gained a disciplined control and an understanding of light, whether photographing a furniture factory, open-heart surgery, or a medieval town in Italy. Since 1976, he has traveled the world extensively on magazine, corporate, and self-assigned projects, photographing lifestyles, cityscapes, and landscapes in Asia, Europe, and North and South America. Having spent several of the past few years working with curators, designers, and facility planners in the art world, Watts has done extensive work in Italy. His favorite technique is using only the first light in the early morning or the last light in the evening to create images that can be soft and pastel or piercing and riotous.

Other photographers and organizations that contributed to *Greater Grand Rapids: The City That Works* include the City of Grand Rapids, Gerald R. Ford Library, Grand Rapids Public Library, Steve Richardson, Steelcase Inc., and Andrew C. Terzes.